Transnational Desires

Transnational Desires

Brazilian Erotic Dancers
in New York

Suzana Maia

Vanderbilt University Press

NASHVILLE

© 2012 by Vanderbilt University Press
Nashville, Tennessee 37235
All rights reserved
First printing 2012

This book is printed on acid-free paper.
Manufactured in the United States of America

Library of Congress Cataloging-in-Publication Data

Maia, Suzana.
Transnational desires : Brazilian erotic dancers in New York
/ Suzana Maia.
p. cm.
Includes bibliographical references and index.
ISBN 978-0-8265-1822-4 (cloth : alk. paper)
ISBN 978-0-8265-1823-1 (pbk. : alk. paper)
1. Stripteasers—Brazil—Case studies. 2. Stripteasers—New
York (State)—New York—Case studies. 3. Brazilians—
New York (State)—New York—Social conditions—Case
studies. 4. Women immigrants—New York (State)—New
York—Social conditions—Case studies. 5. Sex-oriented
businesses—New York (State)—New York—Case studies.
6. Women—Brazil—Case studies. 7. Women—Identity—
Case studies. 8. Women—Sexual behavior—Case studies.
I. Title.
PN1949.S7.M34 2012
305.4'379278—dc23
2011030581

Contents

Acknowledgments

I would like, first of all, to express my gratitude to the women who participated in this project and who shared their lives with me over the years. I greatly appreciate our friendship and their trust in me, and I can only say that I did my best to honor their experiences. Unfortunately, as it goes in most research, I must avoid thanking each of them by name so as to not reveal their identities.

At the Graduate Center, CUNY, the support and mentorship of Ida Susser, Shirley Lindenbaum, and Vincent Crapanzano were of crucial importance. Over the years Ida Susser has been a constant source of encouragement, and from her I learned that differences in ideas and approaches can be not only a source of inspiration but also the basis for creative scholarship. Shirley Lindenbaum's insights and enthusiasm for my attempts to create new forms of representation were a constantly refreshing support. I thank Vincent Crapanzano for encouraging me to generate new questions for recurring issues and for insisting that I dwell on what is not yet known. I am also thankful to Nicole Constable for her generous reading, comments, and suggestions. Also at the Graduate Center, I wish to thank my colleagues, particularly Jimmy Weir, Esin Egit, Chris Lawrence, and Susan Falls. Participation in a number of Brazilian immigration seminars helped me build my research, and I am particularly grateful to Cileine de Lourenço and Maxine Margolis for their invaluable insights and suggestions. For discussions on how to reconcile the vicissitudes of personal and academic life, I wish to thank Nancy Flowers and Susan Besse. In Brazil, Maria Rosário de Carvalho, my mentor since undergraduate school, has been a constant source of inspiration. Her trajectory has taught me, since early on, that intellectual curiosity and creativity do not have to be separated from ethical and political concerns.

This work was made possible thanks to a generous fellowship from CAPES, Brazil. I was also fortunate to be granted a CUNY Writing across the Curriculum fellowship, which supported my fieldwork in New York as I developed educational tools and got to know more of New York City's "other minorities" in Caribbean Brooklyn.

My work would not be the same without the intellectual and emotional support of my transnational friends: Ana Dumas, Elisabeth Senra de Oliveira, Luise Pedroso Kipler, Thiago Szmrecsányi, Natália Campos, John Messenger, Susannah Monty, Selmo Norte, Mário Vieira, Michael Gordon, Anthony Sloan, and Myriam Marques. In New York, David and Edith Mendelsohn, as well as Margaret Smith and her family, made me feel as if I were at home. I am particularly indebted to Eliana Moreira and Rita Carvalho for accompanying me in an enterprise that proved to take longer than expected. With them it was easier to persevere with joy and laughter. For giving me the necessary push to complete the last stages of my writing in Brazil and for helping me to move on, I am thankful to my sister Silmara Maia and to Lucas Peixoto.

My deepest thanks go to my parents, Vavá Maia and Ruth Augusta Moura Maia, for their unquestioning trust and support over the years that I have been living between here and there, for understanding the difficulties of making life-changing decisions, and for accepting my confusion. With Steve Himes, I learned that it is all part of life, and so we have to proceed with patience and love.

Introduction

During the years 2003 and 2005, I often left my house in Brooklyn to meet with one of the dancers I knew, and together we would either take a van to bars or simply walk to the ones near their homes. I had been living in New York since 1995, but it was not until 2001 that I first visited Astoria, in the borough of Queens, where there is a large concentration of Brazilians. Around this time I learned about Brazilian go-go dancers.[1] It was with hesitation that I first visited a go-go bar just around the corner from a friend's house in Astoria. What I most remember from this first visit was the doppelgänger feeling of familiarity and strangeness that often accompanies experiences of displacement. My friend and I spoke Portuguese to each other, and when dancers came to us to pick up our dollar bills, we also spoke to them in Portuguese. In my first visits to bars, I was startled to hear Brazilian Portuguese spoken with such frequency. In the years that I visited gentlemen's bars, particularly in the borough of Queens, most of the dancers were Brazilian, with women from Colombia the second most frequent. At first, I was just curious about how they exhibited their bodies and the life on the edge I imagined them to inhabit. Or rather, I was seduced by these.

At that time, I had received a scholarship from Brazil in order to study Brazilian women in New York, but the project was still not defined. From existing research, I knew that a number of Brazilian women, like other migrant women, worked as nannies, babysitters, waitresses, or housecleaners.[2] I had just finished my master's thesis on Brazilians who worked as artists' models in New York, and I was interested in the intersection between nationality and representations of the body. I worked as a model myself for four years, and it was intriguing to see the different representations in art of Brazilian bodies. In addition, I enjoyed New York's nightlife and was looking for some subject that excited my imagination. From my first visit to a gentlemen's club, I began to consider Brazilian women who worked as erotic dancers as a subject of study.

In Queens bars, semi-naked women wearing G-string bikinis and at times topless parade up and down a small platform alongside the bar. Their work consists of dancing and attracting clients who, sipping their drinks, observe the dancers' performance. Every now and then dancers stop to receive dollar bills from clients, which is the way dancers make most of their money. On a regular night's shift—from 7:30 p.m. to 4 a.m.—about ten to fifteen dancers take turns performing onstage. Each stage performance lasts twenty minutes. When not dancing, a woman is supposed to socialize with clients on the floor and encourage them to buy her drinks, from which she receives a small percentage. Some bars also offer lap dances in which a woman dances for a single client, usually in a corner of the bar or in a separate space. In Queens gentlemen's bars, a dancer can make between $100 and $400 per night, and sometimes more, depending on her performance, the day of the week, and the mood of the bar. Contrary to the common belief that erotic dancing is a form of prostitution, there is no exchange of money for sexual intercourse in gentlemen's clubs, and, in fact, strict city and state laws define the border between prostitution and erotic dancing.[3]

From the beginning, I was particularly struck by the presence of Brazilian women from the middle class. Being a Brazilian middle-class woman myself, I could perceive their class markers in their ways of speaking and moving, in their gestures and mannerisms. I identified with these women on a variety of levels. Often when I went to a new bar, dancers I did not know, clients, and management would see me as a potential dancer—I was of the same nationality, age, and body type as most of the women working in the bars. Soon after I started visiting gentlemen's bars in Queens, I was lucky enough to meet Barbara and Clara, two women from the same part of Brazil that I was from. I became close to Clara sooner, as she has an outgoing and friendly personality, and after our meeting in the bar she was the first to call me. Clara is a lawyer and one of the eighteen women from her extended family who live in New York, most of whom work as erotic dancers. Through them, I met an extensive network of dancers from the Brazilian middle class.

Among the reasons I chose to focus on middle-class women were the delicate nature of my research subject and the stigma attached to being an erotic dancer—I needed to establish trusting relationships with these women. A number of dancers were in precarious life situations and feared giving information to someone they did not fully know. A number of them also had a difficult time understanding the nature of my research and suspected that I was a journalist and that news of their work in New York would be spread among Brazilians in Brazil. I have of course respected their choosing to remain silent. However, there was another reason that led me to work with middle-class women. From the beginning of my research, I knew I wanted to study people who were my equals. Not that my relationship with my subjects was not imbued with power struggles, but I did not want to reproduce a representational system in which I was implicated as an "other."

The question of representation in anthropology and the relationships of power implicated in the making of ethnographies has been the subject of inquiry for a number of years now. I was aware of these issues and was particularly interested in thinking about how ethnographic writing could expand the ways we understand the lives of individuals in society. While living in Brazil and working with Brazilian indigenous populations, I grew dissatisfied with anthropological typification and the erasure of the anthropologist from the scene of research. I thought that the ethnographies I knew did not account for the complexities, dilemmas, and conflicts of the people I encountered in my fieldwork. However, when I came to New York these questions took on greater significance, for I became an "other" myself, a subject of study and an object of curiosity, an exotic of sorts. As a native Brazilian in New York, I became acutely aware of how generalizations work toward encapsulating "others" in a bounded time and space of culture and difference.[4] Such generalizations about distant others, however, no longer apply. More than twenty years ago, James Clifford remarked on how the contemporary anthropological subject has "gone crazy." Traveling between worlds, occupying spaces once reserved for the authorial researcher, anthropological subjects can no longer be associated with values of authenticity and culture. "Entering the modern world, their distinct histories quickly disappear," Clifford noted (1988, 5). Much has been written in the past decades about the predicament of the relationship between researcher and object/subject of study, arguing that an anthropology that constructs cultural difference as distance keeps the other in an allocated space and as belonging to a different time. Despite being a contemporary, the other is created as the opposite of self. The self of the researcher is represented as modern and progressive, while the other is constructed as primitive or, nowadays, as underdeveloped and unmodern.

The women I encountered in gentlemen's bars were fully modern women to me, no longer bounded by any space of authenticity but immersed in a global consumers' society, independent, venturing out at night, drinking, smoking, using their bodies as sites of spectacle and as commodities, beyond the safe net of their families, away from a place that they could call home.[5] Yet these women were caught in a web of representations that persistently slots them into categories that define them in relation to fixed time and space: as immigrants, as Brazilian women, as sex workers. The discomfort I felt about such categorizations was a pervasive underlying tension that motivated me throughout the making of this book.

On June 30, 2005, the *New York Times* reported that, after Mexicans, more Brazilians than any other nationality were crossing the Mexican-U.S. border illegally. According to that article, in two days alone, U.S. Border Patrol agents in Texas detained 232 Brazilian men and women. One city in Brazil issued 140 passports in a single day to Brazilians who wanted to leave the country. The article also noted that, since the tightening of U.S. visa requirements after September 11, 2001, most of those seeking to immigrate are more likely to apply not to U.S. embassies in Brazil but to traffickers in one of the many agencies that offer to smuggle people across the border for $10,000. On December 26, 2005, the *Times* gave its readers a different portrayal of Brazilian immigrants: they were not illegal border crossers but mostly from the middle class—educated people who, because of the ongoing economic crisis in Brazil, came to the United States searching for a better life.

While other, still more positive views of Brazil, particularly with the betterment of that country's economy, have begun to appear, Brazilians, like other migrants, continue to face suspicion in the United States, as immigration laws and debates have as yet failed to fully embrace migrants who live and work in this country. The contradictory views expressed by the *Times* come from clustering under the category "immigrants" people from a wide variety of class and ethnic-racial backgrounds, places, and languages. With an increasing presence in public debate and the media, "immigrants" have become a facile explanation for many of the problems that the United States now faces, along with terrorism and the transfer of jobs and investments overseas. These are all, in the public imagination, the downside of globalization.

Just who are the people crossing into the United States? What are their dreams and aspirations? Do they want to assimilate into the U.S. population? Are they buying into American values, or are they critical of them? Can those who have never cut the ties to their home country in fact be defined as "immigrants"? Are they "immigrants" if they live their lives between countries, with their national loyalties equally divided? What factors must we take into consideration to account for the extensive flow of people coming into the United States and to understand their motivation to make this move?

There is now a substantial body of work about the migration and displacement of Brazilians, most of which rightly points to economic reasons for the move and highlights the 1980s as the turning point in Brazil's recent history. It was in the 1980s that Brazil experienced new political freedom with the end of a twenty-year military dictatorship, as well as a deep economic downturn resulting from the restructuring of the global economy. It was in this so-called lost decade that Brazilians started leaving the country in massive numbers; they have been defined as "economic refugees" (Sales 2003). Critics of neoclassical push-pull theory also point to the internationalization of production, rather than just unemployment or subemployment, as a leading cause for the movement of labor from countries such as Brazil to overseas locations. They also rightly argue that it was not the poor or destitute who first started migrating, but people from the middle class in search of better opportunities (Martes 1999; Margolis 1994). Others (Beserra 2003) point to U.S. cultural imperialism as the creator of a pool of potential migrants. Most of these observers also call attention not only to the better pay and the increase in consumer power immigrants find in the United States but also to the hardships they face, such as the loss of status for middle-class people who must engage in menial work. Ethnographic works have described in detail the immigrants' struggle to find and keep work, to build communities and family strategies, and to create support groups through religious institutions.

This volume builds upon this body of work but departs from it in significant ways. It seemed to me that most studies of immigration were caught up in constructing a nostalgic subject that dwells in displacement and loss, and whose identity is allied too closely with the sphere of work and the remembering of a time past. This contradicted my own experience of displacement and that of people I knew. I am not arguing that experiences of loss and strategies of survival are not common to everyone. However, I wanted to explore issues that shed new light on people's experiences—their desires and their ambiguities. I was interested in how socioeconomic transformations affected the personal lives of women. I wanted to know what happened to their sense of self and the uses of their bodies, to their sense of being in space and time, to their ways of looking at life and their relationships with men and women. Inspired by studies of globalization and sexuality (Constable 2003; Altman 2001; Kelsky 2001; Povinelli and Chauncey 1999; Jolly and Manderson 1997), I started looking at desire and how it is produced between places, in border zones, and in spaces of colonial and post- or neocolonial encounters. Arguing against a construct of "immigrants" eager to catch up with the modernity of the center, I needed new ways to construct subjects: transnational, diasporic, hybrid, nomadic (Appadurai 1991; Braidotti 1994). However, while I share the need to understand these new "nomadic subjects," I am also attentive to specific contexts that create differences among them. Following more grounded studies of transnationalism (Ong 1996, 1999), I am equally attentive to the ways in which race, class, gender, and sexuality work to create cleavages among subjects and to define the experiences of particular individuals as they cross the borders of nation-states.

A number of Brazilian erotic dancers in New York are from various segments of the Brazilian middle class. Most of them have at least a few years of college education and have had independent and relatively successful careers in Brazil. Their ages range from the early twenties to the forties, although most are in their thirties. For the most part, their parents' generation took part in the expansion of the middle class, which was mostly financed by foreign investment in Brazil. For these women, growing up in the 1970s and 1980s in Brazil, consumer power and shopping malls were a given. Our parents had cars and our mothers took jobs outside the home. Foreign, particularly U.S., goods, values, and ideas were common features on our TV screens and in contemporary music, cinema, and dance, and dictated the jeans we wore. As part of the global middle class and its modern leisure practices, we took vacations at the beach and traveled nationally and internationally. In tune with Brazilian modernity, many of these women also used their bodies as instruments to get what they wanted and had developed hedonistic approaches to their relationships to others.

Although socioeconomic considerations were important in their motivations to come to the United States, such Brazilian middle-class women did not conform to the typical immigrant image. Quite the opposite. They had occupied privileged positions in their home countries, representing a somewhat small elite within the extremely unequal Brazilian social structure. Most of the Brazilian populace lives in poverty or below the poverty level, and in Brazil poverty mostly equals dark skin color. As a result of the country's long history of slavery, the Brazilian social hierarchy is racialized: the whiter one's skin color, the more likely one is to occupy a higher position in the class structure. In the United States, many of the Brazilian erotic dancers from the middle class belonged to the whiter part of the Brazilian racial spectrum and occupied a privileged racial position in the Brazilian hierarchy—for instance, they all used to have maids, mostly women of dark skin color, taking care of their homes.

Yet compared to the middle classes from centers of economic power, their middle-class location appears less privileged. Goods and values that are taken for granted in the United States represent luxuries that most Brazilians must strive hard to earn. Particularly with the restructuring of the economy in the 1980s, middle-class Brazilians experienced downward mobility; they could not realize the good life epitomized by models of modernity developed in Europe and particularly in the United States. As life standards deteriorated and violence grew, Brazilian middle-class anxieties about social stability and class maintenance became all too pervasive, while disenchantment about the future of the nation became widespread. It was then that Brazilians started migrating in massive numbers to centers of economic, political, and symbolic power. Once established, this migration became a self-perpetuating process. Despite the betterment of Brazil's economic situation and the prevailing optimism in regard to building a future in that country, Brazilians have not ceased to migrate, now to more diverse destinations easier to access as airlines expand throughout Brazil. Today, direct flights connect many cities of the once-isolated Northeast to Paris, Madrid, and Amsterdam, in addition to Miami and New York. And often these cities represent not destinations but stopovers in expanding geographical networks of travel and migration.

Although Brazilian men and women leave the country in proportional numbers, they use different networks, have different aspirations, and encounter different opportunities transnationally. Middle-class men seem to see their stay overseas as temporary, are more likely to remain within networks of their compatriots, and tend to go back to Brazil after a few years. At home they take advantage of their gender-privileged position in the job market or run inherited family businesses, which they capitalize with money from their migrant experience. Although many women migrate accompanied by husbands and families, the women I met in gentlemen's bars had entered the United States on their own and were living in New York alone or in the company of female friends and family members. At the time of their migration, they were single or divorced, and they are critical of the Brazilian gender system of privilege that excluded them from the good jobs in that country. In constructing their migratory horizon, they have used to their advantage a gendered and racialized discourse of woman's body as national symbol. By appropriating nationalist discourses about the mixture of races as embodied in Brazilian women, their bodies have become an instrument of their move, a subject of commodification and desirability in the centers of power.[6]

However, although Brazilian women dancers use the discourse of an adaptable, malleable body able to venture overseas and to mingle with the foreign, they do not look at such "Western" values uncritically. As I hope to make clear, Brazilian women who work as erotic dancers have a very ambivalent attitude toward the United States and what it has brought, or failed to bring, in the name of modernity. More in tune with what has been defined as postmodern, many women I met were highly skeptical of the values of rationality and progress, and (although aiming to have access to U.S. goods and services) were quite critical of what they perceive as North American consumerist lifestyles. Many women were also critical of North Americans' ways of dealing with their bodies and sexuality, particularly as manifested in the way they eat and dress. While Kelsky (2002) and Constable (2003) found that women from Asia, for example, tend to construct an ideal of North American men as "liberated," many Brazilians, incorporating the national celebratory attitude toward sexuality, tend to see U.S. men and women as "puritanical" or "*mal-resolvido*" (unresolved) in their relation to their bodies. As middle-class women, they had a distinctive view of their bodies, their entitlements, their capabilities, and their instrumentality. Such views of their bodies translated into a knowledge of how desire functions in the global arena: how to go about finding work, where to go, what gentlemen's bars were, what kinds of bodily display and performance of national identity would enable them to make money, and what kinds of people one would be likely to meet or get involved with. Those are some of the themes that I explore in this work.

Contrary to public debate that often links migrant sex workers and human trafficking, poverty, and oppression, this association does not by any means apply to the women in my research. In fact, throughout my fieldwork, I met mostly middle-income Brazilian women who for many reasons had chosen to work as erotic dancers rather than as domestics, the other most common job available to migrant women. Some women told me they found working in another person's house demeaning to their class status. As mentioned earlier, Brazilians from the middle classes usually grow up being served by maids, often women of African descent. Indeed, to have maids in Brazil is a marker of class status and is felt as a basic need for the maintenance of a middle-class family dynamic. To work as a domestic servant in the United States would subvert a deep-rooted class and racial habitus of the Brazilian social structure, perhaps painful for many Brazilians as a signifier of their social downward mobility. In addition, in tune with their middle-class modern tastes, these women find the bar scene and New York's nightlife more appealing and exciting than the isolation of domestic work, as well as better paid.

Yet as a kind of sex worker, the erotic dancer must be viewed along a continuum that includes domestic servants and caretakers that the changes resulting from new forms of economic and social life demand.[7] Dancers are part of the services industry that involves a sort of subjective labor, difficult to define, and that some researchers have denominated "emotional labor" (Hoschchild 1983; Chapkis 1997; Augustin 2003). Characteristically, these jobs involve an intimacy between the workers and those they serve in face-to-face encounters that erase the borders of what can be described as work and what can be described as emotional involvement. Nannies' jobs illustrate the sort of resource that such work requires (see Parreñas 2001). Not only are nannies paid to keep children clean and fed but also they are expected to give the children loving attention, moral instruction, and emotional support when they fall down or when they get sick. A parallel situation exists for sex workers. Besides the allure of sexual seduction as spectacle in the case of erotic dancing, or sexual intercourse in the case of prostitution, also involved is the emotional labor of entertaining and pampering clients' self-esteem, listening to their problems, and providing affectionate support in their lives away from home. In the reconfiguration of both the public and the intimate spheres of life, as Giddens (1992) so thoroughly analyzes, much of what once belonged to the private sphere has come to be realized away from it, mediated by financial exchange—including both child care and sexual and emotional satisfaction. To meet this new demand, particularly in the centers of economic power, migrant women workers stepped in to expand the pool of native women who occupy this highly gendered social role and labor market.

The increasing presence of migrant women in the sex work industry of North America and Europe has generated heated discussions among feminists, particularly those engaged in policy making. As suggested by Augustin (2005), debate has polarized feminists between, on the one hand, those who see immigrants and particularly migrant women in the sex industry as victims of a patriarchal regime, represented both by abusive bosses and unscrupulous smugglers, and, on the other hand, those who argue that sex workers are free agents and that sex work is just another form of employment where workers must make rational calculations in terms of costs and benefits.[8] Subsumed in both perspectives are issues central to the social sciences, particularly the issue of agency (Kempadoo 1998). Both represent simplified views of the conditions and dilemmas such women face in their daily lives, whether one sees them as victims of patriarchy or as willingly crossing borders to pursue careers in sex work. Despite such heated polemic in activist and feminist circles, and while a considerable popular and academic literature focuses on erotic dancers in the United States (Price-Glynn 2010; Barton 2006; Frank 2002; Bernstein 2001; Bernstein and Shaffner 2005; Liepe-Levinson 2002; Burana 2001; Weitzer 2000; Chapkis 1997), there is virtually no ethnographic research on migrant sex workers in the United States.

In this book I document and analyze the choices that such women make, given the reality of their transnational condition, their desires, their work options, their moral dilemmas, their family structures, and the political and economic contexts in which they live. Moreover, rather than studying a professional category of sex workers, I gained insight from my relationships with just a few women into how Brazilian women in general enter and leave this market depending both on socioeconomic contexts and on their own desires. I see erotic dancing as representing certain moments in these women's lives as they accommodate its social position with competing worldviews and life-projects, which takes place in a transnational context—between the United States and Brazil.

Encounters: Self-Equation

Although I have talked informally with numerous dancers over the years that I have been going to gentlemen's bars, in this book I refer to only nine women, a few of whom I was friends with before I started my research. They are members of a network, meeting not only in the bar scene but visiting each other and living or traveling together, and have become significant in each other's lives and in my own. My research is based on informal personal encounters with these women and did not occur over a scheduled period of time but followed the rhythm of the city and of our lives. These Brazilian women were not the other to me, separated by geographical or cultural schisms.

In the encounters and the ethnographic writings typical of the colonial enterprise, the subjects of research often appeared as a generalized other, faceless subjects of governance and knowledge, to be put into categories that served the colonial regime. These writings often overemphasized dissimilarities between self and other and established a distance believed to be necessary for objective research and effective knowing. Rather than assuming the traditional role of an anthropologist, my encounters with the nine New York women took a form I like to imagine as postcolonial. Although Brazil has been free from Portuguese colonial control since the early 1800s, postcolonial thinking and writing shed light on what I was experiencing in my life in New York and on the lives of the Brazilian women I met. After all, these Brazilian women, even if they belong to the whiter Brazilian middle class, are defined, when they come to the United States, as sexualized subjects within a colonial framework that persists to this day. Brazil itself, like other emerging economies and nation-states, is still evaluated in terms of wealth and civilization as defined by Europe and the United States. There is also a postcolonial sensibility about processes of disjuncture and displacement common to those who have lived transnational lives that includes an awareness of how textual representation is connected with issues of power and authority. This sensibility has led me to construct a person-centered ethnography. The portraits of the women in this book as well as the depiction of our encounters throughout the city and transnationally are meant to capture the feelings of the moment, the nuances of their personalities, the contradictions that they were experiencing as they tried to figure out what it is to live across borders.

The first breakthrough in my research happened when I met Clara and Barbara late one night in a Queens bar, as I've mentioned. When they approached us, I was sipping a beer with a Greek American male friend who often accompanied me to the bars on these first visits. I recognized Barbara's and Clara's accents as very much like mine and asked where they were from. "From Bahia," they said. "Me, too." This was the first time I had met women from my home state in the bars, and I felt quite comfortable with them. Most of the women I had known in the bars were from either Minas Gerais or Rio de Janeiro, but now I began to meet women from states such as Goiás and Rio Grande do Sul, and a few from São Paulo. The women from Bahia became my most valuable research informants, and some of them also became my closest friends in New York. We have spent innumerable hours together in bars, in dressing rooms, in cafes and restaurants, listening to music, walking in the park, and lying around watching Brazilian soap operas and gossiping. Throughout my field research my informants/friends from Bahia became my point of entry into the bars, which helped me but also framed my presence in an inevitable way. Other dancers would talk or not talk with me according to their relationship with them.

I do not attempt in this book to represent all Brazilian women in New York, or all Brazilian dancers, for that matter. Rather, my work is bounded by our social locations and the relations that developed among women who shared some aspects of identity. As middle-class Brazilian women, we had a similar life history and some common anxieties about the present and the future, yet each woman is singular in her own way. Although based on factual people, these nine women became characters through whom I would explore possibilities and variables embedded in a larger group of women whom I met. Because the work often focuses on intimate spheres of life and ethical concerns, I created composites in order to protect the identity of my subjects. I not only changed names of places and people, but also included in these portraits characteristics drawn from similar individuals and analogous situations.

Rather than simply an ethnography of the New York strip scene, my research findings apply to Brazilian migrant women who go into and out of situations, encounters, and events as they question what their lives are about. This book is about these women as they fall in love, marry for papers or for affection, and as they confuse both; as they dance for money and for pleasure; and as they reveal both the sexual and the work parts of sex work. Although I conducted extended formal interviews with some women, I found their answers in this context rather flat, tending to reinforce the stereotypes of Brazilian women that it was my intention to question. A significant part of my data relies on the time I spent with these nine women in their daily lives. We visited and called each other frequently, hung out in ordinary bars and cafes, went dancing and traveling together, and helped each other make decisions. My involvement in their lives beyond the bar scene gave me more intimate knowledge of the complex deliberations that women have to make, given the emotional and material considerations involved. Close and continuous contact with these women over time also allowed me to watch the ways in which their relationship to men evolved and the changes in their trajectories of desire. My knowledge of their relationships came from direct observations of important events in their lives and from sharing their reflections as they made life-changing decisions.

Thus, I report informal conversations from my fieldwork that make sense only in context. I depict scenes, which, as Crapanzano (2005) notes, are not mere factual portrayals of events or situations. By capturing elements of color, humor, emotion, frustration, and the momentary, scenes are more capable of conveying subjective—or rather intersubjective—aspects of reality. Some of the reflections that I construct through these scenes originated in a third space that Crapanzano describes as common to all anthropologists—a "third" space where we feel a "fusion" with the thoughts of our subjects. As a "native" anthropologist, this seemed even more to the point. Although my work is not autobiographical, I use autobiographical reflections to better convey the complexity of my relationships with the women I met and the effect that current transnational events have on all our lives—because each of these nine women, in one way or another, has had a significant impact on my own life.

Organization of Chapters

The structure of this volume follows a spatial and temporal logic. It first traces the lives of nine Brazilian dancers while they were still living in Brazil, continues with their move to New York City where they work as erotic dancers, and goes back and forth between Brazil and the United States following the transnational logics of their lives.

In Part I, "Brazil: The Anti-postcard," I explore what it meant for them/us to be part of the at once privileged and unstable Brazilian middle class. What did it mean to be in college in the 1980s and 1990s when Brazil was experiencing both a democratic awakening and a spiraling inflation that reached 1,000 percent a year? What were their goals, their relationships with men and women, their dilemmas and frustrations, their ways of dealing with their bodies, given Brazilian nationalist ideologies and our location within the racial system of the country? In Chapter 2, "Representing the Nation: Class, Race, and Sexuality," I examine how the category of *morenas* to which the women and I belong functions as a signifier of women's capacity to mix not only races, but also cultures.

Part II explores the ways in which Brazilian middle-class women are socially located in the New York context. Looking at identity as it is constructed in space and place, I try to understand how race and identity are reconfigured as these women move between nation-states. Relocating to the borough of Queens represents a profound transformation in these women's racial and class identification. More significantly, they are racialized through the deployment of their sexuality as erotic dancers. In Queens gentlemen's bars and in the larger society, these women are ambiguously reinscribed as "Hispanics," a label that assigns both racial position and class location in U.S. society.

In Chapter 3, "Hierarchies of Bars and Bodies," I examine the social organization of the bars in which Brazilian women find work as erotic dancers vis-à-vis the social geography of New York City's racial and class distribution. In Chapter 4, "Performing Seduction and National Identity," I look at the ways in which dancers' interactions with other dancers work toward reproducing hierarchies of class and race through specific displays of sexuality, a language of morality, and ways of performing national identity. Chapter 5, "Women and Clients," examines how dancers can discern by observation the national, class, and educational background of each client, and the possibilities, limits, advantages, and risks that the various kinds of relationship with clients carry. Unlike dancers who are U.S. nationals, who seem to have more restricted relationships with clients, Brazilian women seek to extend some of their social connections beyond the bar encounter. By emphasizing the performative aspects of dancers' actions and attitudes, I argue that what happens inside the bar has a significant effect on women's lives far beyond the bar scene.

In Part III, "Beyond the Bar Scene," I suggest that what occurs in the bar scene interferes with these women's relationships with others and with the larger society. In Chapter 6, "Ambivalent Relationships," I examine the options available to women in their relationships to various men and the consequences these relationships have for their incorporation into U.S. society. In "Transnational Ties," Chapter 7, I look at the consequences in Brazil of the women's work, relationships, and lifestyles in the United States. In Chapter 8, "Expanding Networks," I explore the lives and dilemmas of three men who, once they became involved with Brazilian dancers in New York, decided to go to Brazil to expand their relationship across borders. In the Conclusion, I consider the implications of the findings of the research and offer personal reflections on the meaning that living between two countries has for me and for the women who participated in my research.

The Women: In Transit

Clara

Clara is one of the eighteen women in her extended family who migrated to New York from the countryside of Bahia in northeast Brazil. Clara's mother, a dentist, has always encouraged her to have a career of her own. Clara, now thirty-two years old, grew up in a middle-class family that identified itself with the markers of modernity, expressed in consumer power, investment in education, and foreign travel. When she was thirteen years old, her parents got divorced, and she moved with her mother and her sister to the capital, Salvador, and spent much time in a smaller city where her grandfather was the mayor. For her fifteenth birthday, her mother sent her to Disney World for a holiday. After high school she went to a private law school, financed by her parents. As she puts it, she lived the normal life of a university student, going to parties, dating, and traveling around with her friends. Clara graduated from law school in 1995, passed the bar exam, and started working as an assistant lawyer for a private company. Still, she could not afford to live on her own, and her mother continued supporting her financially.

After Clara had spent two years struggling with her financial instability and lack of career prospects, her aunt Gina, who had lived in New York for two years with her daughter, arrived in Bahia for a visit. Gina worked as an erotic dancer. Seeing Clara's difficulties in making ends meet, Gina suggested she come to New York and stay with her. Upon her arrival, Clara—and Nadja, a lawyer friend who came with her—immediately started dancing, following the path and advice of her aunt and three cousins who were also dancers. She describes her first year of dancing as "fun." She loved the fast flow of money, the ability to buy new clothes and accessories, to pay her bills, and to rent an apartment on her own. She also loved the party scene. Through the years I have known her, Clara has changed her life quite dramatically. She started going out with an older Greek man and then became pregnant by a white American man who didn't want the child. She moved in with the Greek, who made it his mission to help her with the baby and with her life. He helped her pay for a marriage to an African American to gain legal status in the United States. Then she got together with the father of her daughter, and the Greek became her daughter's godfather. In order to meet her and her daughter's expenses and supplement the household's budget, Clara continued to dance. Although she was ambivalent about the role of housewife, that was what she became after a while.

Barbara

I met Barbara on the same night that I met Clara, and through the years she has become one of my closest friends in New York. Barbara is thirty-seven years old and was born in the same city as Clara. It was actually through contact with the other women in Clara's extended family that Barbara came to live and work in New York. She is from a lower-middle-class family but married the son of a local doctor, thus ascending to a comfortable upper-middle-class life. She had a child from that marriage, which lasted fourteen years. With financial support from her husband, she opened a restaurant but eventually had to close it down in 1999 when Brazil's economy took a turn for the worse. That coincided with the dismantling of her marriage. She stayed in the same city, tried to open up another business, and got involved with a man from Clara's family. Neither the relationship nor the business worked out and, after working at a few low-paying secretarial jobs, Barbara decided that it was time to try something different. Her chances of getting a visa to the United States were not good, but she decided to try anyway, and it was with surprise that she succeeded and saw a radical change in her life working out.

Although born in a city with no more than thirty thousand inhabitants in Bahia, Barbara says she always considered herself a "cosmopolitan." She knew what was happening in the world, kept up with the latest trends in fashion, and could see movies and hear music from everywhere as they came to that corner of the country. She describes her first week in New York as presenting "no real surprises." She had a pretty good idea of the work she was going to do and had brought outfits for dancing. Upon her arrival, she was received by the women in Clara's family, with whom she lived for a time. After a few months dancing in three nightclubs in Queens, she met a man of Hispanic descent who became her husband in a few months. Although one of the main motivations for the marriage was to legalize her stay in this country, the couple also had an intense, yet troubled, love relationship. Her husband's problems with alcohol proved to be a major drawback. Still, she stayed with him for two years, after which she received a permanent green card and divorced him. She now lives with another dancer from Bahia, Nadja, whom she met through Clara, still works in three bars in Queens, and is taking photography classes. "Barbara" is the name she chose for herself because it is the name of her protector, Saint Barbara, who is also the goddess Iansã in the African-Bahian religion, Candomblé. The goddess of tempests, Iansã/Saint Barbara likes only red flowers, with which Barbara keeps Saint Barbara's little statue in her bedroom provided.

Nana

Nana is a thirty-four-year-old woman who has been in my life since our college days in Bahia. She has black hair that reaches almost to her hips and very white skin, a whiteness that she protects from the sun and that contrasts wonderfully with her long dark hair. She is a striking beauty and was always considered so back home. She has a degree in sociology from the same university that I attended, but our paths had not crossed since our undergraduate days. I became an academic and hold some left-wing political ideas. She wanted to make money and developed a stronger sense of feminist anger from having to deal with a market more competitive than the academy. I moved to New York when I was twenty-five and would meet her once in a while during my trips home. One year, in the middle of a street party when we were both already drunk, she asked me: "Is it true that a woman can make a lot of money dancing in bars in New York?" Next thing I knew, in August 2003, Nana called me from Astoria. "I am dancing," she said, "and living with Clara." "Cool," I said. I took the subway the next day to Astoria. I was one of the few people she knew in New York besides Barbara, and now Clara.

Nana and I became closer friends in New York than we had ever been in Brazil. We see or call each other at least once a week, participate in each other's lives, and love and hate each other as any very close friends do. We sometimes talk so much and so continuously about our lives that we get tired and promise not to call each other for a while. But it never works.

Throughout her life, Nana has experienced the free lifestyle of a modern single woman, living first with female roommates and then by herself. The prospect of buying her own apartment, along with her desire to travel and pay off some old debts, were the immediate reasons that Nana gives for deciding to leave Brazil. Despite her relative success in her profession as a state sociologist, her salary in Brazil, about $500 a month, could not support her lifestyle and ambitions. Besides economic and professional frustration, Nana particularly expresses a profound dissatisfaction with gender roles in Brazil and the lack of what she considers desirable and available men. Through her friendship with Barbara, she learned about the work of go-go dancers in New York and about the kind of income she could expect. She started working as a dancer the same week she moved to New York and danced for about a year and a half. Before the expiration of her six-month U.S. visa, she met and married a young white American, Jimmy, through whom she got a green card and became a legal U.S. resident. Nana has recently cut her hair because as she said she didn't want to look Hispanic anymore. Barbara and I disapproved of her remark but said nothing to her.

Ivana

It was a cold winter day when I met Ivana in her basement apartment in Astoria for coffee, after being introduced to her by Nana. She seemed to me so mature, it was difficult to believe that she was only twenty-three years old. She is from the south of Brazil and had been living in the United States for a year before we met in 2002. She was born in a large city but moved to the countryside with her family after she and her brother were kidnapped by a gang for three days and after her father was stabbed in front of their house. The family chose a city of thirteen thousand inhabitants, leaving behind a lifestyle that Ivana would always long for. Soon after, her father, who was a doctor and twenty-five years older than her mother, died of a heart attack, leaving behind Ivana's family and three older children from a previous marriage. Her mother, who was a lawyer but had never worked, suddenly became the family provider for their two children. Not surprisingly the family experienced downward social mobility, despite the help of family and friends. Indeed, it was this network that made it possible for the two children to travel not only within Brazil but also to the United States, where two of their siblings from her father's first marriage were living.

Despite the difficulties, her mother sent her two children to private school in a larger city six miles away. Ivana remembers this daily trip as marking a disjuncture between her lived reality and the promise of a broader world elsewhere. Ivana says that, although people in her small town had some money, their children did not have any ambition beyond following in their parents' footsteps. She, however, had other role models—people who had moved to bigger cities and to the United States. Indeed, her mother's sister lived in New York, where she first worked as a go-go dancer and later had a career as a nurse in a Harlem hospital, and Ivana's older brother worked in a travel agency in New York City. Although moving to the United States was for Ivana the logical thing to consider after finishing high school, she decided to go to law school and applied for work in the city. For a couple of years, she commuted from her town to another city to go to university, and earned about $200 a month working in a city office. In 2000 her brother visited Brazil on vacation and decided to take her back to the United States with him. Although she had a leave of absence from school, she quit her job and had no plans to ever go back to Brazil; she told her mother to give away all the things she left behind and that if she wanted to see her again, she would have to go to New York. For some time, Ivana has dated a Greek man, Chris, thirty years older. She told me that she had empathized with him since the first time he came to the bar where she was working—this empathy, not money, is the reason she goes out with him, she said. Her friends and I worry about this relationship and think that she is too young and is getting too involved with him.

Renata

I met Renata through Nana, whom she met when dancing at La Casa, a gentlemen's bar in Queens, and who became her best friend in New York. When remembering their first meeting, they both speak of recognizing the other's awkwardness about working in the nightclub. They both said that they could immediately recognize that they did not fit there. Thirty-four years old and from a lower-middle-class family in the state of Minas Gerais, Renata had worked as a secretary in a bank for many years in Belo Horizonte until she decided to move to a smaller tourist town in the south of Bahia, Porto Seguro, where she had some relatives. There she met a man whom she lived with for five years. Sérgio had a small business for which Renata also used to work that she described as "going nowhere." The relationship did not seem very promising either. Nevertheless, they decided to move to New York in 2001, partly as a result of an armed robbery of their home that also diminished their business prospects. They decided that Renata would migrate first and meet with her cousins who were already living in New York, one of them working as a go-go dancer.

Renata did not plan to come to New York to work as a dancer. First she worked as a manicurist for a Brazilian salon and also as a housecleaner. She says that she felt rather exploited by the Brazilians who owned the business where she was working, and after a few months she decided to ask her dancer cousin to introduce her to the bar scene. She described her first few times dancing as traumatic, but because she badly needed the money, she decided to overcome her shyness and started dancing in Queens five times a week. It was in a Queens gentlemen's bar that she met Brandon, an Irish American fireman from Long Island. Although Renata's initial plan was to make money and prepare to welcome her Brazilian boyfriend, Sérgio, who would soon join her, all had changed. She told me that upon her arrival in New York, she had started questioning her relationship with Sérgio. When he eventually arrived from Brazil a few months after her own trip, she was already dancing and had already met Brandon.

The lack of a vision for the future and a job—the insecurity of life that characterized her relationship with Sérgio—was even more apparent compared to the prospect of a relationship with a working-class white American man and the secure lifestyle that Brandon could offer. She broke up with Sérgio, and after a few months Brandon invited her to live with him. After moving in, at Brandon's request Renata stopped dancing and started devoting her time to the house, the relationship, and the English classes Brandon paid for. With another six months until her visa expired, a time of much anxiety for her, Brandon finally decided to marry her. They had an expensive wedding on Long Island and another one in Brazil in December of the same year. Recently, Renata found a job as a housecleaner twice a week for a wealthy family not far from where she and Brandon live. She says she will never go back to dancing.

Nadja

Nadja is a thirty-six-year-old woman born in the capital of Bahia, Salvador, to a lower-middle-class family. She worked her way into law school, where she met Clara, with whom she came to New York in 1999. I met Nadja through Barbara, who became her roommate after she got divorced. Nadja's relationship to me was always somewhat ambivalent, ranging from cold and reticent to intimate and confessional. Sometimes, she would start telling me things about her life without my inquiring about it, stressing how hard she worked and how much she made because she had to help her family back home. Over the years, Nadja has sent enough money to Brazil for her father to buy a truck for himself and for her brother to buy a house. She also bought a four-bedroom apartment in an upper-middle-class neighborhood for herself and has opened a clothing store in Brazil, all paid for with money she made from dancing. She is the only one in this close group of women who worked in Manhattan, which explains her more abundant cash flow. While the other dancers make an average of $200 working in

Queens, Nadja can make around $700 on a good night. In Manhattan, however, women work topless and perform one-on-one dances with clients in the so-called Champagne Rooms, in which the boundaries of what is and is not permitted are more fluid. These circumstances may explain Nadja's sometimes paradoxical relationship to me.

Upon her arrival in New York, Nadja lived for a while with women of Clara's family, then rented small rooms in other people's apartments, usually other dancers. In contrast to the other women in this group, whose goal is to establish themselves in the United States and who immediately upon arrival sought the means to do so, particularly through their relationship to men, Nadja tends to see her stay as temporary. Her life is somewhat precarious, as revealed by the way she lives. Her bedroom is packed with cases containing her belongings, from clothes to letters and decorative objects that do not seem to fit anywhere. Although she went on frequent dates with American men from whom she accepted gifts and money, she has never had a steady relationship with any of them.

For years, Nadja has been in a relationship with a Brazilian man from a Rio de Janeiro upper-middle-class family whom all her friends consider a loser. With no steady job and constantly commuting between New York and Brazil, Daniel never wanted to become engaged to Nadja, which was a source of constant strain in the relationship. The other women had a strong incentive to marry—that is, to obtain legal status—which was or was not accompanied by romantic motivation. For Nadja and Daniel, romantic motivation was not enough to push either of them into the decision to marry, meanwhile keeping them from making other possibly more advantageous arrangements. Nadja, however, periodically obsesses and talks about marriage, for she believes that getting married is a necessary step toward becoming a successful woman and fears the stigma of spinsterhood. She has recently gone back to Brazil, where she takes care of her clothing store. However, according to Barbara, Nadja is thinking about coming back to New York and dancing again. It is not clear if she will be able to renew her visa, having let it expire before she left the United States.

Sara

Sara, forty-five years old, is one of ten siblings of Clara's mother. I came to know her through Barbara. She lives in Astoria near Barbara and Nadja's apartment, and Barbara and I sometimes go to her place to watch Brazilian soap operas on her cable TV in the early evening when they were not working. Since the first time I saw her, Sara has struck me as a woman of authority, the result of her strong body and her carriage, which makes her look taller than she is. She has long reddish hair extensions, wears tight clothes and high heels most of the time, and has a fondness for glamorous fake-fur coats. She goes out with men who seem to adore her, and she likes bossing them around. Her apartment is filled with photographs of the women in her family—beautiful women, I comment every time I walk into her place. Sara likes telling jokes, some of which I find distasteful and racist. Sometimes she comes to Barbara's apartment to chat when I am there, and she loves analyzing her body and face and figuring out new ways to improve herself: Botox, lifts, gym visits, facials, new clothes, and new ways of smiling. Her obsession with her body and what I came to perceive as her self-consciousness in performing femininity make me feel uncomfortable and sometimes unfeminine and awkward in my clothes and body.

Before she came to the United States, Sara had a good government job in the transportation department in a midsized town in Bahia through the influence of her family. With the increasing cuts in government expenditures, Sara watched her earnings significantly dwindle over the years. Divorced and with an adolescent son just about to go to college, she decided to join her sisters in New York. She has been dancing for about three years, mainly at Highway on the outskirts of Queens. She says she does not like to work in the same area in which she lives so she does not run into her clients when she is not working. She hangs out a lot in Astoria and has a Greek boyfriend, an Italian lover, and an African American husband, whom she married for papers.

Teresa

I met Teresa one late night at Highway gentlemen's club. I was talking to a few dancers in the basement dressing room when she came in carrying suitcases full of string bikinis, small skirts, and dresses. The women gathered around her during their breaks and took turns trying the outfits on and commenting on how they looked. My presence immediately caught her attention, since I was the only one wearing street clothes. Why didn't I try them on? Although I explained that I was not a dancer, she insisted that I should give it a try and proceeded to choose the outfit that would best fit my skin color and body shape. On this and all the other occasions when we met, she tried to convince me that studying dancers was not enough. She wanted me to try to make some money by dancing, investigating the possibilities of my own body and seductive power.

A forty-seven-year-old woman from a middle-class family from Recife, in northeastern Brazil, Teresa has a degree in psychology and held a position as the chief director of a center for battered women in Recife. She also shared a small clothing factory with a boyfriend, but the love and the business partnership failed after a few years—the immediate reason for her decision to come to New York. She also alludes to her frustration with the lack of social results from her work and with the social conditions of Brazil in general.

When she decided to make the trip, Teresa did not know anyone in New York and had only an address of a friend and a name of a hotel. She did not meet this person, however; instead, a taxi driver at the airport told her he knew a place where other Brazilians lived and where she could certainly rent a room for much less than she would pay for a hotel. So she decided to go to Astoria and stayed in a boardinghouse for the first few months. She worked as a housecleaner until she heard about the possibilities of go-go dancing. Teresa sees herself as a revolutionary in the dancing business. Despite her advanced age for a dancer, during the years she danced in Queens bars, she was, by her account, one of the most successful women in the business. While the other women changed outfits once or twice during a shift, she brought a suitcase full so she could perform different characters each night. How long she worked as a dancer was never clear to me—sometimes she said one year, and other times three or four. (This apparent confusion was common among dancers, as they sometimes have a hard time admitting to themselves and to others to having been in the business for much longer than they had initially planned.)

Teresa danced until she met someone she fell in love with, an Italian man in his fifties who manages a restaurant in Manhattan. They had a relationship for about three years, but he could never share a life with her since he was already married (he did not live with his wife, but for financial reasons he would not get divorced). The ambivalence of their relationship and his inability to commit to her led to their breakup. Now she lives by herself and owns a small store where she sells mainly products from Brazil, as well as a small manufacturing business (just her and one or two seamstresses) where she makes outfits for dancers. She also sells those outfits by visiting the bars late at night.

Justine

"Justine" was her artistic name during the years she danced, and it surrounds her with an aura of mystery; her life has always been equally mysterious to me. We met in the Photography Department at the School of Visual Arts, where we both worked as nude models—we first saw each other as naked bodies. Her lean, tall, dark body intimidated me, and it was not until we met again at a Brazilian night at Nublu, a fashionable bar on Avenue C in downtown Manhattan, that we started to talk. She called me before I could call her. We agreed to meet in Union Square and walked down to the East Village, which is still our favorite space in the city to meet. Justine, the daughter of an upper-middle-class family from Minas Gerais, came to New York the same year I did. She is three years older than I, and a free spirit and an intellectual. We exchanged Anaïs Nin's diaries the second time we met and like to think of ourselves as free feminists, by which we mean that we do not necessarily follow any settled path but like to explore different ways of experiencing sexuality, body, and gender. She has a master's degree in philosophy from a university in Brazil and had dropped out of her

CUNY Graduate Center program, finding it too conservative. I didn't find out that she was a topless dancer in an upscale bar in Manhattan until a couple of years after we met.

Justine used to dance in Manhattan and made enough money to commute between New York and Paris for three years. Then she married for love and papers, worked as a dancer and an artist's model for a few years, and later, with the support of her husband, resumed her doctoral studies. Like many things in Justine's life, her husband and her life with him are surrounded by secrecy. However, she really enjoys talking about her many lovers. That's when she feels that she is transgressing social rules, and when her humor is at its best. With the security of a husband and house, she feels free to meet men from other social and racial backgrounds. Among her lovers are an African American, a man from the Caribbean, an Italian, an Algerian, a Russian, a Frenchman, a Canadian, and a Brazilian who crossed the U.S.-Mexican border and whom we call a "punk from the periphery." ("U.N. pussy" is how Barbara refers to women curious to experiment with men from different national backgrounds.) Justine has a distinct inclination to fall intensely in love with most of her lovers, at least for a few days or months. She has recently divorced and moved to Rio de Janeiro, where she became a university professor and started surfing, an old dream of hers. On the phone, we continue our long discussions about movies, men, women, travels, books, pornography, and the nature of being in the world.

Part I

Brazil, the Anti-postcard

Chapter 1

Middle-Class Trajectories

Would like to address myself, in a straight line,
directly, without courier, only to you, but I do not
arrive, and that is the worst of it. A tragedy, my love,
of destination. Everything becomes a postcard once
more, legible for the other, even if he understands
nothing about it.
    —Derrida, *The Postcard*[1]

As I now travel to Brazil feeling as if I should send a message back to a home that evades a precise geographic location, I stroll through tourist centers looking at postcards that I fantasize about sending—and never do. Images of beaches are juxtaposed with Rio de Janeiro's statue of Christ and semi-naked women's bodies in carnival parades. A number of postcards picture people of darker skin colors, some of them wearing typical regional costumes. What the postcards fail to depict are the polluted waters of the ocean, the shantytowns, and the urban violence so widespread in Brazil. Also absent from the stereotypical views, both those of national celebration and the depictions of poverty as folklore, are images of middle-class people and the landscapes they inhabit. They are just not exotic enough, not authentic enough for the tourist gaze. What is there to attract the viewer in images of shopping malls, traffic jams, airports, and antiseptic office buildings that can be found anywhere?

Brazilian middle-class women hold a paradoxical position in relation to the Brazilian nation, caught between antithetical views of what it means to be Brazilian and what it means to be part of a global project of modernity. As Bourdieu (1984) argues in his study of the French class system, one's position in the social class system is the result of a complex combination of subjective and objective factors. These include variables such as income and ownership of land, houses, and durable goods, as well as one's family history, taste, aesthetic preferences, and relationship to other classes. In the case of the middle class in "peripheral" countries of the Global South (Johnson 1985),[2] other factors must also be considered: the colonial and post- and neocolonial relation to centers of political and economic power, racial configurations, ways of dealing with drastic changes in the politics and economics of a country, and the perceived or real experience of violence and urban chaos (Caldeira 2000).

As members of the middle class from the Global South (De Kooning 2005; Fernandes 2000; Guano 2002), the women in my research inhabit a space between the local reality and the global promises of modernity. This makes problematic their identity in regard to a fixed geography, as supplied by a specific relationship to a nation-state. Appadurai (1990) and Gupta (1992) argue that national identity is just one form of organizing space and that attention should be given to other forms of conceptualizing what Benedict Anderson has called "imagined communities." In Gupta's (1992) assessment of Anderson's work, he points out that the elite and middle class of the Third World do not necessarily identify horizontally with the other constituencies that are part of the same nation-state—that is, the working class, which in Brazil correspond to racialized others of darker skin color. Rather, the peripheral elite and middle class are more likely to identify with the elite and middle class of the First World centers of power. This identification, however, can never be complete. If, on the one hand, the women's location and lighter skin color puts them in a position of relative privilege in Brazil, on the other, their participation in a global middle-class identity is impaired by a disadvantaged position in the hierarchy of nations.

The relationship of the peripheral middle class to the centers of power is subject to debate. In Gupta's work on transnational imagined communities, for example, the elite and middle class of the Global South seem only to mimic their northern counterparts. In contrast, Partha Chatterjee (1993), in his analysis of the Indian case, argues that nationalism in the colonies cannot be described as an imitation of nationalism in the colonial centers but is defined based "on difference" from the centers, in the context of anticolonial struggles, as a "domain of sovereignty of civil society." According to Chatterjee, the idea of nation in India entails two different spheres: the material and the spiritual. In the material sphere, the Indian nation has succumbed to the superiority of the West, as expressed through technological advancement and the accumulation of wealth and power. In the second sphere, the spiritual, not only is India autonomous in relation to the West, but also through this sphere Indian nationalist discourses can critique Western values. Still following Chatterjee's argument, in the process of defining a national sovereign identity, family and sexuality—particularly women's sexuality—become subjects and symbols of a different kind of modernity. In tune with his argument, I also believe that a consideration of Third World nationalism in its historical depth can add to the discussion about the relationship between centers and peripheries.

Growing Up as Global Nationals

As the nine dancers' portraits show, the involvement of Brazilian women in transnational migration practices is not the consequence of just one factor. It is rather the result of a series of events such as the Brazilian economic crisis, the restructuring of the world economy and the disruption of local economies, the massive entrance of women into the labor market, and changes in consumer behavior, as well as shifts in gender relations, sexuality, lifestyle, and expectations. The turns that the women's lives took epitomize a trajectory for many women from the Brazilian middle class. Growing up in the 1970s, we inherited the promise that Brazil would catch up with First World nations, a promise of sharing the world of educated professional women who could travel around the world and experience a modern life. For the most part, our parents participated in the expansion of the Brazilian middle class financed by the influx of capital that flooded Third World countries with development projects. In the 1960s and 1970s, U.S. money, goods, and information invaded Brazilian homes.[3] Brazil's TV Globo, the main television network in Latin America (which was subsidized by the military government), transmitted TV shows and commercials simultaneously in the United States and Brazil (Simpson 1993). Jeans, TVs, refrigerators, vacations at the beach, cinemas, shopping malls, and cameras—these were goods that all middle-class women took for granted and that we associated with the United States.

As I remember growing up in that period, typical middle-class families lived in nice comfortable houses with patios open to the streets; our fathers drove Volkswagen Beetles, soon to be replaced by American Chevrolets. Education was extended to more people, and record players, telephones, and TVs became essential to one's sense of existence and of the fantastic. U.S. television series dubbed into Brazilian Portuguese were part of our reality and daily life; Brazilian soap operas had (and perhaps still have) two soundtracks, one national and the other international. Not being able to understand the words of U.S. songs only added to one's curiosity about distant places and faraway romantic encounters. Mothers like Clara's, a dentist, and my own took jobs outside the house. They were freed from most domestic work thanks to the availability of cheap labor provided by poorer women, usually of dark skin color, who worked as domestic servants. Under the military regime between 1964 and 1985—and particularly between 1968 and 1973, the years of the so-called economic miracle—the Brazilian middle class expanded with the support of state-subsidized projects and the expansion of welfare and the service economy, financed by heavy borrowing from international financial institutions such as the International Monetary Fund (IMF) and the World Bank (Veltmeyer, Petras, and Vieux 1997).

After 1982, when Mexico announced that it would no longer continue to pay back its external debt, the international lending agencies radically altered their policies toward Latin America. The IMF and the World Bank shifted their focus from poverty alleviation investments to harsh pressure on debtor countries to pay back their debt. "Structural adjustment" policies imposed by Washington-based institutions entailed trade liberalization, market deregulation, privatization of state enterprises, and downsizing of the state apparatus. As in other parts of the world, particularly in the Global South (Veltmeyer, Petras, and Vieux 1995), the results of this so-called structural adjustment were a critical reduction of wages and social benefits, a dramatic increase in poverty, and the general deterioration of middle-class living standards. In Brazil, the state's financial crisis and the inability of the banking system to stabilize the country's economy led to soaring rates of unemployment and inflation of more than 100 percent a month in the 1980s.

Those economic transformations coincided with the end of twenty years of military dictatorship (1964–1984). The 1986 political campaign for "Diretas Já" (the public's right to "vote now"), the main theme of Tancredo Neves's presidential electoral effort, marked the first time people were allowed to congregate in large numbers for a political event since the repressive days of military rule. During that period our professors and parents had personally experienced or known of demonstrators running from the police and being arrested and deported, and there was much anxiety about this political turn. But the anxiety that this new generation of protestors felt was accompanied by a great sense of liberation that applied not just to the struggle to vote, but also to the freedom to speak up publicly, to go out on one's own, and to trust in the future. Yet contrary to the expected left turn in the political sphere, the neoliberal language of modernity still appealed to the middle class. In her analysis of the Brazilian middle class in these "transitional years," O'Dougherty (2002) shows how the media constructed Fernando Collor de Mello, a politician in his early forties from the Northeast, as the face of a modern Brazil—young and promising. Representing the neoliberal model, President Collor (1990–1992) gave new impetus to the implementation of the structural adjustment demanded by the IMF and the opening of the market to foreign goods. The middle class viewed expanding the market to imports as an opportunity to catch up with the First World in terms of consumer goods.

In March 1990, in a spectacular radical plan to curtail inflation, Collor announced that personal withdrawals from savings accounts would be limited to 50,000 cruzados ($1,200 US). The remaining savings would be confiscated by the Central Bank and converted into the new currency eighteen months later. In September and October 1990, bankruptcies in Brazil increased 233 percent (O'Dougherty 2002). The country's "modernization" efforts came to a halt as state accounts were paralyzed and work interrupted. Exports stagnated and unemployment skyrocketed; it was estimated that during this period sixty million people were living below the poverty level. From her examination of contemporary media reports, O'Dougherty (ibid.) concludes that the media constructed the middle class as the main victim of this economic crisis and moral chaos, but she argues that in fact working-class people suffered most from Collor's disastrous economic plan.

Adjusting to the Crisis: The 1980s and 1990s

When I asked the women in my research group how they had experienced this period, I was surprised to learn that it seemed to them far in the past. They had heard of many people whose lives were transformed with the sudden disappearance of their savings, but none of the women felt directly affected. Corroborating O'Dougherty's (2002) findings, an important strategy these women used to maintain their middle-class identity during this time was to invest in education. Clara, Nadja, Nana, Justine, and I were attending college in the 1980s and early 1990s, with the financial support of our families. Both Clara and Nadja, for example, described this period of their lives as "a lot of fun." Away from their families, they were experimenting with drinking, dating, studying, and partying, as college students do. However, the strikes that often interrupted classes in the federal universities beginning in the 1980s represented the first cracks in the nation's promised modernization.[4]

Barbara, who lived in a country town and was busy getting married and raising a child, experienced this period differently. The pragmatic Barbara talks little about politics. She remembers the late 1980s and particularly the early 1990s, when she opened a restaurant, as symbolized by the small calculator she carried to check the value of currency from one month to another, or even from day to day. "But that was part of life," she says. "When we think of it now, it all seems crazy, but back then we just had to deal with it and go on with our lives." Despite the country's economic and political crises, Barbara's life was more comfortable than before. She had married into an upper-middle-class family. She had a house to take care of, maids to manage, and a store of her own. Her calculator suggests another strategy that O'Dougherty points to as defining class identity in a moment of economic crisis: "immediatism in buying." Since the Plano Collor, with their savings accounts confiscated by the state and inflation significantly devaluing the currency from one week to the next, people found that buying durable and nondurable goods was a way of investing. Shopping strategies within and outside the country became important activities for the Brazilian middle class.

As I can clearly remember, U.S. appliances such as cordless phones, VCRs, and personal computers became common, increasingly viewed as necessary as people started traveling back and forth to the United States, bringing with them goods, information, and values. Traveling abroad, besides a shopping activity, became a way of investing in symbolic capital as part of one's education. According to data collected by O'Dougherty (2002), by 1997, four hundred thousand Brazilians were going to Disney World annually, a trip O'Dougherty views as a way to participate in an imagined global middle-class experience. What her data do not reveal, however, is that a trip to Disney World was often just an excuse for getting a tourist visa to enter the United States—the Magic Kingdom had become a stopover for a more permanent stay in the United States.

If in the 1980s there was still some optimism in the air, by the mid- to late 1990s, the women in my project were feeling the effects of the economic crisis and the consequences of privatization and downsizing in more dramatic ways. As demonstrated in studies on the consequences of structural adjustment policies, women have been the most affected by the neoliberal turn in Third World countries (Veltmeyer, Petras, and Vieux 1997; Freeman 2000). The way erotic dancers from the Brazilian middle class experienced this period depended upon the way political and economic changes intersected specific moments in their lives. For Clara and Nadja, graduation from law school in the mid-1990s failed to fulfill their expectations.[5] Although the participation of women in Brazil's labor force increased from less than 15 percent in 1950 to nearly 40 percent in 1990 (Plank 1996), this participation was not equally distributed among the professions. Law continued to be a male-dominated field. Clara and Nadja both worked with a male lawyer who systematically denied them the means to advance in their careers, treating them as his personal assistants.

To Sara, who was already in her thirties and pursuing a career outside the home, the economic crisis intersected with her social and job location in no less definite ways. Sara was among the first generation of women from her family to occupy a powerful position outside the home. Thanks to her own skills and with the crucial help of her politically influential family, she took an administrative position in a government office when she graduated at age twenty-seven. In the 1990s, Sara was already divorced and had a son. With the freedom afforded by her social position, she and her seven siblings enjoyed a life of comfort and conspicuous consumption.[6] This lifestyle became impossible with the economic downturn that resulted from the decline in the production and market value of cocoa, the main produce of her family's *fazendas*. Most of the family wealth dissipated, and although they kept their properties and durable goods, the flow of easy cash came to an end. Although Sara's work paid well by Brazilian standards, it was not enough to sustain the lifestyle that she was used to and that she wanted to pass on to her child.

Urban violence increased considerably with the economic downturn, and socializing in public spaces was transformed by fear and violence.[7] In São Paulo, for example, one of the most unequal cities in the world, an upper-class minority hires private security and flies to work in helicopters in order to avoid traffic, pollution, and criminality, while members of the middle class are vulnerable targets for robbery, both in violent and armed forms and in the daily petty crimes of street kids. A few women in my project have experienced this violence firsthand. Among them is Renata, who with her boyfriend owned a small juice distribution business in Porto Seguro. After she was fired from a secretarial position at a local bank in 1992, Renata started a small business selling processed juice for *lanchonetes* (snack bars) with her boyfriend, and was barely maintaining her middle-class standard of life. She had sold her car and now had to use the business truck as transport. Vacations were out of the question. While relaxing on a weekend in their house, where their business was also located, Renata and her boyfriend were attacked by five robbers who immobilized them and took all the money they had made over the week. While other members of the middle class, such as the other women who were in college at this time, lived in apartment buildings protected by doormen and surrounded by walls, lower-middle-class houses, such as that of Renata and her boyfriend, became yet more vulnerable to attacks. Ivana, who was still a child in the late 1980s, had a more dramatic experience of violence:

she and her brothers were kidnapped for three days in their midsized hometown in southern Brazil.

Even if the other women have not undergone such trauma, like most Brazilians they have a pervasive fear that anything can happen, at any moment, to anyone. Fear is one of the most widespread emotions in Brazilian society, and middle-class Brazilians live in a state of constant tension and fear that something might happen either to them or to someone they know. More than just material privilege, comfort involves a certain way of being in the world, of inhabiting a house, a car, and a city. One might say, for example, that owning a car is a sign of comfort. But driving anywhere in the Global South, one is constantly reminded that one owns a car against the poverty outside the car. Street kids, almost invariably of darker skin color, knock on one's window selling water, pens, or cookies, or threatening one's arm with a broken glass—and that, I assure you, in my experience as a native, is not comfortable for anyone. This might sound inappropriate for a middle-class philanthropic scholar or visitor, who understandably is drawn to sympathize not with the driver but with the peddlers, and to dismiss the driver as part of the exploitative local bourgeoisie. In a visit of a few days, one may experience the fear of being robbed as an annoyance, but this fades to just a memory, a snapshot, as soon as one leaves the country. However, as Crapanzano's (1986) study of white South Africans shows, everyone who *belongs* to a violent society is affected by it: the silence, the waiting for something—anything—to happen, as one fears to risk leaving one's home at night, as one fears to drive a car to work.

Doubting Modernity, Imagining the Move

Sitting around the table on Christmas Day in Clara's apartment with some of her cousins and aunts, sharing food and soft drinks while her Greek boyfriend watched TV, we discussed the sense of personal loss that came with our transnational moves. "Me? I suffer so much from a sense of loss that if I stay in a hotel room for over two days, I cry when I leave," I said jokingly, exaggerating my own reactions, as Rayana, one of Clara's cousins, started telling her history of loss. She told us about her despair when, in 1996, she had to sell the house where she lived with her husband and young daughter in order to move to New York. "I stayed in that house," she said, "for two days all by myself, me and the furniture; it was a beautiful house that took us two years to build. I chose each piece that decorated that house . . . [and] I cried nonstop for two days." Although she planned to move to the United States permanently, she could not bring most of her belongings in order to avoid arousing the suspicion of customs agents. With the increase in airport policing of borders and the restriction of migrant arrivals, carrying a large amount of luggage containing enough for a lifetime abroad is not advisable. One must convey the intention of staying for a brief visit as a tourist. One of the few things not likely to arouse suspicion is music. CDs were the only personal belongings, besides her clothes, that Rayana brought with her—light, small, and easy to carry (now one can of course just bring in an iPod). She told me that the music on these CDs was so much a part of who she was that she "could not live without them." I asked Rayana for permission to take a look at her CDs. Not surprisingly, she had some of the same music that the other women and I either had brought with us or were familiar with.

One of the songs we played that night was "A Novidade" [The novelty].[8] First released by Paralamas do Sucesso, a rock-and-roll band from Rio de Janeiro, this tune was an immediate success. It was a fitting metaphor for what Brazilians, particularly young Brazilians from the middle class, felt about the deep inequalities in Brazilian society and coming to terms with their own privileged locations. The song tells the story of a mermaid who appears on the beach and surprises the beachgoers, a paradox whose upper body represented beauty and poetry and whose lower body was a fish that could be eaten. The middle class desired the upper body of the mermaid, which one could access only from a privileged social position. Yet the enjoyment of beauty was impaired by the blatant reality of what the other half of the mermaid represented for those who saw the tail as the possibility of a meal. At the end of the song, what would be a dream becomes a nightmare, and the mermaid was torn apart by the two struggling sides. Poetic contemplation for some and hunger for most was a reality that did not escape the perception of Brazilian middle-class youth.

Coming of age in the late 1980s and early 1990s, Rayana, like all of us, directly or indirectly participated in the political protests of what became known as the "transitional years." During our college days, which coincided with the first elections in the country and the subsequent impeachment of President Fernando Collor de Mello in 1992, Rayana and Nana actively participated in public protests, and I would meet Nana often either in the streets or in smaller political gatherings at our university. The School of Humanities—which included the social sciences, philosophy, and psychology—was one of the main centers for organizing the movement, being traditionally on the left. The protests would run into the night, exercises of a political and personal power struggle. They would invariably end in beer drinking in the DCE (Students' Central Directory) quarters or marijuana smoking in the hills close to school, before the city slums spread to the neighborhoods surrounding the university. Later, with the increase in robbery and police persecution of the slum dwellers, which would send stray bullets and people running from the police through classroom doors, these areas became off-limits for smoking and socialization.

In meetings and also in the larger arena of Brazilian society, the Brazilian middle class was rethinking the promises that came in the name of modernity as it experienced both democratic opportunity and severe economic crisis. Despite the economic downturn, the 1980s were an effervescent moment in the history of Brazil, particularly for Brazilian youth. As they adopted new ways of life and consumption, Brazilian young people also became uncomfortable with their place in the world, their family structures, sexuality, and the inherited inequality in which they participated. In the School of Humanities, which Nana and I attended, Marx continued to be mandatory reading for the activist left part of the movement, while others were reading Simone de Beauvoir, Sartre, Guimarães Rosa, Nietzsche, Kafka, and Fernando Pessoa, among others in the Western canon, and carrying on group discussions about existentialism and nihilism. UNE and the public library organized film series—we saw movies directed by Bergman, Godard, Eisenstein, and, particularly, Glauber Rocha. As Xavier (1997) shows in his study of the "cinema novo" movement in Brazil, central to Glauber's work was the issue of national identity in a peripheral country. Produced in the 1960s, films such as *Terra em Transe*, released in English as *Anguished Land*, and *Deus e o Diabo na Terra do Sol*, released in English as *Black God, White Devil*, for example, criticized the Brazilian elite's mimicry of First World ideals and expressed profound disbelief in the models of modernization.

However, it is through the music produced in the 1980s and 1990s that we can clearly see the pessimism that affected Brazilians coming of age in these two decades.[9] In the wave of the so-called democratic opening (*abertura democrática*) and the amnesty that brought intellectuals and musicians back to the country, Brazil experienced a burst of musical production. In the 1980s, Brazilian rock-and-roll music became a mass media event, the result of unprecedented market expansion in music production and distribution. As argued in a number of works, music in Brazil has been at the core of national identity, and Brazilian music, along with cinema, visual arts, and theater, had to grapple with the issue of what could be considered essentially Brazilian and what had been incorporated from elsewhere. However, while earlier movements in the arts were somewhat obsessed with building a separate identity for the nation (Dunn 2001; Vianna 1999), 1980s Brazilian rock expressed profound ambivalence toward the nation as well as consciousness of a larger, interconnected world—not necessarily a Disney World picture, but a more noir scenario. Brazilian anthropologist Goli Guerreiro (1994) analyzed the music of some of the most popular Brazilian bands of the 1980s and 1990s and classified their songs according to recurrent themes such as daily life, identity, love/sex, and politics.

In the 1980s, significant numbers of Brazilians and Brazilian youth moved to urban centers. The mushrooming of Third World cities and the increase in poverty and criminality deeply influenced the lyrics of most songs. The streets, the "asphalt," replaced the house and the beach as favorite song themes.[10] Images of cars, a multiplicity of information, and streetlights were common representations in much of this music (Guerreiro 1994, 53). In the lyrics of bands such as Barão Vermelho, Capital Inicial, Ira, Ultraje a Rigor, Paralamas do Sucesso, and Titãs, panic, obsession, vertigo, depression, distrust for the future, disjuncture, and the unconscious were common to a narcissistic self who could reach others only in furtive encounters. Love and passion were experienced as temporary, and playfulness came to characterize intimate relationships. Marina Lima, a young singer in the 1980s, openly talked about her homosexuality and free love, and combined criticism of deep-rooted family values with what could be considered postcolonial consciousness. In the song "To Begin With" (by Marina Lima and Antonio Cícero), Marina questions who will be able to collect the pieces of a broken old world order based on family, nation, and religion, and affirms that there is no longer a way out.

Marijuana and particularly cocaine became the preferred party drugs, and the growth in drug trafficking fed the urban slums where poverty was concentrated (Alexandre 2002; Marmo and Alzer 2002). Consumption of drugs and a sense of danger in the streets were portrayed in many songs of the period. "Silent Nights, Nervous Calm" is how Lobão, a student of classical music turned rocker, describes getting ready for a party while *"aplicando,"* which could be translated as "injecting" (a general word for drug taking), when surprised by a police raid. State and society appear increasingly polarized in these songs (Guerreiro 1994), and government institutions are portrayed as corrupt and unable to deal with the complexities of a new world order. Adding to the general sense of disenchantment, AIDS claimed the lives of many, including two of the most important rockers in Brazilian history— Cazuza and Renato Russo. Cazuza, the son of an upper-middle-class family from Rio de Janeiro, was one of the first media personalities to publicly proclaim his homosexuality and to openly refer to his recreational drug use. He fiercely criticized the nation and its corrupt politics in a song that became the theme of a popular soap opera in prime time on Globo Television.[11] Entitled simply "Brazil," the song inquires who would be the owner and partner of a nation that does not show its real face to the common citizen. Renato Russo, the leader of Urban Legion, became something of a prophet of Third World consciousness. An anti-imperialist discourse developed alongside a sense of impotence— a sense that, even if one despised it, one was still part of a world system fed by values imported from the centers of power, particularly the United States. If the 1980s, as economists hold, was the "lost decade," this generation saw itself as the "lost generation," unsure of itself and of its role in the future of the nation.

Musicians and artists expressed disbelief in a rational life and in an organized, modern system, which we, as a nation, were unable to achieve. Highly influenced by bands from the English-speaking world, Brazilian bands were formed mainly by young people from the middle class, mostly white, well educated in private schools, and with access to global goods and information. A common noir aesthetic and awareness of urban decadence were intertwined with skepticism about the future of the nation. By the late 1980s and into the 1990s, people of our generation started leaving the country. The United States was a preferred destination. A network and a common language of participation in global modernity, however impaired, had already been established. Places like New York felt, as Barbara said about her first days in the city, "like home."

Chapter 2

Representing the Nation:
Class, Race, and Sexuality

In Brazil, the construction of national identity came with the reappropriation of two central categories of the colonial discourse: race and sexuality.[1] Brazil—a country that received more African slaves than any other in the world—never had an official policy of racial segregation. Mixing was encouraged by the state in various periods of history, and Brazil has a significant racially mixed population. Particularly when slavery was abolished and when European evolutionist theories of race became prevalent, Brazilian thinkers and the state had to come to terms with the country's perceived unique racial makeup, as compared to Europe's and North America's. What became known as "racial democracy" in Brazil resulted from an effort to transform what European thinkers defined as a mixed, mongrel race into a source of national strength. While in earlier writings racial mixture was a source of degeneracy, in the seminal work of Gilberto Freyre it became a source of national pride: Brazil lived a "racial democracy" in comparison to racist German Nazism and the racial segregation of North America.

However, the discourse of "racial democracy" not only left unresolved but also may have aggravated social inequality in Brazil, to the disadvantage of the African-descent population. In Brazil, the lighter shades of skin color still correspond to the more politically and economically privileged groups, while the darker shades correspond to the less advantaged. Nevertheless, racial mixture discourses are crucial to Brazilians' sense of self and ways of experiencing the body (Parker 1991; Correa 1996; Pinho 2004). They are embedded in the ways Brazilians think of themselves and their relationship to others, relationships that increasingly cross the borders of nation-states. In fact, it is an argument of this book that it is through a particular language of mixture that Brazilian women articulate a discourse about modern sexuality, a malleable body, and a particular manipulation of racial relationships by which they envision their migration to the United States, yet at the same time reproduce Brazil's structures of inequality.

Brazil's elite and middle class have always wrestled with their identities vis-à-vis the elite and middle class of European and North American centers. The formation and historical development of Brazil as a colonized country has been tied to a world of goods and values located outside Brazil. During the first few centuries of colonization, the Brazilian economy was based on sugar cane plantations and cattle farming, organized in an oligarchic structure of large farms and plantations serviced by slave labor (Viotti da Costa 1985). Production was directed to the export of raw material and the import of manufacturing goods. Although a middle stratum of the populace participated in the service sector, not until the abolition of slavery in 1888 and the transformation of the oligarchic social structure did a middle class develop in a more significant way. By the turn of the twentieth century, the Brazilian state had expanded and the industrial subsidiaries of coffee production burgeoned.

The transformations introduced by industrialization, urbanization, new forms of technology, transportation and communication, and the growth of the educational system came hand in hand with a discourse about modernization and an increasing concern with the racial makeup of the country. As Brazil was grappling with its economic inferiority vis-à-vis industrialized nations of the Northern Hemisphere, Brazilian thinkers were trying to find paths that would lead Brazil toward a place among other modern nations. The eugenics theories prevalent in Europe in the late 1800s argued that centuries of racial mixing were responsible for the creation of a mongrel race that, left to its own devices, would forever impair the development of a nation. Preoccupied with the "racial degeneration" of its population, the Brazilian government and intellectuals saw a need to "whiten" it (Hofbauer 2006; Skidmore 1993). After the abolition of slavery in 1888, government laws forbade Africans to enter the country, while European migrants were recruited in their countries of origin and given subsidies to settle in Brazil. According to Lesser (1999), between 1872 and 1949, four and a half million foreigners entered Brazil (particularly Portuguese, Italians, Spanish, and Germans, but also Japanese and Middle Easterners), settling mainly in the South. In the process of whitening the Brazilian population and importing a supposedly more skilled labor force, the Brazilian state and elite failed to incorporate the freed slaves into the fabric of the society.

At the same time, paradoxically, Brazilian nationalist thinkers were selectively searching for elements of folk expression in indigenous, and particularly Afro-Brazilian, cultural manifestations as the authentic constituents for forging a national identity. In the various founding national narratives of the twentieth century, the concepts of race mixing and of a distinct Brazilian sexuality were crucial elements. Foundational Brazilian elite thinkers such as Paulo Prado, Sérgio Buarque de Holanda, and—the best known outside Brazil—Gilberto Freyre theorized about the construction of the Brazilian nation as the result of the mixture of three races: the indigenous, the Portuguese, and the Africans. By reappropriating colonial categories defined by early European travelers and writers, Brazilian authors also connected notions of race and representations of tropical sexuality, conceiving of racial mixture as the result of contact between white colonizers and native women and especially African slave women in an atmosphere of excessive sexual license.

If in earlier writings racial mixture was a source of degeneracy, in the seminal work of Gilberto Freyre it became a source of national pride. Far from a characteristic that would impair the development of the country vis-à-vis European nations, racial mixture became a symbol of modernity, a proof of Brazilian malleability and ability to adapt to the complexities of a new world order (Vianna 1999; Pinho 2004). It was in this formative period of the nation that the *mulata*, samba, and carnival became the chief symbols of Brazilian racial mixture, epitomizing the festive and sexualized essence of the Brazilian nation (Parker 1991).

While a national identity was being forged upon the sexualized image of Afro-descent women, Brazilian women of lighter skin colors were entering modernity in a very different way, as historian Susan Besse reveals in "Modernizing Patriarchy in Brazil" (1996). Besse focuses on the effects of modernization on the lives of upper-class and middle-class women from Rio de Janeiro and São Paulo between the years 1914 and 1940. Using ample documentation, Besse examines the demise of the patriarchal model founded in the large extended families of the planter aristocracy and considered the cradle of racial mixture, as theorized by Gilberto Freyre. She documents how new consumer practices and values inaugurated a new configuration of the Brazilian socioeconomic and racial hierarchy and reinforced the separation between races. New patterns of social interaction emerged, and middle-class women started venturing outside their homes, strolling along streets illuminated by streetlamps and eyeing the new store windows displaying the latest in European and North American fashion (Besse 1996, 6). Brazilian audiences were introduced to Hollywood and American personas, such as the working girl and the sexy flapper. The magazine *Revista Feminina* (1914–1927) debated women's emancipation and initiated women into the mysteries of the marketplace.[2] Its articles discussed issues that ranged from fashion to sexual satisfaction, as well as world history and politics, geography, science, arts, and Asian and African dress, claiming for Brazilian elite and middle-class women a cosmopolitan inclination.

While the *mulata* was imagined as a national symbol, middle-class women became the symbols of another nation, a modern nation, occupying the whiter end of the Brazilian racial spectrum. In an article on Brazilian beauty pageants of the 1920s and 1930s, Besse (2005) notes and elaborates on the interaction between notions of race, gender, and class in defining the Brazilian national identity. To her, beauty pageants constituted an arena in which different ideals of femininity and modernity were played out against each other, revealing the clash of cultural references and competing views about the project of the Brazilian nation.[3] Carnival parades and beauty pageants appeared simultaneously in the 1920s and represented parallel and antithetical views of the nation. In both cases, Brazilian women represent the embodiment of the mythical marriage of the three formative races: indigenous, European whites, and African blacks. However, while supporting the ideology that racial mixture not only is characteristic of Brazil, but also gives the nation a unique source of international attraction, beauty pageants encouraged conformity with more modern (read Western, North Atlantic, and whiter) ideals of beauty.

The Modern *Moreno* Body

Inhabiting this dual frame of reference, Brazilian middle-class women have come to represent two somewhat contradictory and antithetical views of the nation.[4] One is modern, clean, technologically advanced, in tune with First World consumption practices and fashion, educated, and white. The other, darker in skin color, is politically and economically backward, chaotic, and unmanageable. Yet the latter carries the signifiers of a more "authentic" bodily culture, as manifest in public celebrations of sexuality. The racial category *morena* can be understood as an attempt to articulate the tensions in the shifting identity of middle-class Brazilian women, having as references both local and global racial configurations.

Formerly dismissed by most researchers or clustered with *mulatas* in references to the nonwhite population of Brazil, *morena* as a racial category has increasingly caught the attention of scholars (Guimarães 2002; McCallum 2005; Piscitelli 2007; Norvell 2001; Pinho 2009).[5] Building upon these current studies of race in Brazil, I am concerned not only with unraveling racial classifications, but also with understanding the semantic contexts that give meaning and social relevance to the use of particular racial identifications. In his anthropologic study about the middle class in Rio de Janeiro, Norvell (2001) notes that "*mulata*" is the word of choice to talk about the race of the nation as a quasi-abstract entity. *Mulata*, as a racial category, implies racial mixing through the sexualization of black women or women of dark skin color and has played a crucial role in the social imaginary of Brazil since the formative years of Brazilian nationalism in the 1930s. As Norvell also notes, nowadays in Brazilian middle-class contexts, *mulata* denotes excessive sexualization and in conversation usually refers to a person who is not present. To people from the middle class, the term "*mulata*" has come to represent Brazil as a racial and sexual celebration of mixture associated with the lower class, from which they feel alienated. Still following Norvell's argument, another racial term better fits the social location occupied by middle-class people—"*morena*," which also conveys the idea of racial mixture, but a mixture that might have occurred prior to colonization. Its origin lies in "Moorish," and goes back to the Portuguese conquests of the Arabs in North Africa. Thus, *morena* represents a Europeanized mixture that became nationalized and "improved" in the Brazilian tropics.

Along the spectrum of black and white, and taking into account factors such as socioeconomic background, the women presented in this book, being from the middle class, tend to occupy the white part of the spectrum. Ivana was the only one who promptly responded that she was white, a whiteness that is defined not just by her skin color but by her place of birth, the south of the country, an area populated mainly by European immigrants. Even Nana, who takes much care to keep her skin fair, said after pondering for a while that she was actually mixed, and vaguely remembered an ancestor or two who were of indigenous descent. *Misturada*, mixed, is the self-perception of most Brazilians. We have been taught since our early years in school that Brazil is a land of the mixture of races. All our textbooks present the official tale of the formation of the Brazilian nation as the mixture of three pristine races: the European, the African, and the indigenous populations. But the specific result of mixing these three races is a complex, myriad combination of minutely descriptive racial expressions and understandings. When asked about their own race or color, middle-class Brazilian dancers are most likely to self-define as *morenas*.

When I asked Clara about her race in an interview, she said: "*Branca, mas eu sou mesmo é morena, brasileira, morena*"—"White, but what I really am is *morena*—Brazilian, *morena*." Clara did not seem interested in discussing race and racial classifications with me.[6] Race was for her a given, an unmarked social position in reference to Brazil. At no point in our interviews or our informal conversations did Clara touch upon the issue of racism in Brazil, except once when I confronted her with a direct question: "Is there racism in Brazil?" She answered: "Yes, there is a lot of racism in Brazil." Then she moved on to talk about something else. The only other time that she referred to racism was in reference to the United States. In her perspective, the lack of racially mixed people and the visual separation between blacks and whites were proof that the United States had much to learn from the Brazilian model of racial contact and mixing. But even that was a remark she did not elaborate on.

When Clara answered "*branca* [white]" to my question about her race, she was giving me a category of the Brazilian census, which offers only five choices for defining one's race: *branca*, *parda*, black, indigenous, or yellow (for Asians). *Parda* is the only category in which *morena*, as well as *mulata*, could fit. But Clara could not put herself in the same box as *mulata*. In fact, by answering "*branca*" she positioned herself in opposition to the other categories in the Brazilian racial classification system. Immediately afterward, however, she said: "*morena, brasileira, morena.*" "*Morena*" in this case is directly associated with her trans-national position and consciousness: *brasileira*. The movement that coupled in the same speech act "white," "*morena*," and "*brasileira*" is the movement of calling on frames of reference that cross the borders of nation-states. Adopting the approach that race is not a fixed marker of identity but one that varies as people inhabit particular spaces, it is im-portant to note not only the discursive details of Clara's speech, but also the social contexts in which her racial identity is defined.

Although I cannot know with exactitude the details of Clara's life in Brazil, I know from my own experience as a member of a similar class that in spaces such as schools, parties, and vacations middle-class people, mostly of light skin color, are more likely to relate on equal terms only to other light-skinned people. In her research on race in Sal-vador, the same city that Clara and a number of women in my project are from, McCallum (2005) finds that on such occasions, whiteness is the most valued attribute, based on the practices and aesthetic prefer-ences of the participants. Casual clothes, blond hair, and suntanned skin are preferable, while the presence of servants—most of dark skin color—makes one feel a "belonging" to whiteness. On those occasions, *morena* does not indicate a racial mixture but a suntan; it might, in fact, function as a marker of class, since it indicates leisure time spent on the beach.[7]

Nevertheless, racial identifications change as one moves from one place to another in a city, or from one moment to another in the span of a day. In Salvador, a city that is estimated to have one of the largest populations of African descent in Brazil, the contact between races is all but continuous. Members of the middle class, constituting a some-what small elite, are very often served by people of darker skin color. In their homes, domestic servants cook, clean, and take care of the chil-dren; at school and at parties, the presence of doormen, drivers, and waiters of darker skin color makes salient the markers of middle classness. In these "spaces of privilege" the *morenidade* of the middle class is closer to the hegemonic values of whiteness and leisure time.

Yet there are occasions in which whiteness is not the hegemonic ideal. In cities like Salvador, a tourist center, people from diverse backgrounds often meet in public celebrations where blackness as a signifier of a more authentic race and culture is the most valued color/race. On occasions such as carnival and the numerous street parties that take place in Bahia, people from the middle class and of light skin color incorporate attributes that associate them with a common "mixed-race" entity as the genuine symbol of the nation. The category *morena*, in these contexts, comes to signify not just a tan color, but also an ability to embody the sensuality resultant from the literal or symbolic mixing of races. One of the few contexts in which the term *"mulata"* might be used among middle-class people is during carnival, when sexuality is valued as a spectacle. According to Norvell's conclusions about the fluidity of race categories in Brazil, women of all classes and complexions can become *mulata* during carnival, as the category implies moments of abandon and a sort of possession by the spirit of the nation through the overtly sexualized movements of samba (2001, 190).[8]

Moreover, in public events such as street parties and carnival, another presence is missing from the works of non-Brazilian researchers, which, in my view, reveals their unmarked membership in the First World middle class. Increasingly in most urban centers in Brazil, foreigners, particularly from Western Europe and the United States, share the streets with local people from the middle and working classes alike. The encounters among these people from different class and national backgrounds constitute occasions in which race is reconfigured, regaining a global frame of reference. How Brazilian middle-class women, as embodying contradictory symbols of the nation, articulate their relationship to foreigners reveals the ambivalence of their social location within Brazil as well as on a more global level. In street parties, *morenidade* becomes a racial positioning both in relationship to local people of African descent and to global foreigners, whose whiteness differs from the whiteness of the Brazilian middle class. On one hand, the racial category *morena* embodies selective sexual attractiveness that approximates that of *mulata* women, without having to compromise middle-class ideas of class within Brazil. On the other, the category *morena* also embodies the modern, malleable body able to adapt to different realities, and to mingle with different nations. Thus, *morenidade* can be seen as an embodied discourse through which Brazilian women envision both their relationship to white bodies from the centers of power, as well as, and ultimately, their move to where those bodies can be encountered.

Here again, I use a personal narrative to explore the ways foreigners were perceived in Salvador, Bahia. In various situations I have heard commentaries by Brazilians about aspects of the North American body and sexuality that with interpretative license we can see as unmodern. The Brazilian perception of the awkwardness with which North Americans hold their bodies begins in Brazil, when attentive participants in street parties scrutinize foreign bodies as they walk by. I remember vividly sitting on the sidewalks of Bahia drinking beer and observing tourists as they paraded up and down and rehearsed a dance step or two. For the most part, tourists and anthropologists alike leave us middle-class people alone. We are not authentic enough, not dark enough, for their tastes. Tourists go to Brazil, particularly to Bahia, to see people of African descent, believed to be the authentic inhabitants of the exotic vacation destination that they are paying for. As Collins (2004) points out in his study of Salvador's historical heritage, the Afro-descent population is constructed, both by Brazilian and by foreigners, as the embodiment of cultural inheritance. As middle-class people, nearly invisible to the foreign gaze, we sat around observing passing tourists, beginning with their shoes, seeking to combine comfort and beauty as they struggled up and down the old cobblestones of Bahia's hills (beautifully described by Ruth Landes [1947]). White sneakers with long white socks always looked ridiculously hot to us but seemed to represent comfort to many North American tourists. Their white skin turned pink in the sun, unlike our off-whiteness. Their pink skin only added to the awkwardness of their bodies, revealed particularly when they danced. Nana and I at times commented on how unmodern they were, how puritanical their bodies and their ways of moving, and how Brazilians were more able to inhabit the complex structure of the new world racial order through our bodies.

Justine, in contrast, used the discourse of the modern body to assert her distance from Brazil and to articulate her desire for the white. Justine's dark skin does not reflect African descent but has been carefully cultivated throughout her life by limited exposure to the sun in the early hours of the day and late afternoons. While living in Brazil, Justine liked to play volleyball and swim, before or after a day of school or work. It is possible that her Portuguese ancestors had mixed with indigenous populations, which may account for her dark skin and her smooth, very black hair, which she likes to keep long enough to touch her hips. In the 1980s, Justine studied philosophy; although politically very well informed, at school she disliked the confusion of people in the streets and abstained from participating in groups or shouting slogans. Coming from a protective upper-middle-class family of aristocratic manners, her biggest challenge was to cross social and national borders by engaging with men from other backgrounds. She recently told me casually at dinner in an Indian restaurant in New York that she used to leave the university early, and as other students went to meetings and protests, she hung out in Copacabana with *"garotas de programa."* This is a term that in Brazil means anything from prostitutes to escort girls to girlfriends or companions—in the case of Copacabana, for foreign tourists. Justine liked the adventurous lives of these women. University students were too limited, in her view, and she enjoyed meeting people of other nationalities and experiencing other forms of sexual encounters. Her taste for the foreign included an intense interest in European cinema. It was at a movie festival that she met an Italian filmmaker, twenty years her senior; their five-year relationship ended only when she moved to New York. Justine decided to come to the United States, combining her desire to end this relationship in a definite way, to pursue her graduate studies, and to continue her search for a more fulfilling life. Justine's *morenidade* and her upper-class social location, as we will see throughout the book, informed her desire to encounter bodies from other nationalities and social backgrounds in adventurous relationships as a way of exercising her modern ability to mingle with others.

Despite popular views that portray people from the Global South, or "peripheral subjects," simply as eager to embrace U.S. values and goods as modern, and therefore better, this has not been the case either for

me or for the women I have met. The United States and the modernity
it represents affected us in more ambivalent ways. Not just economic
necessity or an uncritical desire for modernity moved such large numbers of Brazilians to migrate, but also a profound change in sensibility,
in their ways of perceiving the world and themselves as part of it, and
of experiencing their bodies and the forms in which they relate to others. Rather than just accepting goods and information from the outside,
and rather than accepting modernity as an unproblematic goal, Brazilians, particularly Brazilian youth, also developed a deep ambivalence
toward what they were experiencing. Beginning with the 1980s structural adjustment of the economy, their prospects for a more modern
life started to dwindle, while violence increased in the country. As expressed in the Brazilian rock music of this period, disenchantment and
pessimism toward the future of the country became widespread. Brazilians started to imagine other places with which they had developed
an identity even stronger than their identity with Brazil. This identity
grew stronger in the 1990s and 2000s as a network of migration and
travel was established and as people began to increasingly construct
their identity from a transnational frame of reference. This trend did
not stop even after Brazil's economic situation improved. Such a global
identity, however, is impaired by Brazil's subaltern position in the hierarchy of nations.

Thus, on one hand, middle-class Brazilians occupy a privileged position within the country. On the other hand, they occupy a subaltern
position vis-à-vis values constructed in colonial or post- and neocolonial
centers of political and economic power. The paradoxical position of
the Brazilian middle class, unable to identify either internally with the
darker-skinned working class or externally with a global middle class, is
revealed in the racial vocabulary of mixing central to Brazilian identity
throughout history. The racial category *morena* conveys the flexibility
and manipulation of a complex Brazilian racial configuration that must
be understood in reference not only to Brazil but also to the global racial order that will encompass Brazilian women when they move to the
United States.

Part II

The Bar Scene

Chapter 3

Hierarchies of Bars and Bodies

How do the nine women in my project, from different segments of the middle class and occupying the whiter spectrum of Brazil's racial configuration, find themselves placed in the New York context? How are their bodies reinscribed by the transnational move as they come to occupy specific positions in the labor market and to inhabit specific spaces in the city's racial, gender, class, and sexual hierarchies?

The process of racialization is a continuous building of differentiations based not only on skin color or other apparent body stigmata but also in relationship to other axes of social positioning, particularly class, gender, and sexuality. Ideas of what constitute race or class change according to context. Here, I am interested in exploring the ways bodies, as they move through transnational spaces and spaces of the city, are inscribed by markers of class, race, gender, and sexuality, and how those markers acquire different meanings. Through ethnography of three gentlemen's bars in Queens and one in Manhattan, I examine how recent socioeconomic transformations in New York City have contributed to the creation of new hierarchies among gentlemen's bars and among dancers who work in them.

I recap here the stories of the nine women in my project as a reminder of what brought each of them to New York, and to dancing. When Clara decided to come to New York in 2000, she followed the path that her aunt Gina had taken three years before. Gina, in turn, had followed Silvana, who had been in New York since 1995, when she came with a friend, also from Salvador. In Salvador, Silvana and her friend were newly divorced and unsure about what to do with their lives. They were in their midthirties, held administrative government jobs, and had children. They lived in upper-middle-class apartments served by maids and doormen. They had cars, frequented good restaurants, and loved nightlife. The downward class mobility that they experienced as a result of divorce and of the increasing squeeze of their wages came at a time when their desires, as now free women, expanded. They came to New York, at first, to "check it out," staying with another woman from Bahia who had come with her husband to Miami and after getting divorced, had moved to New York and started dancing.

Clara arrived in New York with Nadja, her best friend and a colleague in the same law office. Sara and Barbara followed almost simultaneously in 2002. Nana came in 2003.

Renata also came via a family network. Before moving to New York, as I have mentioned, she lived and ran a small business with her boyfriend/partner in the tourist town of Porto Seguro, where some of her relatives lived. It was in Porto Seguro, a center for national and international tourism, that Renata started entertaining the idea of migration. Five of her cousins were already living and working in the United States, although Renata said that it was not quite clear exactly what kinds of jobs they held in New York. She had heard about housecleaning, working in salons or stores, and babysitting, but nothing about dancing. She and her boyfriend decided that she would come first and stay with her cousins; then, if things went well, the boyfriend would rent out the store and follow her.

Teresa did not know anyone in New York, but she had a couple of telephone numbers of friends of friends. She had some savings in Brazil and an unpaid leave of absence from her work and did not intend to migrate but also to "check out" what kind of life she could have in the States and what kinds of jobs would be available to her. As she said to me, she "had nothing to lose." At JFK Airport, she met a Brazilian gypsy cabdriver whose work was to greet the newcomers and offer his transportation services. Teresa gave him the address of a Manhattan midtown hotel familiar to Brazilian middle-class people who used to come to the city for shopping, particularly in the 1980s. Probably sensing that her stay, as an unaccompanied woman, might last longer than those of the usual visitors and shoppers, the driver instead took her to a Brazilian boardinghouse in Astoria, in the borough of Queens. It was in that boardinghouse that she learned both about housecleaning and about go-go dancing.

Ivana's only brother was already living in the city, but it was through her aunt that she learned about dancing. After just two weeks in New York, Ivana met other women of her age who took her to a gentlemen's bar in Astoria. At first, her family thought that she was too young to dance and tried to stop her.

Justine was received in New York by her uncle, a bank investor, and his family. She at first pursued her graduate studies and moved in with some friends in the East Village. After two years, she began working as an erotic dancer in an upscale gentlemen's bar in Manhattan.

New York City: Changing Geographies of Desire

As Brazilian women were entering the gentlemen's bar scene, New York City was being transformed into the financial center, a global city from which the world economy is managed and regulated (Sassen 2001). This has led to the gentrification of areas of New York City, a process that has been articulated through the regulation of the city's sex industry, with the result that there has been a hierarchization of gentlemen's bars that differentiates those in Manhattan from those in Queens.[1] Particularly during the conservative government of New York mayor Rudy Giuliani (1994–2002), the ban on sex-related industries in gentrifying areas was managed through campaigns against pornography that led to a process of "zoning the city" according to sexual practices that used a language of morality, equating public, commercial, and alternative sexualities with criminality and unruly behavior.

In a conservative climate accompanied by the mass arrival of immigrants, American citizens who saw their standard of living shrinking with the loss of secure jobs joined corporate and real estate forces to reclaim the city in the name of traditional values and quality of life. In an analysis of quality-of-life discourses used by New York City's government to justify the expulsion of sex-related businesses from areas such as Times Square, Papayanis (2000) exposes the lack of evidence for the association of such enterprises with criminality. She argues quite the opposite, that sex-related businesses that moved to decayed areas like Times Square in the 1960s and 1970s because of their low market value actually helped upgrade these areas. That is, the rise in real estate values in Midtown Manhattan in the 1990s was facilitated by the presence of sex-related businesses. This shift followed the fiscal crisis of the 1970s; as gentrification got underway, these businesses were expelled both under zoning laws that marginalized them and by high rents imposed on them by real estate interests that dictated, through their ties with the government, the zoning of the city.

In 1995, in the middle of much heated debate over pornography, the City Council and Planning Commission approved New York's new zoning code, which became a turning point in the way public sexuality was organized and managed. Other cities have dealt with the geographical location of sex-related business in two ways: by concentrating them into red-light districts (Amsterdam and Bangkok) or by dispersing them to lessen their impact on any specific area of the city. Arguing that the concentration of such businesses was the reason for the decline of quality of life and family values, and anticipating a renovation of the large Times Square area, city government opted for the latter strategy. Thereafter, spaces for commercial and public sex came under the category "adult entertainment business."[2] The new zoning laws barred sex-related businesses from operating within five hundred feet of residences, schools, houses of worship, and hospitals; those that did not comply were closed or removed. By 1998, most sex-related businesses in Manhattan had been forced to relocate. Once the heart of New York City's sex-related business, Times Square has been gentrified, pushing small gentlemen's clubs, peep shows, and stores selling pornographic material to the outer boroughs.[3] The number of sex-related businesses in Times Square dropped from 120 to 19, according to "Sex Shops Face XXX-ile: Smut-Free Zones Win Court's OK," in the *New York Post* of February 25, 1998, with many converting a large parcel of their space or materials into nonadult use in accordance with the zoning laws. XXX-rated rental places now devote a portion of their space to mainstream videos and tourist paraphernalia, and others relegate peep shows and nude performances to spaces far from their entrance (usually a curtained-off room). Some gentlemen's bars now segregate nude women from those who wear clothes.

Only a few of the most upscale gentlemen's clubs benefited from the new zoning laws; most moved to Queens, Brooklyn, and the Bronx, areas that also received the bulk of the city's recent migrants.[4] What followed this reorganization of the city's sex industry was a redistribution of bars and bodies along class and ethnoracial lines, as well as their proximity to ideal body types in terms of weight, age, and shape. Thus, the gentlemen's bar scene was divided between upscale Manhattan clubs and the neighborhood bars of the outer boroughs, a distribution refracted in the social composition of the bars' clientele and dancers. The law and its capillary powers have had an impact not just on the location of the bars, but also on the dynamics within the bars. The way the dancers dress, the distance maintained between clients and dancers, the way clients and dancers touch, the exhibition of nude body parts, and the types of performance are also under government jurisdiction, delineating the kinds of relationships possible among dancers and between dancers and clients.

Queens Bars

Upon her arrival in New York, Clara visited four gentlemen's bars where she might consider dancing, all located in the borough of Queens, where some of her aunts and cousins were already working. Clara's relatives introduced her to the managers and helped her communicate better with clients. The hiring system in the bars is casual, and as in other cases in the informal economy, employers prefer to work with networks of employees through which an older worker becomes responsible for a new one.[5] Managers are often willing to hire new dancers, as their client base is sustained by the allure of a changing variety of bodies and faces and employee networks are usually determined by nationality. Because of language barriers, not uncommonly managers ask a more experienced dancer to give tips to new ones in terms of how to dress, to walk, and to move her body, and other important details of performance.

Although some bars in Queens can be considered as upscale as the ones located in Manhattan, most are neighborhood bars. They are much smaller than the bars in Manhattan, and relationships between dancers and clients follow a different set of rules, dispositions, and etiquette. In Queens on an ordinary night, about eight to fifteen women work in a bar, a number that might increase on weekends or for a special occasion, a party, or a holiday. The women work a nearly eight-hour shift (7:30 p.m. to 4 a.m.) and, if they arrive at the bar when it opens, are paid from $25 to $45 a shift. This sum has dropped considerably in recent years, and this bonus may be eliminated altogether.[6] During their shift the women dance for about twenty minutes and then socialize in the bar for forty minutes until their next set; typically three women dance at one time on a stage. The stage consists of a long platform surrounded by the bar counter, which separates clients from dancers. Dancers make their tips mostly in the form of dollar bills when dancing on the stage or when socializing with clients and encouraging them to buy drinks, on which they receive a small percentage. Dancers in these Queens bars earn from $100 to $400 a night, depending on the mood of the dancer, the day of the week, the time of year, the weather, events in the city, or the general economy. As is true for other jobs in the informal economy, the work of dancers is somewhat seasonal, and the bar is not responsible for compensating dancers during slow days or seasons.

Usually each dancer arranges her schedule with a manager a month in advance. In both Queens and Manhattan bars, the negotiations between manager and dancers at the moment of booking are a source of tension and a way in which the power of management manifests. Besides considering the tastes and preference of clients, the manager decides how many nights to give to each dancer depending on his own evaluation of the dancer's performance, how long she has been dancing, and her availability. In Queens, some bars have instituted a new rule that a dancer is responsible for clients' buying at least five drinks a night; dancers who do not comply with this rule cannot get new bookings. The management also observes the behavior of dancers through the night and their interaction with other dancers, bartenders, bouncers, and, particularly, clients. Dancers who are ill humored, who have difficult relationships with other dancers, and who argue among themselves are not booked again. Above all, dancers who do not interact with clients or who argue with them, for whatever reason, are not tolerated.

A common complaint among dancers is that managers never take their side when there is an argument or disagreement between them and the clients. Dancers, in fact, learn very early that they must negotiate directly with clients as best they can, since the mediation of management will probably benefit the client. Disagreements with clients are most likely to occur in the negotiation of sexual limits. Some clients are known to dancers for their aggressiveness. When buying drinks for the dancers, they may try to touch their buttocks or breast, or they may use foul language and gaze excessively at certain body parts.[7] During the night, the manager spends time in the bar, drinking and talking to dancers and clients, and is attentive to the general atmosphere and the specific behavior of both parties. He listens to the comments and reactions of dancers and clients. As he develops his knowledge of the scene and its participants, he judges which dancers and clients will bring in the highest profit and contribute to the festive atmosphere of the house.

In the Queens gentlemen's bars, bartenders are invariably women and most of them are Hispanics. Some have danced at some point in their lives and grown tired of it but still find the bar scene profitable and best suited to their lifestyle. The bouncers and doorkeepers exercise a strong symbolic presence in the bars, helping keep the clients in line and guaranteeing that unacceptable behavior does not happen inside the bar. Occasionally, bouncers have to intervene in fights among clients or arguments between clients and dancers. Bouncers and doorkeepers are also symbolic figures in the mediation between outside and inside the bar. Other people who make their living from the scene are drivers (mostly from car service companies or individuals who drive exclusively for dancers, usually owning a van) and salespersons who sell dancers' outfits (some of them, like Teresa, have been dancers and have developed a relationship with a bar and its dancers, who became their clients).[8]

Because dancers have a tight day schedule, salespeople periodically go to the bars, usually late at night when the dancers have already made some money, carrying with them samples of their product. They usually show the pieces in the dressing room, where the dancers take turns trying them on and buying them or placing their orders for adjustments in style, color, and fabric. Dressing rooms are small and purposely underfurnished in order to encourage the women to be constantly socializing with the clients when not dancing, encouraging men to buy them drinks. Yet dancers do have to spend some time in them while preparing for their performances; there they change their clothes, talk, apply their makeup, count their money, gossip, and rest. When (un)dressing, the women have almost to step on each other's toes and make an effort not to touch each other's bodies. In fact, the etiquette of bodily display and the distance that dancers keep from each other are part of how hierarchies among dancers are constructed, and also function to reinforce the differences among bars.

After considering the advantages and shortcomings of the bars, Clara decided to work in three of them—Blue Diamond, La Casa, and Highway. Despite their similarities, Queens bars differ according to their location and the city laws under which they are regulated. Blue Diamond is located in Astoria and, because it is near a residential area, is a go-go bar, which means that no topless is allowed and no lap dances offered. The women wear small tops and minuscule shorts or skirts or G-string bottoms; they make their money in tips when dancing on the stage. With the gentrification of Manhattan, parts of the five boroughs have also experienced upgrading and increasing prices in the real estate. Astoria, occupying the first strip of land across the Queensborough Bridge from Manhattan and with easy access by major subway lines, is part of this new upgrading, which is also reflected in its gentlemen's bars. The owner of Blue Diamond is a Greek man, and the majority of the clients are Greeks and Italians, many of them from an older generation of migrants. While some of the Italian clients belong to the second or third generation of the more established ethnic communities in the area, the Greeks mostly moved to this neighborhood following World War II and the Greek Civil War (1946–1949). Greeks and Italians are usually the wealthiest of the clients and the traditional patrons of gentlemen's bars in Queens. They are often owners of restaurants and other businesses, or construction subcontractors. Although their income level is high enough to propel them into the American middle class, they seem more comfortable among the working class or in the company of other migrant groups, such as Albanians and "Hispanics."

La Casa is the second bar in which Clara works. Since the bars must offer a variety of dancers each night, dancers usually rotate among two or three bars through the week. Although the owner of La Casa is also Greek, the manager as well as most of the clientele is from Colombia, joined by regulars from a variety of other Latin American countries—Peru, El Salvador, Dominican Republic, Guatemala, and so on. La Casa, located in a highly populated area of Queens Boulevard, where there is a mix of residences and businesses, is also a go-go club and follows the same zoning rules as Blue Diamond. In Astoria bars, Greek or Albanian songs are played according to the nationality of the patrons. In Corona and Jackson Heights, salsa, *cumbia*, and *batchata* music are usually played for a mostly Hispanic clientele. In order to cater to the taste of clients, the two latter bars also have more dancers from other Latin American countries, such as Colombia, Puerto Rico, and Dominican Republic.

Nana, Barbara, and Ivana also worked both at Blue Diamond and at La Casa. The argument that they gave for preferring to work in these bars is that no topless is required. This, according to them, makes the atmosphere somewhat more "familiar" and "respectable." Another important consideration is that the bars are located near their homes or to subway stations. Despite these similarities, however, these two bars occupy different spaces in the hierarchy of Queens bars. As Clara also puts it, Blue Diamond's environment is, among all the bars, the most "amicable," "festive," and "familiar," while La Casa is, "I don't know, more Hispanic; it has a heavier energy in the air." In Astoria the dancers tend to be younger, of lighter skin color, and with body types closer to the mainstream ideals of beauty. Nana, for example, with her very white skin, smooth long hair, and sophisticated manners, at age thirty-two was one of the most successful dancers at Blue Diamond, despite her sometimes "hostile" attitude toward other dancers. Clara and Nana, with festive attitudes and light *morena* middle-class Brazilian bodies, had no problem fitting in at Blue Diamond; neither had Ivana, age twenty-one when she started dancing. This was not the case for Renata. Although Renata was the same age as Nana and Clara, her body did not correspond to mainstream ideals of height and shape. She was somewhat shorter than the other women, her body weight was not so well distributed according to mainstream standards, and she had buckteeth. The owners of Blue Diamond never called her back after her audition, and she started working at La Casa and Highway.

Highway is situated in a more desolate area, close to abandoned buildings, warehouses, and parking lots. In accordance with city zoning regulations, the women in bars situated in such locations dance topless and also perform lap dances, intimate dances offered more privately to individual clients. At Highway, there are no separate rooms, and lap dances are performed in a corner of the bar, relying on the discretion of other clients and dancers.[9] Most clients at Highway are of Greek, Italian, Irish, or Portuguese descent, men from the working class who live in the nearby Long Island suburban locations. They are mostly unionized electricians, firefighters, public transportation personnel, or men in the construction business. The men come alone or often with friends from work. They also must have a car to get to Highway. Located in places of more difficult access, bars like Highway are considered by both clients and dancers to be more "edgy." A Greek American client in his early forties and a liberal professional described them to me as "sleazy." He said he likes it this way; he likes the scenario of decadence and the underground atmosphere. Both Nana and Ivana told me that they would never work at Highway, while Clara and Barbara worked there only for short periods of time and said that they prefer not to. As opposed to the more lively festive bars of busy areas, which display younger bodies, Highway has more women in their forties. Dancers whose bodies do not quite fit the standard ideals of height and weight as set by mainstream society can also more easily find work in bars such as Highway, located on the outskirts of Queen.

Another reason dancers prefer not to dance at Highway is its location—close to a highway and accessible only by car. The women who work there must either have cars, make transportation arrangements with other women who have cars, use gypsy cabs (usually owned by other migrants from Latin America), or make arrangements with the van drivers who offer special night services for dancers. Three of Clara's aunts have cars and they make arrangements among themselves, exchanging transportation for other services or for cash—usually less than the fares charged by vans, owned by other Brazilians, or by gypsy cabs, usually owned by Dominicans or Colombians. In line with the age and body type hierarchy of the bars, Sara and other women in her family from the same generation work at Highway, while Clara and her friends work at Blue Diamond and La Casa.

Manhattan Bars

Justine had no problem being hired at one of the most upscale clubs in Manhattan. She was twenty-eight years old when she started dancing and became one of their most profitable dancers. Speaking good English, as well as Portuguese, Spanish, French, and Italian, Justine attended to the upper ranks of tourists, businessmen, pop stars, corporate executives, and international and national politicians. She was a perfect combination of internationalism and exoticism, fluid enough to grab the imagination of bar patrons and to make them pay generously for her company. Brazilianness is inscribed in her body by many means. She represents a valuable mixture, according to Brazilian and international parameters, the result of the "right" combination of race, class, and discipline of her body. Extremely conscious of everything she puts in her mouth or on her skin, Justine eats only what she considers healthy food—lots of fruits and vegetables, fish and chicken only once in a while, never red meat. She loves coffee and wine but never has milk or beer, because "they make people fat." Justine has enhanced her naturally thin, dark, tall body by cultivating a strict diet and a physical as much as an intellectual discipline throughout her life. There is not a hint of fat in her stomach or butt, and her expression is consciously serene to prevent unnecessary wrinkles or unpleasant stress marks.

Nadja, age thirty-three when she started dancing, did not have all the markers of upper classness, such as the ability to speak various foreign languages. Her body did not have the natural race and class markers customarily demanded by Manhattan bars either. Still, coming from a more modest family background, Nadja soon decided that in order to make the kind of money that she thought she needed to advance in life, she had to dance in Manhattan. She started dieting more rigorously, wore a hair extension, and had a breast augmentation. She also had liposuction on her buttocks and thighs and invested in elaborate outfits that would balance the "excesses" of her exoticism and better suit the sophisticated atmosphere of the Manhattan bars.[10]

Both Nana and Clara, who started dancing in their early thirties and had the appropriate body types, visited Dolls' House in Manhattan. Although they were accepted by the management, both declined to work there, arguing that the atmosphere of Manhattan bars was much too aggressive. They particularly did not like the fact that they would have to offer lap and table dances and told me they preferred the "familiar" atmosphere of Queens neighborhood bars.

There are bars in Manhattan that are more like neighborhood bars similar to those in Queens, just as there are bars in Queens that are more upscale. However, the high costs connected with doing business in Manhattan makes most bars there more likely to be upscale gentlemen bars. Located in privileged areas of the city, they cater to a whiter clientele of businessmen, Wall Street brokers and investors, tourists, and international politicians. To continue attracting this upscale clientele, these bars must combine the allure of foreign women with the sophistication demanded by their patrons. They employ mostly white American women, as well as women from Western European countries such as Spain, Italy, England, and Denmark.[11] Following the preference for light-skinned bodies as the most valued in the global racial hierarchy, the presence of women from Eastern Europe and the former Soviet bloc is significant. Adding to their exotic allure, Manhattan bars also hire women from a variety of Asian countries, such as Thailand and the Philippines. If they do accept women from Latin America, they make sure these women are compatible with the social class markers and body types that suit the clientele, as Justine and Nadja do. At one point during my research, rumors spread that there was such a surplus of Brazilian women in the bars that management was no longer accepting Brazilian applicants.

The spatial organization of upscale bars is also different from that in neighborhood bars and invites a different set of contacts between dancers and patrons. Because the bars are in commercial areas, city regulations allow the dancers to perform topless and to offer personalized services such as table dances and lap dances, which might be performed in separate areas, the so-called Champagne Rooms. The way dancers are displayed in upscale bars also differs from neighborhood bars. Usually the women do not make money by receiving dollar bills while dancing on the stage. They dance in elevated spaces scattered throughout the bar and some small circular platforms provide a pole for solo dancers. The stage dance functions to advertise the dancers. There they work their performance of seduction by exchanging gazes and performing their special numbers, identifying the clients for whom they will shortly offer a table or a lap dance. Patrons sit in comfortable lounge chairs around small tables, sip their drinks, and talk to each other while observing the dancers on the stage or as they work the room offering lap and table dances.

A large number of dancers work in these clubs. At 8 p.m., when dancers from the afternoon shift exchange places with the dancers from the night shift, there can be sixty to seventy dancers in the larger Midtown Manhattan gentlemen's bars. Since dancers must pay a fee of about one hundred dollars to dance in upscale bars, the management places no strict limit on the number of dancers who can work in them. Dancers themselves must decide at what point the competition makes working at a club not worthwhile. Indeed, a bar with an excess of women plays into the clients' fantasy of too many bodies and too much pleasure, and fits the archetype of an orgy. The bar becomes a space for conspicuous consumption and luxury, as well as reinforcing privileged upper-scale masculinity. The patrons sit calmly and comfortably in their lounge chairs as they closely inspect the bodies and performances of the dancers and choose from the large number of women the ones that most fit their taste. In groups of four, five, or more, clients comment to one another about the women walking around. They approach the dancers they like when the women come to offer dances. Meanwhile, dancers are also talking to each other in small cliques organized by nationality or empathy, observing which patrons look wealthier and most likely to buy more dances and give extra tips. Because of the larger number of women dancing and the more competitive atmosphere, dancers must be quite aggressive in selling dances. They can waste no time just sitting around while not on the stage.

After coming down from the stage, the women approach the clients and offer a dance, either a table dance where the client is sitting or a lap dance in a reserved room or space, the Champagne Room. According to city laws, patrons cannot touch dancers, and dancers must touch patrons only on their shoulders and legs for the purpose of balance when dancing. However, while table dances are regulated by the gaze of the administration, as well as that of other dancers and clients, lap dances are not. At the time of my research, each table dance cost about $20 for a song or a few minutes, $15 paid to the dancer and $5 to the club. Usually a person or a group buys more than one dance. At the time of my research, the Champagne Room costs $500 an hour—the woman keeps $300 and the bar $200. Men often tip the dancer $100 more. Usually the customers stay for more than one song, and what in fact happens in the rooms depends on the agreement made between client and dancer. Whether more intimate sexual contact occurs or whether the patrons are allowed to ejaculate is a source of constant ambivalence in the women's conversations among themselves and with me, as the distance between fantasy and prostitution is ever more blurred.

Whereas in local bars, clients may establish intimacy and familiarity with the dancers, men who frequent Manhattan bars seek male bonding and an opportunity to display power and money. As described in Allison's (1994) case study of hostesses in Japanese clubs, such men go to bars in groups and are in competition. They may also use the visit to seal business contracts, and sponsors (usually a single employer) may cover their expenses in order to bond with employees. What has been called corporate masculinity is less concerned with a man's satisfying his desire through a relationship with a dancer than with the way his contact with a dancer plays out in the eyes of his partners in business.

Unlike the dressing rooms in Queens bars, those in Manhattan are quite spacious and well lit, and have individual lockers for the dancers. These more upscale bars also have a "house mom"—"a woman who looks after the girls, takes care of them, and makes sure that they look and behave well," I was told by one of the dancers, a tall, skinny blond from Poland, who came to ask for a tampon when I was sitting around with Nadja in the dressing room. As in gentlemen's clubs across the United States, a house mom organizes the schedule of the dancers in partnership with the manager. She inspects dancers' makeup, G-string bikinis, and house wear. She is also the only one who is allowed to sell outfits inside the bar, although some dancers negotiate with her and bring outfits to be sold there as well. The house mom controls the movement and the appearance of the dancers and is responsible for explaining to newcomers the rules of the bar and the secrets of seduction. She also orders food, makes calls, and answers the phone to give information about the bar. She receives each dancer's fee for the house, $100, and the fees for herself and for the DJ, $20 each. In fact, the women have to pay $140 a day just to work in the bar. "That is a lot," I said, when a house mom in Tantalus, a Manhattan bar, explained this to me in the dressing room, as I played with a hairpiece and she fixed and re-fixed her makeup. "Yes," she replied, "but some women always make good money. Nadja, for example, she works well. One has to be quite aggressive to be able to work here, you can't be shy. You have to make the men buy dances, and if they are not sure, you sell it anyway." Unlike other dancers I met, Nadja thinks that not being able to speak English adds to her success. On a very good day she makes about $1,000. The house mom spoke perfect English and it wasn't until I heard her talking in Spanish that I asked her where she was from. She is from Domini-can Republic and studies at Parsons School of Design. She quit dancing about a year ago, after dancing for three years. She talked about school, while I kept reading the signs hanging on the mirrored walls:

Rules of the House

Do not touch yourself
DO NOT REFUSE DRINKS OR SHOTS
You are being watched for this!
Pedicures and manicures are Mandatory!!
Ladies should always look their best
No massage from dancer to client
A professional massager has been hired

Fines

No show for shift: $200
Late: $50
Leave early: $50

The rules of the house and the disciplines of the body are stricter in Manhattan than in Queens, as I learned on one of my visits to High Times. Nadja instructed me: "You tell the bouncer that you are Nadja's cousin and you are there to see her." "Cousin" is a category that in the bar scene refers to a friend of a dancer who comes along when a dancer goes out with a client or who visits a dancer in the place where she works. I put on leather boots, black clothes, and a little makeup, and took the train to Manhattan on one of the coldest nights of the year. By the club entrance there were two men who looked Italian American, and I said that I would like to see Nadja. The older one, who was wearing dark glasses, told me to wait for a minute and then let me enter. Nadja was sitting between two other very blond longhaired dancers on a couch overlooking the main space. She greeted me and introduced me to the other girls, the only two Brazilians besides Nadja working in the bar that night.

I sat between them, very uncomfortable in a jacket and clothes since they were just wearing little tops and long, sensual, tight dresses, very high heels, and a lot of makeup. I sensed that my presence was awkward. Unlike the women in the bars in Queens, the dancers here looked more like the body types we see in calendars. We talked for a bit but the gaze of the bouncers was too focused upon us, and Nadja told me she was going to do a dance so they would not bother us. I sat with one of the girls while Nadja went to offer a dance to a group of four men and one woman who were sitting in the main space. Two other women were taking turns dancing on the stage but not attracting much attention.

Nadja told the man for whom she was performing a table dance to buy me a drink so the bouncer wouldn't bother me. He agreed, but my presence was very awkward, and sure enough the bouncer came with my things and said I couldn't stay there. It was clear that I was interfering with the men's enjoyment and group bonding. The bounder said that if I was not going to dance, I should go upstairs, and I decided to go to the dressing room to wait for Nadja. A Mexican busboy walked me through warehouse-like corridors to a stairway and then to the dressing room. He asked my name and said, "Welcome, I hope you start dancing here." It was sweet, but by then I was feeling weird in a way that I never felt in Queens bars.

A complex articulation of race, class, sex, and space creates new hierarchies of bodies in the bars of Manhattan and Queens. Factors such as language, the availability of support networks and institutions, as well as discrimination practices within the real estate market explain why migrants tend to concentrate along ethnic and racial lines. By moving to certain areas, they become incorporated within larger groups. In Queens, for example, Brazilians tend to be clustered, along with other dancers, in the category of "Hispanics/Latinos," a subordinate structural position within the larger U.S. society. However, these larger identifications as inscribed in the general geography in the city become highly contested when one looks at the on-the-ground daily experiences of these dancers in their interaction with other dancers, clients, and management. It is in specific situations in the scenarios of gentlemen's bars that we can observe how women from various classes, racial and ethnic backgrounds, educational levels, and places of origin work side by side and how new, transnational hierarchies are reconfigured.

Chapter 4

Performing Seduction and National Identity

On a summer day a dancer leaves the street when there is still daylight and enters the bar as if she were entering a cave. Amid dim lights, black and mirrored walls, and the smell of stale beer, she carries her bag or backpack or rolls a small suitcase containing the props for her performance: high transparent heels, G-string bikinis, small dresses, and makeup. Although the props that Brazilian dancers wear often come from Brazil, they are not so different from those of other dancers. Here and there, the colors of the Brazilian national flag are combined with casual necklaces or ankle laces made of some indigenous material. These pieces are often sold by American outlets in New York, as their agents go around the world collecting signs of exoticism with which people in the global centers adorn their bodies. In New York City, these same pieces are sold to dancers from the periphery, who then re-exoticize themselves in the eyes of the center and in their own eyes. In the mimetic plays that characterize dancers' performances, those floating signs of exoticism become attached to particular national bodies and are resignified in the game of seduction that happens in gentlemen's bars.

This game of seduction can be described as theater and dancers' work as acting or, rather, performance. Dancers assume a role while they are in a bar, and in order to assume this role they must go through a transformation, much like that of an actress going onstage. Indeed, the wearing of costumes and heavy makeup, and the adoption of a fictitious name for a bar persona, reinforce the idea that the bar is a separate space of theatrical performance. But the acts performed by dancers, unlike those of actors onstage, are not restricted to the bar. Although occurring in the context of the bars, dancers' performances have continuity over time and space. On one hand, the performances seem highly standardized—the dynamics of a gentlemen's bar involve patterns that are independent of the individual performers. The audition as an initiation rite, the slow walk of the dancer, the greetings— all seem part of the script that structures the functioning of the bars. The identity "dancer," able to seduce a client through a performance of gender and sexuality, is formed through the repetition of highly stylized gestures and bodily movements (Butler 1997; Schechner 2002). On the other hand, in the postcolonial and transnational context of New York's bar scene, besides having to follow a series of standardized acts as an abstract "dancer," a woman's performance must also have a particular appeal, something that distinguishes her from the other dancers. For a migrant dancer, the first and most significant source of identification and differentiation in the transnational context of gentlemen's bars is nationality. Her identity as a dancer, as a woman, is immediately marked by her nationality, which becomes both a stigmata that defines her identity, and a prop for the performance through which this very identity is constituted.

Nonetheless, a dancer's performance must balance the demand for an erotic exoticism supplied by the appeal of her nationality with her particular class, educational, and lifestyle background. Dancers' body movements while on the stage and their "speech acts" while on the floor are ways of performing gender, nationality, class, and race simultaneously, axes that build distinctions between dancers both inside and outside of bars. Within the bar scene, Brazilian middle-class women seek to distinguish themselves from two other groups of women: "the Hispanics" and Brazilian women from working-class backgrounds. The play of identity and distancing is embedded in multiple and complex uses of symbols, bodily movements, discourses, and representations— particularly regarding sexual control and morality—that maintain or reconfigure class separations and processes of "racialization."

Walking into a gentlemen's bar, one may notice small groups of women who mostly socialize among themselves. The women in small-ish Queens bars probably know all the other women dancing on the same night, at least by name and nationality, but associate mainly with women from their clique of friends. These cliques seem at first to be somewhat malleable, with women talking to various groups as they come and go from stage to dressing rooms and while working the room. However, as one looks a little closer, these cliques are demarcated from each other. Since the majority of dancers in Queens bars are either Colombians or Brazilians, nationality is the foremost dividing line, although language also appears significant. Dancers from other parts of Latin America, such as Dominicans and Puerto Ricans (the other two most common nationalities), tend to be clustered with the Colombians as "Hispanics."[1] However, "Hispanics" is a category that expresses more than language or nationality. For Brazilian dancers from the middle class working in gentlemen's bars, identification with the Hispanics constitutes a process of racialization that should be avoided. Since silence on issues of race is characteristic of middle-class Brazilians, instead of talking directly in terms of race, women distinguish themselves from others by using a language that accentuates class markers such as education, manners, and etiquette regarding bodily display and movement, as well as contact between dancers and clients. In addition, in the sexualized atmosphere of bars, a language of respectability and morality is often used to demarcate class and racial boundaries.

What kinds of outfits to wear and how to wear them, the ways to move one's body, attention to the ebb and flow of a night's dynamics, the gaze, the display of specific body parts, what is considered acceptable and what is not—all are part of the discipline and knowledge necessary for the realization of a dancer's performance. How did the Brazilian dancers from the middle class construct their performance in relationship to the performance of the other dancers with whom they share the bar scene? How do they learn, as Teresa once put it, "to seduce in order to make money" in a way that does not conflict with their other significant identity axes? How do they demarcate and negotiate their sense of self and identity as they recreate themselves as erotic dancers?

Becoming Foreign to One's Own

The Audition

The work of becoming a dancer is a labor of learning how to possess a certain kind of femininity that is able to seduce a client through a performance of desire—a desire that is mediated by fantasy and imagination. The process of learning how to be a dancer is not easily theorized by the dancers themselves but is experienced as they go along, testing what works and what does not work, both when they are on the stage and when they are talking to clients. The audition, which a dancer has to go through before she officially starts to work in a bar, can be seen as a rite of passage, a crucial moment in her introduction to the scene and in her construction of a new persona. Since the most common way for a woman to enter the dance scene is through another dancer or a relative or friend, these people constitute her main source of information and guidance for what to do and not do. During the audition, the manager asks the woman a few questions—Has she danced before? Does she know how the bar works? Normally the manager will trust the person who is introducing the new dancer to tell her the rules of the house and show her around, as well as to give her tips on how to dress, how to perform, and what to expect.

To start dancing is to learn a symbolic system, a language, through which a dancer communicates what she is or what she wants the other to fantasize that she is. The movement of the body is an active performance through which her identity is signaled, formed, and negotiated (Desmond 1997). Movement styles are ways in which social identity is inscribed in the body throughout one's life history and background. What happens in the bar scene is an adaptation and resignification to the demands of the bars of what is embedded in the "natural" movements a woman has learned throughout her life. In the bars, she must rearrange gestures, postures, and movements to convey particular messages to viewers. Viewers, remember, are not only clients, but also other dancers, who are constantly analyzing the social positioning of every dancer in relationship to the others. In addition, and perhaps even more importantly, the dancer herself—in the mirror where she sees herself while performing—is a careful viewer whose scrutiny she must attend to.

As I observed and as dancers themselves have explained to me, a dancer's first day follows quite a ritualized pattern. The aspiring dancer will go to the dressing room, where other dancers are already getting to perform, taking off their regular clothes and putting on their bikinis, doing their makeup, arranging their hair, fixing details of each other's clothes. They then should leave the room, three by four meters, to free up the small space for other dancers. In the sexualized atmosphere of the bar, it is considered good manners not to touch the naked bodies of other dancers and to maintain a minimum distance from each other. This unspoken rule particularly applies to women who are not part of the same clique. Cliques are very clearly demarked in the dressing rooms. Dancers talk mainly to the women they know and identify with, and with whom they may share makeup, outfits, comments about clients, information about the management, and updates about their personal lives.

On a woman's first day in the bar, other dancers who are part of that dancer's clique or of the network who introduced her may speak one or two words of encouragement while she is preparing herself in the dressing room. They may make comments such as: "Oh, it's easy!," "There is no secret," "You will enjoy it, it gets better with time," "You will learn fast." These words of encouragement will be accompanied by dancers' observations about the bodily display and movements of the new dancer. Ready for her performance, the woman leaves the dressing room accompanied by her dancer friend or some other person in the same group. She then sits by the bar, chatting and waiting for her turn to go up on the platform. Usually, the manager arranges for the aspiring dancer to be onstage at the same time as her dancer friend. For extra encouragement on her first day of work, the house, the other dancers, or the bartender offers the new woman a dose of tequila. All dancers say this helps very much in one's first move toward the stage. The consumption of alcohol, the preferred drug in the bar scene, functions as a disinhibitor and stimulant to a dancer, not only on her first day but regularly thereafter.

Nervously, the new dancer tries her first step on the platform, observing the reactions of clients and other dancers and her own feelings of what can and cannot be done. Sharing different spots on the small platform, the other dancers may dance a little closer to her, smiling and playing with her, showing her what to do while working on their own performance and getting tips from clients. Although the new dancer might have observed how the tipping and the seduction process occur from offstage, this is the first time that she is actually dancing. The movements of different body parts, particularly the pelvis—such as thrusting, undulation, and rotation—are carefully studied and function as markers, signs, and symbols by which a dancer is evaluated in hers and others' eyes. What might have seemed easy to her as an observer (the movements of the body, face, and eyes) now becomes a conscious part of an act—an act that differentiates a dancer from those who do not belong to the same class or ethnic group. Now, she must observe and try to discipline herself in the game of seduction without losing her sense of what is morally acceptable, as manifest in the movements of the body. Meanwhile, the manager and other dancers observe the new dancer closely. The first time, the aspiring dancer performs just one or two sets, so the manager can have an idea of whether she is capable of doing the job. Even though there are no clear criteria for what constitutes a potential dancer in the eyes of the manager, women who come to the bar showing the right attitude, naturally, have a better chance than the ones who do not. Such an attitude, rather than a spontaneous quality of a dancer, is constructed over time.

Before going to her first audition, the woman must be minimally prepared for what to expect. Most women talk about imagining and rehearsing in their minds and in front of the mirror numerous times what they think might be sexy and able to attract the attention of others. Depending on how urgent is the need for a woman to start dancing, she may rehearse her display for weeks, months, or even years. Women who know beforehand what to expect from a bar are also more prepared for the performance. Some women come to the United States with the clear purpose of becoming a dancer. All the women in Clara's network had a close relative or friend who, in a trip back to Brazil or in international calls, had explained in minute detail what being a dancer entails: how much they make, the apparatus that is necessary, the shifts, the relationships with other dancers and with clients, and the rules of the bars. The first time I met Nana in her basement apartment in Queens, just a few weeks after her arrival in New York, she showed me the outfits that she (well advised by Barbara) had brought from Brazil.

She had a suitcase packed with G-string bikinis, small shorts and tops, wraps, high heels, and a small purselike black bag to collect the tips. Nana had bought them in Brazil for their supposedly ethnic quality, despite the fact that they are very similar to products one can find in New York. The pieces used in the performance are also bought in Brazil—because they might be cheaper there, and because one knows better where to buy them at home than in a new country. Soon, however, they discover that they can buy similar products in New York from home manufacturers such as Teresa.

Other women have a less clear idea of what dancing in a gentlemen's bar means. They may not have any close friends or relatives who dance, or if they know someone, the person might have been reticent to discuss dancing. Both Renata and Ivana had relatives who danced in New York, but the subject was taboo within their families in Brazil. Although one of Renata's cousins worked as an erotic dancer, Renata did not know that until she came to New York. Because Renata was considered a married woman, her cousins did not think it appropriate to share this information with her. Not knowing what Renata would think of her, her cousin did not want to expose herself unnecessarily. On her arrival, Renata stayed with a third cousin, who worked as a hairdresser in a Queens Brazilian salon, and her husband, who worked installing cable TV for a Brazilian company. She started working as a manicurist in the same salon as her cousin. It did not pan out. Renata did not make the kind of money that she was expecting and that was necessary to support herself in New York and save for the future. In addition, she did not get along well with the cousin with whom she was living. On the advice of another cousin, who worked as a dancer, Renata entered the bar scene.

> Suzana: How was your first experience dancing?
> Renata: It was terrible. A disaster. The first bar that I went to
> was La Casa. I went with my cousin who used to dance there
> before she started dancing in Manhattan. So she went with
> me to introduce me to the manager who she knew from
> before. She said she was going to take me there because it was
> a tranquil bar. When I walked in and I first saw the women
> dancing on the stage and the clients giving them money like
> in a show, I could not believe it; I did not know what to think.

I said I cannot do this; I have no courage for that. How am I going to work with this kind of people? What am I doing here, for God's sake? I didn't want to stay there. Then the manager talked to me; the other women came too, they gave me a shot of tequila in order to relax.

Suzana: And had your cousin arranged the outfits for you?

Renata: No, I bought them myself, but she explained to me all beforehand; she told me what I should do. In my first night it was all very scary but she stayed there with me, and at some point she said: "Now you go—if you can't handle it, never mind, but just give it a try." I was in the bar for over an hour already and then I took a shot of tequila and went up on the stage. I didn't see anybody. I pretended that there wasn't anybody in the bar. I started dancing and the clients started giving me money but I couldn't face anybody. I didn't even look at the men. It was terrible. Then the manager said: "You can come down off the stage." I was so embarrassed, it was a relief; I had done it and I survived. After this audition, he told me what days I could work there, so I started dancing. It was very difficult at first, but I had a goal in mind—to make enough money to be able to go back to Brazil—and I told that to myself: I am doing it for the money, and there's nothing really bad about it, I am just dancing here. Then, little by little, I got to know the other women, watching each woman's style; I am a very discreet person, and I observe. I don't like gossiping, each person does what she thinks is the best. I learned a lot from the other women in terms of how to make money.

Ivana's family thought that she was too young to be exposed to information concerning erotic dancing. Ivana had heard about dancing only in the form of rumors. In those rumors, dancing was represented in a less sexualized way. When explaining their night-shift work to people outside the bar scene, dancers say that they work as bartenders and may even say that they dance on the counter to "*animar*," or cheer up, the clients.[2] That was the story Ivana's aunt told her family, and that was the expectation that Ivana had in mind when she decided to visit a gentlemen's bar with her new girlfriends from Astoria. Less prepared than the dancers who came warned about what to expect, women like Ivana and Renata have a harder time coming to terms with the business of dancing. They do not have the right outfits, and they probably have not rehearsed parading on the extremely high heels that they must wear. Instead of buying their first dancing apparatus in Brazil at a much lower price, for example, an unprepared dancer must buy it in New York after she arrives, when she has very little disposable money. Because of this, she will have fewer outfits in the beginning, which may make her performance a little poorer than that of someone who has a better idea of what attracts a client. More importantly, these women did not come psychologically prepared to perform in ways that may be more effective or efficient in terms of making money. They have to learn the hard way.

Disciplining the Sensual Body

I talked to Mayra in one of her first nights in the bar, a plump woman in her late twenties from Rio de Janeiro, with hair dyed blond and an appetite that made her finish all the snacks in front of us on the counter twice. The other women were making fun of her and showing her how to move her hips so she would not seem so stiff when dancing. She laughed and did not take the comments too seriously. As with other dancers, she asked me why I was not dancing, to which as usual I said that I was at school and doing research. This answer never stopped dancers from insisting on my starting to dance. Although most Brazilians think that going to school and having a degree is a legitimate goal in life, they also think that this is not enough, particularly if you are living in the United States. They argue that education does not guarantee a good life in Brazil. In the United States, so the argument goes, you have a chance to make money and arrange your financial life for when you go back home. Besides, they argued, you are hanging out in bars anyhow. When Mayra did not accept my excuse that I was going to school, I said: "I don't know, maybe *eu não dou para isso*, I am not fit for that, I am kind of shy, a little bit." "Yes," she said, "if you are shy, you can't do that. I was never shy, I always liked showing my body, wearing shorts, dancing in the streets."

When I made a comment about my hair, which was somewhat short, she replied: "Ah, now I know, you have a problem with your hair. But your hair is fine. Besides, if you really don't like it, you can always put an extension." Since women with long hair are considered more sensual, several women put extensions in their hair. The importance of having long hair as a symbol for sensuality and the lifestyle it emphasizes was illustrated by Tatiana's case. After working as a dancer for three years, Tatiana, a twenty-seven-year-old woman from Minas Gerais, became a born-again evangelical and decided to stop dancing. She said that the first thing she did when she converted was cut her hair to shoulder length. She explained to me that by doing this, she would prevent herself from falling into the temptation to go back to dancing. To Tatiana, having short hair ensured her new lifestyle as a born-again. Even if she wanted to dance again, the absence of a fundamental prop, long hair, guaranteed that part of her sensual persona would be missing. Likewise, Nadja, after deciding to go back to Brazil, called me to say she had cut her hair like mine. She said she liked a more "professional" look. I was surprised to see her with long hair when I went to meet her in a bar in Manhattan later that week. "Well," she said, "I am staying for another month until after Christmas. I tried to dance with short hair, but it felt weird, so I got some hair extensions."

To be able to dance, and to expose one's own body to the scrutiny of clients and other dancers, one must deal with whatever uncertainties about one's body one may have. As was clear from Mayra's comments, from the perspective of dancers, any uncertainty about appearance might stop a woman from dancing. But one can learn to accept the disliked parts of one's appearance or can modify one's body into what is defined as more desirable. Although it might seem that any person can dance, this is not the case. In order to be a successful dancer, a woman has to undergo a disciplined investment in her body and appearance. Other women were constantly talking about Mayra's "bad" eating habits. When Nadja was looking for a job in a Manhattan bar, she was once told that she first needed to lose some weight. Dancers must control their weight and must be fit enough to endure an eight-hour shift every night. Sara and Barbara, for example, go to the gym three times a week.

Taking advantage of her transnational location, Sara even has a personal trainer from Brazil with whom she talks via MSN messaging so she can fit her work schedule into her exercise schedule.

"Ladies must look their best," reads a sign in the dressing room of one of the bars. Dancers must always be carefully shaved or waxed. Other investments include manicures, pedicures, and artificial tanning. These daily investments in their bodies are closely inspected by managers, owners, clients, and other dancers. Dancers may also have breast implants and liposuction, the most common cosmetic surgical interventions for dancers. Clara had liposuction done on her stomach area and silicone added to her buttocks, while Nadja had liposuction on her buttocks and stomach area and had silicone put in her breasts. Sara, into her forties, besides having silicone in her breasts and liposuction on her stomach and parts of her back, had Botox treatments on her forehead and filled in her cheeks. If a dancer has legal papers, these procedures can be done during a trip to Brazil, at much lower prices.

The Slow Walk and Seductive Gaze of a Dancer

I have heard from people who have visited the bars occasionally out of curiosity that dancers in Queens are not so pretty and that their performances are "lame." Occasional visitors, unfamiliar with the subtleties of the bars' dynamics, may say that dancers are lazy and do not make much effort to get tips from clients. What they fail to see is that clients not only do not fall for the prettiest women, but also do not fall for those that give the most energetic performances. Indeed, many clients like women who move slowly, so they do not feel threatened and or pressured to look at them incessantly. Women must learn the subtle play of seduction that attracts different kinds of clients.

Once, for example, I was openly admiring the performance of a Colombian dancer who, as I learned afterward, was a salsa instructor. "She is a great dancer," I said to Barbara, who was sipping a glass of water next to me and has much experience with the dynamics of these bars. "That's an exaggeration and a waste," she told me. "Look, she is not getting almost any tips at all. Clients do not like when women move like this, that's too much. Besides, this is an eight-hours shift. If she continues dancing like that, she will get tired in a little bit. I will sit here while the guys are getting drunk, and then by the end of the night, when most of the women are exhausted and the guys do not care about anything else, I go and I make my money. I don't stress out in the beginning of the night. That's stupid."

In fact, the strategy Barbara uses often works well. Bars function in ebbs and flows of excitement that dancers must observe so they can make the most profit without burning out by the middle of the night. The early hours of a shift are almost invariably slow. That is the reason managers must pay a fee to dancers to make sure they come early. Dancers who come to bars more than half an hour late are not entitled to the pay. Yet some dancers prefer to give up this small fee (the value of which has been shrinking as the competition to work in the bars increases) and arrive later. Clients who go to bars in the earlier part of the evening are likely to be stopping by on their way home from work to have a drink or two. They may give a dollar or two to each dancer on the stage, but they are not up to a night of fun and spending. Their purpose is just to relax after a day of work, and their budget might be twenty to thirty dollars for the hour or so they spend there. In this time they may chat a little with the dancers, but usually they just sit by the counter, comfortably sipping their drinks. After these early birds depart, the bar slows down.

After 11:00 p.m., clients who are out for the night start coming. While men who come from work tend to arrive by themselves, men who go out for the night tend to come accompanied by their friends. Groups of two or three friends start coming steadily and by 11:30 the bar is usually pretty much full. By midnight on a good night, one can count as many as thirty to forty clients. Most of these clients are regulars and know the dancers, who greet them by name (most often fictitious names) and engage in familiar conversation. They ask about their life, their business and family, without getting into any compromising details. Dancers also comment on how their clients look and about their mood that night, mostly in broken English: "You are looking good today," or, "Is there anything wrong with you today? You look sad. How was your week (end)? Are you enjoying the summer?" And so on. This is the time of night when dancers are also more careful about their performance. Some change outfits after midnight, adding a tone of novelty and surprise to the atmosphere.

Apart from the movements of the body, the choreography of the eyes is the most important part of the play of seduction between clients and dancers. It is through making eye contact that the dancer captivates the client and earns a tip. The dancer cannot be either too aggressive or too coy with her gaze. A client also may ignore her gaze if he is not interested and look away or in the direction of another dancer who might be more attractive to him. But it is considered most appropriate for clients to relate to the dancer performing in the area near where they are sitting.

> Teresa: I began with working on my gaze. I was rather a shy woman before, and if a man looked at me I would look the other way, or look down, or pretend I didn't see that he was looking.
>
> Renata: It's like this. You go up on the stage and a man looks at you. You can sense if he likes you by the way he looks at you. Then after you go down off the stage you sit by him, talk to him, and give him some attention. Men go to bars because they are needy; they need attention. In a way you are an actress there. Unfortunately, this is the truth. This is a work in which you have to lie to men, you have to make them believe that they are going to have you, that you are going to go out with them for other things, do you understand? So, you talk to them, tell them things that they like to hear. The other women taught me a lot what to say, and I watched how they did. You can stroke their faces, and when you see the same clients again, you should look happy to see them, you should show that you remember them, that you missed them, things like that. Even if in the inside you are like, I hate you, I just want your money, you jerk. The thing is to convey to them that they are important; this is how you make money. And it goes without saying that there are women who actually go out with clients.

The Sexualization of the Brazilian Body

The performance of seduction must combine two sets of elements. The first is constituted of standardized acts or scripts. The general display of dancers and the overall structure of gentlemen's bars in New York seem to be pretty much the same as those in other places in the United States (see Price-Glynn 2010; Frank 2002; Bernstein 2001; Barton 2006). The audition, the rules governing the house and the kinds of contact permitted between dancers and clients, the forms of bodily display, and the overall structure of seduction follow quite standardized scripts. However, the representations and meanings that might be attached to the same acts are markedly different. In the transnational context of New York, exoticism is a second and equally important element in defining the performance of a dancer. The evocation of an exotic sexuality becomes a dancer's work, an excavation of that which a dancer considers necessary to incite the desire of a client. Desire, from the psycho-analytical perspective (see Cowie 1993), is a relationship to a fantasy. Dancers are simultaneously props and inciters of fantasy. The work of auto-exotization, as Savigliano (1995) in her work on Argentinean tango puts it, is the work of imagining the fantasy of the "colonizer." In Brazil, the appropriation of the colonizers' narratives and fantasy was central to the construction of national identity. In the gentlemen's bars, the presence of Brazilian women evokes a chain of associations that echoes a post- and neocolonial context. Becoming a Brazilian dancer means working at the level of representation and subjectivity that transforms Brazil into a source of fantasy and desire.

However, dancers disagree over what constitutes exotic sexuality. Of the women in this project, Teresa, who has a degree in psychology, had thought about the questions involved in performance most thoroughly. I will concentrate now on the aspects of her life in which Teresa has dealt directly with the issues of perception of her body and sexuality as play, display, and seduction. Teresa talks of her upbringing as a middle-class woman, the daughter of a strict military officer, growing up in northeastern Brazil. Although she has a dark complexion and curly hair that could put her in the category of black or African descent in the United States, and in my own categorization as a *mulata* in Brazil, she refers to herself as *morena*. As a middle-class young woman, she did well in school, had a few boyfriends, and later decided to study psychology in college. Teresa worked as a housecleaner in New York until she heard about go-go dancing. She said that even though she never thought of being a go-go dancer, the work of cleaning houses was insufferable for her. Teresa said she had never cleaned even her own house before, and she dreaded what the cleaning products did to her hands as much as she disliked the isolation of domestic work.

Nevertheless, it took Teresa nearly a year to start dancing. With a degree in psychology, she inquired into the nature of men's and women's sexual mores. Knowledgeable about the effects of dress and of self-presentation in the production of desire, she started doing research on what outfits would play to men's fantasies. She explained the process of becoming a dancer to me in this way:

> First, I needed to do research about what it meant to be sexy to me, what it meant to be a woman who worked with her sexuality. I would put on a G-string and high heels and just spend a lot of time in front of the mirror, walking up and down in my place, hours in a row, until I felt like I knew how to do it right. I bought many different kinds of outfits. I had to learn how to be that kind of a woman. I was already a normal woman, but now I was a performer, a woman who seduces for money. Because when a woman is beautiful, you know, with blue eyes, that's fine, but that's not what dancing is about. The important thing in dancing is to arouse men's fantasies. Then you have to put some high heels on, corset, stockings, all that. My idea is that I was a *vedete*, like in Sargentelli shows—do you remember, these *mulatas* with beautiful clothes? I knew that I could not be just a normal person—a normal person I already was. I needed to have another persona there.[3]

To Teresa, dressing the exterior body was not all she needed to do in order to transform her *self*. Simultaneously with the work of presenting herself to the gaze of others, she had to work on the level of imagination and fantasy. Although Teresa usually referred to herself as a *morena*, to arouse men's fantasy she felt the need to define herself as a *mulata* in the context of the bar. To be a *mulata* requires more than a certain skin color or hair type. *Mulata* also implies a certain voluptuousness of the body and the feeling of "abandonment" that one experiences through the movement of the body in events such as carnival (Norvell 2001). Teresa's evocation of the image of Sargentelli's *vedetes*, who were mostly *mulatas*, relates to the deep-rooted representations that intersect in the formation of Brazilian racial configuration as spectacle.[4] Sargentelli was the owner of a famous nightclub in Rio de Janeiro. In the 1970s and early 1980s, he became a celebrity in Brazil. In his nightclubs, capitalizing on the allure of carnival, Sargentelli put on spectacles of mostly topless *mulatas* wearing G-strings, which became icons of the Brazilian sex tourism industry inside and outside the country. Teresa's reference to the body and sexuality of the *mulata* and to Sargentelli is part of the process of her reinterpretation of symbols and images excavated in the imaginary of the nation in order to fashion her new self across national borders, mimetically incorporating icons of Brazilian sexuality and race.

The approximation of Teresa's *morenidade* with the body of the *mulata* in this context also echoes her own particular location with reference to Brazil. Three elements may contribute to this approximation. First, Teresa's skin color is darker than that of most of the women in my research and her hair type reveals, according to Brazilian standards, that her color is not a result of tanning but of racial mixture. This would not have much importance if her class location were not also slightly, but significantly, lower than that of Clara and her network of friends and family. The fact that Teresa sells outfits to other dancers in the bars puts her in a position of serving them, and thus in an inferior position in the social hierarchy of the bars. Finally, Teresa's age, forty-seven, brings her closer to a time (the 1970s and early 1980s) when Sargentelli's iconic *mulatas* were not yet associated so closely with sex tourism practices (Norvell 2001). None of the other women in this project used the word "*mulata*" to classify themselves or to describe the kind of persona they assumed in their performance.

Most Brazilian women in these bars cannot dance the samba, the kind of dance and musical style associated with the figure of the *mulata*.

In fact they may feel more comfortable with recent hip-hop songs, and some do not know what to do when DJs of their own accord play what they think might please Brazilian dancers, usually versions of samba. Depending on their social class and place of origin in Brazil, as well as their age group, the women have varied musical and dance preferences. Some, like me, grew up listening to Brazilian and foreign rock-and-roll music in the 1980s. As we have seen, this music not only defined the way we moved our bodies but also strongly influenced our way of being in the world and represented a certain skepticism toward the Brazilian nation and the symbols used in nationalist representations.

Brazilian Buttocks

Tommy, a young American of Italian and Irish descent, started going to bars more often after he met Nana. It was also after meeting Nana that he went to Brazil for sex and tourism a few times. Once, I was sitting with him and Nana in a bar watching the dancers when Nana pointed to a black woman nearby, and said to Tommy: "Look, just the kind you like." This was a somewhat racist remark, but I did not say anything. Tommy continued sipping his beer while looking at the woman and finally said: "Nana thinks that I like *pretas* [blacks], but I don't, not like this, ugh. I like mixed—dark, but mixed. I like when they have a black women's ass, big and up, and I also only like brown nipples. I can deal with pink nipples, but not black." In his work on representations of female sexuality in the nineteenth century, Gilman (1985) calls attention to the ways in which the body parts of the colonized become synonymous with race under the colonizer's gaze. Regarding presentations of the Hottentot Venus, Gilman demonstrates that her buttocks become symbols of black sexual excess and degeneracy and the subject of erotic fascination.

To cater to the fantasy that most foreigners have of Brazilian women's behavior on Brazilian beaches, dancers must modify their beach-going habits. If a dancer comes from a middle-class *morena* background and frequents middle-class beach areas, she must go to the beach early in the morning because she must a wear G-string to avoid problematic tan lines, and G-strings are not acceptable beachwear for respectable women in either Brazil or New York.[5] In middle-class beach areas of the city of Salvador that I frequent, for example, it is rare to see any woman on the beach wearing a G-string bikini. In fact the beachwear in these areas has tended for the past few years to become a little less revealing, although the cut of the bottoms in Brazil is V-shaped, while in the United States it is round, covering most of the lower buttocks.

In Brazil, particularly in Bahia, a dancer can go to the beach either by herself, with someone who knows why she needs to wear a G-string, or with someone naive enough to believe that this is just a matter of taste. With few people on the beach, she can find a secluded area where she can lie down and sunbathe to achieve the right tan. Since there has been a trend for the last few years for people to socialize on the beach until early evening, another option is to go to the beach only late in the afternoon, when the sun is down and will not leave her with undesirable tan lines. That is what Nana does, since she has never liked the sun in any case.

In the United States, most dancers I know rarely go to the beach, and when they do, they go to more secluded areas. Accompanied by friends who understand the demands of their job, they can wear G-string bikinis without feeling frowned upon. Certain areas of Rockaway Beach in New York, for example, are known to be Brazilian areas, where, according to foreigners, the women "typically" wear G-string bikinis and where people like music, drinking, and dancing on the beach—strange, by U.S. standards.

Transnational High Heels

In one of my trips to Brazil, in a shoe store I saw a pair of high heels made of a transparent material, just like those dancers wear in New York bars. As I was trying on shoes, I decided to try those on too, and laughing at my own clumsiness asked the saleswoman how any woman could walk in them. She laughed with me and said she didn't really know, adding for my information that the women who buy them don't use them in Brazil but seem to like to use them "*no exterior*," or overseas. Some women come here with foreign men, she said. That's how we know.

Distinctions of Class and Morality

Given that the first large group a dancer belongs to is that of her nationality, Brazilian dancers immediately join cliques with other Brazilian dancers, and Spanish-speaking dancers with others of the same language and nationality. Besides this division, however, differences among dancers might be less perceptible to an outsider. These are differences in terms of class and race as defined transnationally, that is, with reference to the women's lives in their home countries. As was true for members of the middle class living in Brazil, in the United States race continues to be a subject to be avoided. Differences tend rather to be perceived and spoken about in terms of class and morality, a practice that does not preclude racism and the perpetuation of racial hierarchies, however, either in Brazil or among Brazilians in the United States.

Compromising Morality

In Queens bars, where from twelve to twenty women work each night, cliques of dancers socialize among themselves while analyzing the behavior of other dancers. Between 9:30 and 10:30 p.m., when the bars are almost empty, dancers talk to each other, go to the dressing room to rearrange their outfits and makeup, call their friends, play video games on their cell phones, show pictures of their relatives and friends, or just sit around sipping juices and eating the food they order from nearby restaurants. This is an important time for socializing, for sharing information about other bars, and for talking about life. Gossiping, as a form of social organizing traditionally associated with women's forms of knowledge, is a common pastime for dancers. While sitting around the counter or when counting money, redoing makeup, or resting in the dressing rooms, women comment on other women's behavior while asserting their own position of difference.

For a dancer, assuming a persona that conflicts with her other subject locations is highly problematic both in terms of her morals and of her location within the larger society. The clash between what is considered acceptable and what is invested with extrasexualized performance is often articulated through a language of morality. More than once, I heard dancers thoughtfully describing their situation as "living on the edge." But living on the edge of what? The differences between the kind of product they sell and what could be considered prostitution is constantly in question and functions as a marker of social differentiation within the bar. This process can be illustrated by the interaction between dancers and clients and with other dancers.

Even though interactions between dancer and client are restricted by a set of scripts, what happens in fact is subject to rules of discretion, etiquette, and morality that the dancers themselves define in negotiation with their clients, and under the gaze of other dancers. The stylistic details of a dancer's performance depend on what she finds comfortable, and varies according to a dancer's sensibilities. Moreover, the limits on what is permitted keep being pushed as the competition among dancers becomes fiercer. Dancers who have been in the business for a long time (some of them for as long as ten years) comment on how the style of dancing has become more "*apelativo,*" or edgy. When there were fewer dancers working in the bars, the atmosphere was more relaxed and women did not need to do as much as they do now in order to earn their dollar bills. As more women, particularly migrant women, enter the sex industry, there is a tendency to go beyond what could be considered proper. Women may have to show more of their bodies than they desire to or get involved with clients more than they would like to.

Dancers' schedules are set periodically, either monthly or biweekly, and this process (of setting the schedules) constitutes a powerful way of disciplining the dancers into more aggressively interacting and drinking with clients, since managers will book dancers who are more willing to be compliant with the interests of the bars. Although a dancer can order water or soda, these drinks do not produce either the symbolic or the bodily and psychic intoxicating effects that follow the rules of fun and the tease of desire that are part of the performance. Experienced dancers must balance drinking enough to comply with the game of seduction and knowing when to restrain their daily alcohol consumption for reasons of health and sanity. This is a very fine balance, since clients with disposable money are more than willing to buy drinks for dancers and to push the boundaries of what is permissible. Accusations about other dancers' excessive drinking are a common way to assert differences of class among dancers.

The appropriate ways of negotiating with a client are a source of controversy and reveal the ways dancers define class and racial differences by using the language of morality. Because, in Queens bars, dancers make their money in the form of tips when dancing on the stage, clients put dollar bills in their hands or place the bills between a dancer's breasts or under the string of her bikini. The details of these negotiations are a crucial part of the performance and define the exchanges between client and dancer. Exchanges that occur offstage, when a dancer is not dancing, also influence how much a client will give a dancer when she is on stage.[6] For Clara, dancing is fine and fits with her ideas about partying and national celebration; however, touching or being touched by clients is unacceptable to her. For others, some touches are fine but they draw the line at rubbing their bodies against a client's genitals. For still others, this is fine as long as they do not have go out with the clients. Although such limits might shift depending on the relationship a dancer has with the client and on bar regulations, women very often accuse each other of transgressing the limits of the morally acceptable. I very often saw women acting in a way that they would not consider appropriate in some other context. Nevertheless, the allegation that "other" women are behaving inappropriately serves as a symbolic separation of bodies from different racial and class backgrounds, not just nationality.

Education: A Marker of Class and Race

As noted before, middle-class Brazilian women separate themselves from two other groups of women: from "Hispanics," and from other Brazilians from the working and lower-middle classes, some of whom are of darker skin color. Excerpts from an interview with Clara are revealing of this process of "distinction" within the bar:

> Suzana: So, what is the difference between Hispanics and
> Brazilians? Do you think we are all part of the same culture?
> Clara: In no way. I think that the Hispanics are *povinho* [little
> people]; they are much more underdeveloped than Brazilians.
> Suzana: And who are the Hispanics—anyone who speaks
> Spanish?

Clara: No, not really. To me Hispanics are Colombians, Ecuadorians, Mexicans—that part of the world. You know by the way they walk, in the bars you know by the way they talk, they are fraudulent, they are repulsive, with exceptions.

Referring to a Brazilian woman who used to date a Greek man with whom she came to have a relationship, Clara tells me:

I met him in the bar; he is friends with the owner. He had just broken up with this other Brazilian dancer. I could never understand that relationship because I knew the woman, a girl from the Rio's shantytowns; she used to do coke, smoke pot, and had a child with an unknown father. She left the child with her mother in Rio. *Gentinha mesmo*, little people. She wasn't a bad person, just low level, couldn't speak for two minutes without cursing. And he did a lot for her; he knew what kind of person she was. She was twenty-one and he, forty-eight. And she couldn't speak English—how did they communicate? I never understood that.

The manager told Janice one evening that she was not booked for that night, but since she was there and apparently had nothing else planned, she just hung around in the dressing room. It was early in the evening and I was also in the dressing room watching the dancers get ready to perform. As a Brazilian, I could immediately perceive by her way of talking and her bodily manners that Janice was from a working-class background. Besides, she had her hair dyed completely blond. For a middle-class Brazilian woman, the right way to lighten one's hair is just to add blond highlights. Janice looked much older than the thirty-two she claimed. That night I was in the bar with Nana, and as soon as she had a chance to talk to me in private, Nana commented that Janice had come to the United States from Mexico. This was a very significant piece of information, which Nana passed on to me not only because she thought I needed it for my research, but also to assert her distance from Janice. Throughout the night I observed the way Nana and the other women who were part of her clique ignored Janice, despite Janice's effort to be close to them. Nana also told me that Janice had been charged with engaging in prostitution while working in a bar in New Jersey. Nana coupled this information with a moral discourse on appropriate behavior and education. For Nana, as for other dancers in my research, a dancer's being able to speak English and her educational background are common markers separating classes or races within the bars.

A little later that night, when I went back to the dressing room, Janice was very talkative. Without my asking much, she proceeded to tell me some of her life history. She told me she had been in the States for about two years and started dancing right after her arrival in New York. Janice said that in the beginning she worked from midday to 8 a.m. and then from 9 p.m. to 3 a.m. "I could hardly walk," she said. "I just worked and worked." Janice's financial need to come here became even clearer to me when she told me she had a ten-year-old son and had recently paid for a repair in her son's father's house, where her son lived. "His house," she said, "would get all wet inside when it rained." Only quite poor houses get rained on inside, and naturally none of the women who are part of my research have had such experiences. Janice had brought with her a bag full of go-go costumes that she distributed among the other dancers. She said that some of them used to belong to her sister and some were her own, but she had gained weight and they did not fit her anymore. Despite her generosity, the other dancers still somewhat ignored her. Nana, even after receiving a couple of G-string bikinis from Janice, still gossiped about her. While we were sipping a beer later on at the bar, she told me that Janice still goes out with clients. "*Deus me livre* [God protect me], this is a miserable life, just working, killing herself to support her family in Brazil. She has no life of her own, she never went to school and never learned English. It is unbelievable these women here, they make so much money and they don't make anything of their lives."

Performance and Performativity

Although there is no set of rules that the dancers have to follow, or clear criteria with which to judge performance, managers as well as dancers and clients agree that some women are naturally more able than others

to do the job. Besides care of the body, outfits, and other ap
of performance, there is an intangible quality that translate
ability to seduce a client. This quality is represented by a wa,
ing and holding oneself, a way of walking and looking, that is intrinsi-
cally sensual and that makes some dancers more successful than others.
Transnational processes affect all steps in the construction of a dancer
and her performance of femininity, race, and class across nations. The
ways dancers are introduced to the bar scene greatly affects the relationships they develop there. The networks by which they enter the
scene also define what cliques they belong to, and the kinds of moral
prescriptions under which they will be performing. The demarcation
among dancers happens not only according to language and nationality, but also class and race. Differentiation and hierarchization among
dancers are manifest and reinforced through practices of the body and
bodily display, behaviors and preferences, and expressed by a rhetoric of
morality, respectability, and education. These are strategies that affect
dancers' incorporation into larger racial categories.

In the U.S. context, Brazilian women must enter one or another of
the historically defined racial categories. Factors such as class and race
locations as defined in the country of origin greatly affect the ways in
which migrants are incorporated. A Brazilian woman will be classified
as Latina (or Hispanic, the most common category in the bars), remain
in the differentiated category of Brazilian, or even be classified as white
depending not only on her color/race but also on the labor market she
enters. In the case of erotic dancers, when women from different racial
and class locations work side by side, the articulation of "distinctions"
functions in a variety of ways. When Clara uses the expression *gentinha*,
or little people, to refer both to Hispanics and Brazilian women from
the working class, she is in fact deploying a language of morality in order to distance herself from the racial lumping that would put her together with people she does not consider her equals in terms of race or
class.

Although dancers' work happens in the separate, ritualistic space of
the bars, their performance spills out into other moments and spaces
outside them. Their performances also have the effect of reiterating or
redefining social roles and subject locations, for identity is constituted
through the repetition of known acts. With time, performances may af-

fect the identity of a dancer not only when she is performing in the bar scene, but also outside it in unexpected ways.

Changing Bodies, Changing Selves

On a winter night in 2003 I met Silvana for the first time, and coincidentally it was also her first time working in a bar. Silvana, twenty-one years old, then had curly dark hair and sat shyly in a chair not by the bar, but in a more secluded area, where she sipped her *guaraná*, a Brazilian soda, and talked to Nana and me. She said she was from the countryside of Minas Gerais and missed her home and her parents. Silvana could hardly walk on her high heels and relaxed only when I tried to walk on them myself and almost fell down, to her amusement and that of the other dancers. She spoke almost no English, and that night she sat with me and did not talk to any clients. During her sets, Silvana would walk unsurely to the platform and not quite look at any man or any other dancer. Every now and then she would look at herself in one of the wall's mirrors and smile at me. I encouraged her, and on her breaks she would come sit with me again. We developed a kind of intimacy and bond that night, and I wished her good luck and got her telephone number for a future interview.

A month after our first meeting I met Silvana again at Blue Diamond. I literally did not recognize her. She had straightened her hair and highlighted it with blond streaks. Her eyebrows were plucked thin, and she was comfortably holding her body on extremely high heels, although she was not there that night to work. In fact, Silvana was there in the company of an older Greek man with whom she had started going out and "having fun." She still could speak only a little English, but she was sitting next to him and sipping a drink while other dancers stopped by to chat. She was somewhat confused when she saw me, although I praised her hair and her new manner and commented on how good she looked. The intimacy and trust of the first night, however, were gone. Still, I decided to call her for an interview a week later. Knowing dancers' late-night schedule, I called her in the middle of the afternoon and found her just waking up. Silvana was tired and irritable, and explained to me that she was no longer working at Blue Diamond. She had a problem with one of the clients, who had thrown a drink at her, and she was really upset because the manager did not do anything about it and did not defend her. Silvana was now dancing in New Jersey and was working every day. She had no time for an interview and told me to call her another time. When I called her a second time a few weeks later, she was in the supermarket going through the checkout line. I could hear the change in her voice, from that timid girl I met on her first night in the bar to the busy woman she was now. Silvana kept saying something like "that's it" in her broken English, trying hard to show me how her language skills had evolved. She had even less time for me now than when I called before. When I later called again, she was in a van that was taking her to her job in New Jersey. I never learned her story and why she needed to work every day of the week and reduce her life to the bar scene that way. With her present schedule, she will have no time to go to school, a plan that she vaguely referred to—rather to please me, I think, than as a realistic goal. Neither will she have time to socialize with anyone outside the bar scene. At twenty-one, Silvana did not seem to be aware of all the things that were happening to her. Her body and self were changing faster than she could keep up with.

Chapter 5

Women and Clients

Men frequent gentlemen's bars for a variety of reasons. Some want a few hours of socialization and drinking before going home to their wives, to whom they might be happily married. Others, unmarried or divorced, may just want to pass some time before going to bed after a long day at work. They enjoy the company of dancers, buy them drinks, talk for a little while, and then go home. Still other men, particularly in the case of Manhattan clubs, go to bars as part of what Allison, in her study of a Japanese gentlemen's club, has denominated "corporate masculinity" (1994), a performance associated with the hegemonic and mostly white executive man who goes out with his business partners mainly as part of a company's male bonding practices. Going to bars, as Frank (2002) argues, can also be seen as a tourist practice. Men may go to bars to experience the excitement of the controlled risk associated with traveling to other countries. Without having to leave town, they travel to its geographic and symbolic edges, where they can encounter foreign bodies.

Here I focus not on the motivations and perceptions of customers but on dancers' points of view—how they see clients based on their observations of clients' positioning, attitudes, and behavior within the bar scene. The kinds of interactions that a dancer may have with the various customers depend upon her perception of a customer's "performance of masculinity."[1] The way a customer holds his drinks, how he tips, how he gazes at women, and his general bodily display and manners are signifiers that dancers must decipher. Like the dancers, customers come from a variety of ethnoracial, national, and class backgrounds. As much as clients racialize dancers in the bar scene, dancers classify clients according to racial and class-based categories. When talking to a client, in addition to displaying her body a dancer must develop a discourse that differentiates her from other dancers and that defines her appeal. Nationality is the foremost marker of identity that a dancer embodies. From my observations, mention of Brazil appears in dancers' conversations with clients in two contradictory ways: as a source of happiness and freedom, and as a place of chaos and violence. A dancer emphasizes these different aspects of the Brazilian nation depending on her own class, racial, and educational background, and depending on the kind of interactions and relationships she considers proper with different kinds of customers.

Relationships with Clients:
The Allure of Brazilian Dancers

When a man starts going to a gentlemen's bar, he is in the eyes of dancers just a customer. This man may have been just passing by and stopped for a beer, or he may be searching for a new bar or a new dancer, and this may be the first of a series of visits. A dancer must maximize her relationship with a new customer in terms not only of their interaction on a particular night, but also of the potential for his continued visits.[2] A dancer's success on the stage and in the bar in general depends on the relationships she develops when socializing with clients. Coming down from the stage, and even though accompanied by another dancer or client, a dancer may keep making eye contact with a potential new customer. Alternatively, a dancer can walk directly up to a potential new client and ask if he would like her to sit with him. Almost invariably in Queens bars the question that follows the first exchange of names is, Where are you from? In fact, a Greek American client who has been going to bars for some twenty years told me that one of the common pastimes among friends who frequent bars together is to guess where a dancer is from.[3]

Knowing where a dancer is from just by looking at her demonstrates the familiarity of the client with the markers of each nationality. This display of knowledge about the global geographies of desire in New York bars adds to his own image of worldliness. The conversation then continues, always around the same subject: place of origin. The next question would be, How long have you been here? Between questions and answers there would be pauses, so as not to exhaust the subject and to maintain the suspense in which the play of seduction is realized. At the same time, this small and slow talk gives both parties the chance to read the body language of the other and signs of advancing the interaction. A drink or two are consumed in half-silence, the accompaniment to smiles, the movements of legs crossing and uncrossing, gazes exchanged, and maybe a few questions about the weather or similar innocuous subjects.

After this initial encounter, it would be time for the dancer to get on the stage again. If the encounter was successful, the play of seduction will continue as she dances, with exchanges of looks or gazes, generous tipping on the part of the customer, and generous attention on the part of the dancer. On her next break, the dancer may go back to sit with the same client, but she is more likely to keep him waiting a little longer. While working the room, sitting and talking with other clients and dancers, a dancer exchanges fortuitous and seductive gazes with the potential customer. This strategy will extend the time the customer spends in the bar, increasing both his expenditure and his anxiety to talk to her again. If the dancer is pushy and sits with the same customer constantly, she exhausts the potential for a continuing interaction too early. If this happens, the client is likely to leave the bar too soon, before the promise of a relationship plays out. Nonetheless, a dancer cannot keep a customer waiting for too long. After one or two breaks in which she keeps him interested by looking at him seductively while sitting with someone else, the dancer goes back to sit with him. Acknowledging smiles are exchanged and the customer buys the dancer a drink while she crosses and uncrosses her legs and perhaps now lets her arm casually touch his. At many points, conversation between dancer and customer is kept to a minimum, and the performance happens on the level of body language, particularly if the dancer's or client's English is still tentative.

The conversation continues with questions such as, How do you like it here? Do you live nearby? What do you do? What did you do back home? If the client has been to Brazil, or even if he has not but wants to show his geographical knowledge, he may ask where in Brazil the dancer is from and then tell a tale or two about his adventures or a friend's adventures there, comment on music or a movie, or tell a casual anecdote that is related to the country. The allure of Brazilian dancers comes not only from their performance when on the stage, but from the evocations of Brazil when dealing with customers on the floor. Sitting with clients, each must develop both a body language and a discourse that distinguishes her from other dancers. Since her nationality is the foremost marker of her identity in the transnational context of the bar, a discourse about the Brazilian nation is inevitable, albeit often broken, flat, or inconsistent. I distinguished two main types of discourse in dancers' interactions with clients.

One kind of discourse celebrates the beauty of Brazilian landscapes and bodies, and the friendliness of its people. Despite the fact that few women would say that they really enjoy dancing (quite the opposite—I regularly heard them complaining about it when not with customers), when asked how they feel about dancing almost invariably the women say that dancing feels natural to them, since that is what they normally do in Brazil. They often refer to the Brazilian climate, the festive environment, and the natural exhibition of their body and beauty back home. Even when they look extremely bored, while talking to clients they may stress stereotypical images of beaches and a place where everybody is happy and partying all the time. Expressing Brazilian warmth, they do not mind kissing the clients on both cheeks or stroking their backs amicably.[4]

The other discourse about the nation that dancers use with clients speaks of economic crisis and political corruption, of disenchantment, and of personal difficulties in surviving in a place of chaos and violence. As Teresa once told me: "You should never tell a customer that you are dancing because you like it, that you want to have fun. You must tell him that your family needs the money and that you can't make this money even as a lawyer or a psychologist there." Brazilian dancers must play with the different elements available in the national discourses as these elements intersect with their personal narratives of class. In this small extract, we can see that Teresa made sure to mark her status by revealing her professional background at the same time that she asserts her financial need.[5] The appeal of a Brazilian dancer from the middle class consists in a very fine balance in the "erotic of the exotic" as it takes place in the bars. She is supposed to enjoy dancing, yet this should not be the reason she dances. She dances for financial reasons, yet she must assert her class position. A dancer's educational and professional background is indicative of her location not only within the class and racial structure of Brazil, but also in reference to a global racial order.

A client chooses a dancer according to a desirable balance between class and race that will reinforce his male privilege. He may want a touch of class in his dancers, but he may feel threatened by a dancer with a higher social status than his. A dancer also must choose among clients the ones that do not hurt her sense of class position. Dancers closely watch customers' performances of masculinity from the moment they walk in a bar. The way clients hold their bodies, if they come alone or with company, the way they dress, talk, or smoke—all are revealing of their class and ethnic-racial location. If there is a point of convergence in the very fine negotiations in the first encounters between a customer and a dancer, the client will give her generous tips as a sign of his continued interest. This new customer might also give his telephone number to a dancer, and he will leave the bar knowing what days of the week his new favorite dancer works at a particular bar.

A relationship with a customer may develop in different ways. From my observations and conversations with my dancer friends, I distinguished three main categories into which dancers place bar patrons: clients, amigos, and psychopaths. These three categories correspond to dancers' perception of clients' class and racial global location, as manifested in the gender and sexual appropriateness of their behavior.

Clients vs. Her Clients

"Clients" is a large category in which dancers place men who go to bars with a certain frequency, which can range from every day to once a month or every couple of months. Relationships between clients and dancers may remain distant, but they most likely will develop some kind of intimacy over time. The bars' loud music and hectic atmosphere limit the type of conversation they can engage in. Favorite dancers and clients know each other's names (likely fictitious), about their work, their country of origin, and sometimes about their family or love life. Clients buy drinks for dancers who sit with them while they observe other dancers on the stage. This interaction can remain at the same level for months or years and may or may not develop into something else.

Once a client starts favoring a dancer above other dancers, he becomes "her client." Each dancer has a number of clients—her clients. This does not by any means imply exclusivity from the perspective of either the client or the dancer. A dancer may have a number of clients that go to the same bar on the same night, and a client can also have a number of favorite dancers. Favorites among dancers and clients change quite often. For a few weeks or months a client may prefer one dancer above all the others. He will let her know by looking at her meaningfully while she is dancing on the stage. When it is his turn to tip, he will not only give her a generous tip, but also smile and ask her name. She will smile back if she likes him and will continue looking back at him even when she moves to another area of the platform, although with some discretion, since she is supposed to interact with the men in the area where she is dancing.

An experienced dancer will keep as many clients returning to the bar "to see her" as she can manage. "To see her" here does not have a literal meaning but expresses an intention that gives the client a vague excuse in his own eyes and in the eyes of the dancers for his going back more frequently than he could justify otherwise. The role expected of a client who has a preferred dancer/client relationship is to give the dancer more generous tips than he gives to the other dancers and to keep buying her drinks at the bar during her breaks. If it is an established relationship, a dancer can always count on one of her clients to buy her drinks and to give her enough tips so she does not have to work the room as much. A dancer can also rely on her clients on a bad night when she is unlikely to make much money.

Dancers consider older Greek and Italian men the best clients in Queens bars. They tend to be men who have a significant amount of disposable money. Restaurant owners or owners of construction companies, in terms of income, these men can be considered part of the American middle class. However, they do not identify with the habitus associated with their income level. These Greek and Italian clients often lack a college degree and have not acquired a taste for concerts, books, or movies that are part of the Western canon. In Queens bars, as opposed to Manhattan bars, they can identify with other foreigners like themselves and not feel awkward about their working-class background. They usually spend generously on their favorite dancers in exchange for attention and for the pampering of their relative male privilege. The bar becomes their main space for socialization and the dancers their closest companions.

The relationship between a middle-class Brazilian dancer and an older Greek or Italian man may develop outside the bar, with the bar scene as a reference for meanings and expectations. It is common for clients to give their telephone number to dancers, hoping or expecting them to call and to go out for a dinner or drink outside the bar. This is a very careful negotiation between dancer and client.[6] A way for a dancer to gain financially from a date with a client is to tell him that in order to meet him outside the bar, she will have to miss a day of work, implying that the client should compensate her accordingly. A good client is aware of this expectation, and after their encounter outside the bar, he may slip into her hand what he calculates is fair compensation, in the case of Queens bars, usually two folded hundred-dollar bills. An experienced client will not necessarily expect any sex from this exchange. This encounter outside the bar scene is more similar to the work of an escort than of a prostitute. The money given is to pay not for sex but for the display of a beautiful female companion, which will serve more to enhance the client's public persona than to cater to his private sexual urges. The women must be sensually dressed for these occasions. Another way for a dancer to maximize this exchange financially without having to receive cash for her services or company directly (and thus to be thought of as blurring the line between dancing and prostitution) is for her to make clients buy her presents, particularly in form of clothes or jewelry.

A client who has a restaurant or bar may also patronize a number of dancers by inviting them to come to his business with their friends, which in the bar scene are called "cousins." It is common for a woman to tell a client that she will be accompanied by a cousin—another woman who will add to the spectacle of sensuality and power that the man wants to engage in. Besides taking his favorite dancers to expensive dinners and compensating them financially for the night of work missed, a client must also give them presents, which can range from less expensive (although never cheap) shirts and dresses to a plane ticket to Brazil or even a house there. The quality and price of the gift depends on the relationship and the ability of the dancer to convince the client of her need. Although the details about dancers' lives may vary greatly, if they want to maximize the profit they can get from the relationship, dancers must not only tell their clients that they are working as dancers because they need to but also exaggerate the extent of their need. At some point in the course of a relationship, a dancer may say (which may or may not be true) that her mother back in Brazil needs an urgent operation; that her house, here or there, needs to be fixed; that she must pay for school; or simply that she needs better clothes if she is going to such nice places with him. The men might not believe everything their favorite dancers say, yet they know that if they are dancing it is because they need to, and they realize they must be generous if they want to keep the relationship going. If a client is considered cheap, there is no reason for a dancer to go out with him unless he offers other qualities to compensate for his lack of financial generosity.

When Teresa needed a knee operation, for example, Frank, her Italian former client and boyfriend/lover who later became just her friend and bar client, did not hesitate to pay for her ticket to get the operation in Brazil and for the surgery itself. In fact, after years of negotiating her friendship/client/lover relationship with Frank, Teresa eased out of the relationship only when he gave her a house by the beach in northeast Brazil. Although Ted, a Greek American client I knew, did not find lap dances particularly arousing, he did not refuse Clara's request for extra money to pay her income taxes.

The relationships between Brazilian middle-class dancers and Greek and Italian older men are a source of constant negotiation. Such men are generous in tipping and gifting, which is the reason a dancer wants to keep them always nearby, preferably as her client or sponsor (as we see the next chapter). However, despite their middle-class income level, Greek and Italian older men do not carry the markers of distinction that conform to Brazilian middle-class standards. The main reason is that they do not have college education, which is crucial to the definition of class position by the dancers in my research, most of whom were university graduates. Further, although they are in the highest ranks within the bar scene (above the Hispanics and the Albanians, as we will see later), they are not white enough. They are still foreigners who are not fully integrated with U.S. institutions and codes. They are still, as Nana poignantly once told me, "on the margins."

Manhattan Clients: Corporate Masculinities

Working in Manhattan, Nadja has access to wealthier men than she would in Queens. I do not know much about Nadja's relationships with her clients. I have accompanied Nadja to work only a few times in Manhattan bars and could not stay in the lounge where dancers and clients interact. It is a rule of some of the more upscale bars that single women cannot frequent the bar on their own. The times I accompanied Nadja or met her in Manhattan bars, I would greet her and her friends in the bar, look around briefly, and then go upstairs to the dressing room to socialize with other dancers. The other times I went to more upscale bars in Manhattan and also in downtown Queens, I was accompanied by male friends. Couples who go to these bars keep basically to themselves. They make comments to each other about dancers and seduce each other through the dancers. They may also talk to dancers when negotiating a lap dance or a table dance, but they very rarely socialize with other people in the bar.

The atmosphere in upscale bars does not invite conversation between bar patrons not related in their business or personal lives. The overstimulation and nonstop consumption seem to make conversation not only secondary but also unwelcome. The music is too loud and the rotating lights have an intoxicating effect that allows one to catch only fragments of speech. Introductions are brief and movements of the body, dress codes, and gazes matter more than anything else. As an outsider who has gone to upscale Manhattan bars just a few times, I particularly noticed clients style of dress—corporate masculinity: plain expensive suits and ties, much like Wall Street fashion, and short, well-groomed hair. A number of bouncers and bar-related male onlookers dressed in black and standing by the entrance set the appropriate behavior and dress code. They greet newcomers and longtime patrons and make sure their presence is acknowledged. Customers consist of brokers, international politicians, managers at transnational corporations, and tourists who come to experience Manhattan's nightlife. Justine, sensitive not just to class markers but also to intellectual sophistication, told me that she has spoken with quite a few professors and that some of her favorite pop stars used to frequent the Midtown Manhattan bar where she used work. The expenditure required in these bars discourages lower-income clients, as well as clients who do not conform to the patterns of spending and the performance of corporate masculinity reinforced by the bars.

Like Justine, Nadja keeps relationships with her clients separate from her private life. Unlike Justine, however, Nadja does not object to going out with clients or accepting valuable gifts from them in return. Blurring the line between being a dancer and an escort, Nadja accompanies wealthy men to dinners and other social events on occasion. For that, she does not receive direct cash as escorts do, which Nadja would view as inappropriate. She prefers to receive compensation for her companionship in the form of presents. Nadja's room is always packed with half-open boxes filled with new expensive clothes, shoes, and jewelry. Once, as Barbara and I were sitting on Nadja's bed and watching her get ready to go out, Nadja showed me a pair of Manolo Blahnik shoes that cost about $600 and a new Coach bag that cost $850. "O bofe"—a Brazilian expression for a man one does not respect—as she calls her clients, "bought them for me." "Uau, I have to learn how to do it," Barbara said. "Me too," I said. "What is the strategy?" "Ah, querida," Nadja boasted:

> You have to learn how to do it. When a client invites me to go out, I say: "I would love to but I will need very nice clothes if I am to accompany you." They know what this is about, and they like that too. They like going with you to a store and then you choose, choose, and call them. They come and pay. It is that simple, he can afford and he is happy to do so, and I am happy too. Then we go to expensive dinners either alone or with his friends and eat very expensive food and drink very expensive champagne and wine.

The client she is referring to here is an older white American investor, "really handsome," according to Nadja, who "just wants to have fun sometimes." They go out to dinners in very expensive restaurants, drink and eat well, and then he pays for her cab back home. He seems to be married, according to Nadja. I asked her about the social dynamics of these dinners, since she has never made much effort to learn English and she even exaggerates her inability when she is around some clients. Nadja answered that her body language is much more effective than her discursive language, and I do not doubt it.

Amigos

The first time I met Popeye, he was playing pool, drinking, and smoking cigarettes.[7] I was talking to Nana, waiting until she spotted a client who could buy us drinks. "Ah, there is one there," she said after a visual search. Critical as she is of the bar scene and as aware as she is of class markers, Nana can sit by herself for a long time if she does not think that the men available are suitable. For that reason, Nana is seen as snobbish by clients and by dancers outside her clique. She sits with a client only if she thinks that the man has some *nível*—literally, "level." Having level, in Nana's eyes, is determined by a man's social and educational levels as manifested through his manners and the way he treats dancers. Nana does not tolerate clients who try to touch dancers or who engage in conversations considered inappropriate or rude, such as talking about sex or talking to dancers in a purposefully indifferent way as the client carries on a conversation with friends. Popeye is considered "acceptable" by Nana, and we walked to the other side of the bar to greet him.

"This is Popeye, he is my friend, *meu amigo*," Nana said, introducing me to Popeye as we took seats next to him. "Nice to meet you." Popeye immediately asked what we wanted to drink—two beers. He ordered the drinks from the bartender and went back to his pool game. Nana and I continued our conversation, not quite interacting with Popeye, when Sheila, a dancer from Rio de Janeiro and loosely part of Nana's clique, came to join us from the other side of the counter.[8] Sheila wanted to comment on Popeye: "These men are really funny. Look at this Popeye. He used to come here once in a lifetime; now he comes here every other day." Nana agreed:

> He is very lonely. He just retired and has nothing to do with his time. He told me that some days he walks for five hours just because he has nowhere to go. Here, he can talk to us, have a beer, play pool, and then go home when he gets tired. Before, he used to buy us a lot of champagne, but now he only buys drinks sometimes. He spent a lot of money. Some guys are nice.

Popeye, as the dancers named him, referring to the cartoon character, is an American man of Italian and Irish descent who enjoys a good standard of living as a unionized electrician. He is in his midfifties and divorced, and he has a married daughter who lives in New Jersey whom he visits once a month.

According to Nana's calculation, Popeye now spends a maximum of a hundred dollars every time he goes to the bar. This is enough for two drinks for him and a few drinks and tips for dancers. "That's not much for him," Sheila said. "If every man does that, we go home happy with some money in our pockets, and they go home happy, too." "Plus," added Nana, "men like Popeye, you see, he helps just by being nice. He makes my night shorter; eight hours at night in this bar is not easy, and with men like him it can be pleasant. He just plays pool and talks with us sometimes, he is not demanding."

For his income level and profile, Popeye could well become a client of any dancer he wishes. He prefers, nonetheless, to remain just a "friend." A friend is a client who differs from a dancers' client in a number of ways. While a dancer's client is expected to have a more continuous relationship with a specific dancer, a friend is not. Popeye, for example, goes to bars when he needs company. He comes to the bar to talk, have a beer, play a little pool, and go home. He never calls any dancer and is not concerned with which dancers work each night. Popeye does not go to bars to see anybody in particular. He is friendly to all the dancers and tips them generously. For Popeye, there are advantages in going to a go-go bar instead of an ordinary bar, where with his timid personality, he would most likely have to have a beer on his own and struggle to exchange a word or two with a bartender or with the guy sitting beside him. In a go-go bar, Popeye has the attention of beautiful, pleasant women who are fun to be with. In exchange for these women's attention, friends like Popeye tip generously, while not committing to be a continuing financial source. Friends like Popeye, from his manners and ways of tipping, are convenient relationships to have in the bar scene. In addition, the whiteness of his social location as part of the American working class makes Popeye "acceptable," as Nana put it.[9]

A second form of friendship a dancer establishes in the bar scene is with a patron who, according to the dancers' judgment, does not fulfill the conditions that would make him a client. He may not have the necessary amount of disposable money or he may be of an ethnic-racial makeup that puts him hierarchically lower than a dancer. This was the case in Tati's (a designer-dancer from Rio de Janeiro) friendship with Carlos.

As I sat around the counter with Barbara and Tati, Barbara commented: "The other day I saw that guy who is your friend; isn't he Hispanic?" "His parents are from Honduras but he is American," Tati said, trying to explain her relationship with him while at the same time excusing the fact that Carlos was Hispanic. Avoiding close relationships with Hispanic dancers (as we have seen) and with Hispanic customers in this case is a form of avoiding racialization. By affirming Carlos's birthright of American citizenship, Tati is clearly demarcating Carlos's, and consequently her, separation from Hispanics. As she said: "He is Hispanic but not like other Hispanics who are undocumented." Despite his ethnic origin, Carlos is an American; in addition to having papers he is supposed to have domain over American codes and lifestyles, which makes him superior to Hispanics and thus acceptable as a friend, according to Tati's standards. "He has helped me a lot," Tati said. "How?" I asked. "He is a friend, he gives me money—before he would give me showers but now he gives in my hand; it is more discreet and the other women don't look at me with evil eyes."[10] "Yes, but sometimes when one gets showers the other men also get *empolgado* [carried away] and you start getting more money—besides, guys like showing off that they are giving money," Barbara commented. "That's true," Tati replied, "but he is discreet. Besides, he helps me just by being my friend, you know, someone that you can count on." "Like what?" I asked. "Like if I need a car to go somewhere, for example; little things, if you need to talk."

Bar patrons can well start as friends, evolve into clients, and then revert to friends. This was the case of Ivana in her relationship with Chris. When she first met him in La Casa, their relationship started as a friendship that began in Ivana's first months in the bar scene. Although Ivana has an aunt who used to dance, she entered the bar scene pretty much on her own. (Her aunt had stopped dancing years before Ivana entered the bar scene and now works as a nurse in a Harlem hospital.) She was informed about what to wear and where to buy her clothes, and had a general idea that she had to go up on the stage and dance. However, she did not have anyone who went to bars with her and could teach her the nuances of seduction or what she should or should not say or do to please a man and at the same time maintain her limits. Chris, a man in his early fifties who is a frequent client in gentlemen's bars, took on the task of giving Ivana tips about dancing and about life in New York. Being new to the bar and to the city, Ivana appreciated his help when he invited her for a coffee in a Greek café in Astoria. He became a friend; sometimes he would call her to see how she was doing and she would call to say hello and to let him know where and when she was dancing.

Particularly when dancers are new in the country, like Ivana, or if they do not have other activities outside the bars, the men and women in the bars become their closest friends in the United States, the only people they can rely on in case of need. They may enjoy the company of someone who can show them around, buy them lunch or dinner, and also teach them some English. Amigos can also be a valuable source of advice and information about how to negotiate with other men in the bar scene, drawing from their own experience. When Ivana started relying on Chris as a stable source of tips and information inside and outside the bar, he became her client. When this relationship evolved into a romance, and their time outside the bar took on importance beyond the bar scene, Chris became her sponsor. (See the next chapter for more on sponsors.)

Psychopaths

I was at a dancer's birthday party eating a piece of cake by the counter
when Carmen, a Colombian bartender, gave me a beer and said that it
was sent by a youngish guy sitting across the stage from me. I smiled
and raised the beer to thank him. Carmen said: "In a little while he will
come to bother you, you can bet." I said, "No problem." The client came
over to where I was in a few minutes. I exaggerated my Brazilian accent
and started talking about the usual bar subjects—where you are from,
how long you have been here, how do you like it, and so on. Demos
told me he was from Albania and that he came to New York six years
ago, following his brother, who had a construction company. While
Demos and I were talking, one of his friends came and gave me a money
shower. I did not quite understand what was happening and actually
thought that it was quite rude, since I was not dancing. It was not clear
to me whether the guy who sent me the shower wanted to encourage
me to stay with his friend or wanted to have a more collective game of
seduction.

I gathered the money around me, thirty dollars, and placed it on
the counter. Demos asked if I wanted to smoke a cigarette outside so
we could talk better. I put the money in my pocket and went with him.
Outside the bar, we met an older Greek man who works in the bar
and who had gone to change money in the laundry across the street.
He joined us and we talked about soccer and Greek-Albanian relations. "Who cares where one is from? Here we are the same," the Albanian said, while he jokingly punched the Greek in his stomach. The
Greek returned the punch, a cigarette hanging from his mouth. After
the Greek man left, Demos started boasting about his success in the
United States. He told me he had bought a house in Howard Beach for
$1 million and, by pressing a device on his car key, showed me his new
Mercedes-Benz parked across the street. "Gray is my favorite color in
the world," he said. "It is a nice color," I agreed. "Really beautiful car."
He continued:

> Before, I had a Cadillac and I crashed it; it was my favorite car.
> After I lost it, that's when I started smoking. I had stopped for
> three years. When I came to America, I said I am only going to

work, no more parties, drinking, cigarettes, but then I started again. I had a Brazilian girlfriend once, a dancer, for three months; she was such a bitch, the most bitch woman, she wasn't serious. Before I had a Colombian woman for two years, but it didn't work out, I was very jealous; she would call me at eight in the morning—what the hell she would call me at eight in the morning if the bar closes at four? Why, you tell me? It didn't work out. I like Howard Beach, but I would like a house in Long Island; when I get married and have kids I will have a house in Long Island. But Howard Beach is closer to the city. I have no business with the city.

Demos asked me what I did for a living and I said I was a student and that I worked in the library. He said that that was good, "more respectable work; here women are not respectful, not a good place." "Why?" I asked. "Men don't respect women here. Some do. But it is no good." We went inside again and he ordered me another Corona and a Red Bull for himself, and his friends offered shots of tequila to everyone. He asked the DJ to put on some Albanian music, and the DJ alternated Brazilian, Greek, Hispanic, and Albanian music from then on. Demos's Albanian friends were by then totally taken with the high of spending conspicuously. As Greeks do in Greek bars in Astoria, the bartender would throw napkins in the air and, inebriated, they would change more hundred-dollar bills for singles and throw them at the bartender and at the women around. More shots of tequila were passed around, this time offered by Ricardo, a Brazilian manager.

I was already quite drunk and stumbled to the dressing room, where I talked with Tati for a while about jealousy and life. I said I thought that jealousy was like a sickness that a person had to treat. Tati had told me that she was a very jealous person and that her boyfriend had broken up with her because of it. Nana came in and said that the Albanians were looking for me. I went back to them and more tequila shots were ordered. At this point Demos left, after throwing a hundred dollars in singles in the air toward the bartender. The Albanian man who had given me the money shower asked me to sit with him. I moved to his side and he offered me a drink. We did not seem to have anything to say to each other, and he soon asked me if I wanted to smoke a cigarette outside and see his car. I said, "Not tonight." He offered again, and when I declined he brusquely got his jacket from the chair, said good-bye, and went to sit on another stool far from me. To pull myself to-gether, I went back to the dressing room. When I told Nana and Tati what had happened, they said: "Psychopaths, they are all the same. The Albanians are really the worst—ruthless."

Brazilian dancers' classification of the Albanians as psychopaths must be understood in a context that, although manifest in the bar scene, has transnational implications. First, dancers define men as psychopaths based on their observations of clients' behaviors toward them, toward other men, and toward the bar owners. To Nana and Tati, an Albanian's performance of masculinity, such as Demos's friend giving me a money shower even though I was not a dancer, is illustra-tive of his class background and occupation. Albanians come to bars in groups, and dancers believe that they are involved in the new Ma-fias.[11] Albanians occupy a lower status than Greek and Italian older men, according to dancers. In addition to being younger and part of a more recent wave of immigration, Albanian men occupy an inferior po-sition vis-à-vis Greece in the hierarchy of nations. Thus, although they seem to be from a similar class background as the Greek and Italian pa-trons, Albanians are not desirable as either clients or friends of Brazil-ian dancers from the middle class.

"Some guys are nice. But look at those three addicts there," Nana commented to me about three youngish Albanian guys on the other side of the counter. They sat, ordered their drinks, and didn't say one word to each other, and none of them gave any tips to the dancers. "They just sit there. Albanians," Nana repeated. "The bartender is going out with the one in the middle," Ivana said. "What a waste," Tati said, approaching us. "Garbage. How can these women fall for these guys in the bar?"

The term "psychopath," however, does not refer only to Albanians. To dancers, any man who behaves in an intimidating way and who makes them feel threatened is also considered a psychopath. Sitting by the bar and watching the dancers on stage, I talked with Ivana about her new roommate. An older Greek man passed by and made a com-ment about Brazilians. We looked in his direction, and he made a gesture by blowing on his fist. We missed the cultural reference of the gesture, but it was obviously aggressive toward us. Later, the guy shouted at Ivana, exaggerating his facial expressions as if trying to shame her. It was Ivana's interval to dance and she did not say anything. When she finished, she called me to go to the dressing room with her. In the dressing room, she said: "This guy is a psychopath." Ivana told me that the other day he gave her a twenty-dollar bill and told her he would be waiting for her around the corner. Ivana said all right but of course never went there. Ivana thinks that this is the reason why he was angry. Soraia, a dancer I had never met before, had seen the exchange and came to ask what had happened. As Ivana told her the story, they commented on the risks that they take in this work, complaining about the low pay: "Besides exposing yourself and your body, you still have to take these risks." Although the man who had shouted at Ivana was Greek, they commented about a fight that had broken out the other day between two Albanians and an American man when the police had to come and intervene. "The Albanians are dangerous, they all part of the Mafia, and some guys who come here are even being searched for by the FBI, for the killing of some members of the Italian Mafia. Dangerous types," they said, ending the conversation.

When I went to get my things and said I was leaving, Ivana came back and said: "No, order two more beers. I need the tickets, have one more." While we sipped our beers paid for by an Italian client, the psycho came by and called Ivana a liar again and made gestures with his hands. Ivana was very upset: "What you talking about? What you want? I don't give you anything, I didn't say anything." The Greek said she did not have anything to give him and left. Ivana shouted, "Garbage!" in her broken English and was a little shaken for a while. "That is the kind of things you have to take here," she said. I drank my beer and left, wondering if the guy would be waiting for me outside.[12]

Part III

Beyond the Bar Scene

Chapter 6

Ambivalent Relationships

It was a rainy summer day when I went on a trip to a Long Island beach accompanied by Nana and her husband, Jimmy, and Renata and her fiancé, Brandon. Not a tree passed without comment from the three of us Brazilian women, in Portuguese. How everything was green and beautiful and peaceful. We compared what we saw with the houses, the landscape, and the architecture in Brazil. Everything in Brazil seemed inferior, inadequate, and violent. Having been assaulted at gunpoint in her house and business in Brazil, Renata is particularly sensitive to the marks of social tension. To her, the open greenery of suburban Long Island front yards and the pastel houses seemed like a dream. They seemed like a dream to Nana and me, too, something we had seen in a movie. Houses and particularly beach houses in Brazil are walled-in condominiums or have come to feel like prisons. The large French sliding windows that would cool the house in the hot days of summer have been gradually replaced by jalousie windows, which help keep out thieves, then by bars on the outside.

We stopped for a late lunch in a diner and then went on for drinks in an Irish pub. The night was pleasant. I went outside to smoke a cigarette and watch people passing. I must have stayed outside for a long time, for when I came inside the bar again, the four of them—Nana, Jimmy, Renata, and Brandon—were already tired and talking about going to a hotel for the night. Fine with me, I said. On our way, Brandon commented, referring to a passerby, a Mexican man: "America is a great country; you immigrants don't know what you are talking about!" None of the other three people said anything, and I had to contain myself to remain silent. I did not want to spoil such a pleasant day with political commentary, and I already knew Brandon's political views. We decided to have a last drink in the hotel bar. Between beers and loud talk as the night worn on, I overheard Brandon ask Renata: "Do you know how much I made this year?"

With the exception of Justine, who came to the United States to pursue her graduate studies, the other women in this project came to New York on tourist visas—six-month permits to stay in the United States but not to work legally. A woman who makes the decision to stay even after her visa expires knows, from friends or family, the legal risks she assumes. If she leaves the United States, she will be unable to re-enter because of her prior illegal stay. If, knowing this, a woman decides to overstay her visa, she has basically two options: either she stays and makes as much money she can and then goes back to her country, never to reenter the United States, or she gets married and regains legal status. For migrant women who come to the United States to work as erotic dancers, the possibilities for meeting friends and prospective husbands are usually limited to the bar scene. Even though some dancers go to school and engage in leisure activities in New York, their busy night schedules limit their social life. As opposed to native U.S. dancers who are immersed in a larger network of family, friends, and acquaintances and a wider range of social situations in this country, most Brazilian women are likely to have personal encounters mainly with clients from the bars, and these encounters will be affected by the women's legal and material considerations in this country.[1]

However, that these relationships are so embedded in political and economic factors does not mean they are devoid of emotion and affection. Although their chances to meet partners are somewhat limited to the bar scene, the women are unlikely to establish personal relationships with just any man who goes to the bar. Rather, their choices are determined by two sets of considerations. On the one hand, as we have seen, the encounters that dancers have with men in the bar scene are mediated by their views of a man's racial and class location as manifested in their manners and in appropriate displays of sexuality and gender. On the other hand, women must attend to their own desires, which occur against a backdrop of political and economic factors and are related to complex and at times contradictory ideas of romance, love, and adventure.

Unlike the cases reported by Constable (2003), in which ideas of romantic love were central in the construction of Philippine and Chinese women's relationships to U.S. men, Brazilian women, very rarely mentioned love, or romantic love, for that matter, in our conversations. Modern ideals of self and body, along with nationalistic playful understandings of sexuality as celebration, have contributed to Brazilian women's hedonistic ways of defining themselves. Such hedonism is for various women combined with competing sensibilities that include gender skepticism, religious beliefs, moral constraints, a taste for adventure, a longing for marriage and emotional comfort, and transnational considerations of proper and desirable family values. These women, we must remember, are experiencing situations for which they have no models or traditions to follow. The recent intense global flows of capital, information, and people have created unforeseen conditions and situations. In what follows I explore some of the new and varied forms that the women's personal relationships take, given the transformations that took place in their material conditions and subjective lives as they crossed the borders of nation-states.

Sponsors

Clara

Clara was the one who first mentioned to me the category "sponsor." That was still how she saw Demetris, despite the many forms that their relationship has taken through the years that they have known each other. Demetris, twenty years her senior, was a regular patron for more than ten years of a bar where Clara worked and had been previously involved with other Brazilian dancers. In common with other Greek patrons in Queens, Demetris had his own subcontracting construction firm and a reasonable yearly income. When Demetris saw Clara, a young dancer fresh on the bar scene, he started the game of seduction by tipping her generously. Accepting this to be part of the game, Clara told him the nights when she would be working, and Demetris started going to bars more often when he knew she would be there. In exchange for her beautiful and young company, Clara began to accept generous tips and gifts from Demetris, and he became one of her clients for over a year. With his help, Clara rented a basement apartment in Astoria on her own. That was a significant move in their relationship. When Demetris started frequenting Clara's apartment and began to pay some of its expenses, there was a shift in the fine balance between what occurred in the bar scene and outside it. Demetris became more than just her client. Now he became also her lover and sponsor. As a sponsor, Demetris was no longer supposed to have other favorite dancers, at least not in the same bars or on the nights when Clara danced. Clara was also supposed to be his exclusive dancer when he was in the bars.

While keeping this relationship with Demetris, Clara continued the discovery of her new self in the city. She made new friends and had affairs with other men, mainly from the bar scene. After a year in New York, Clara started entertaining the idea of staying in the United States more permanently. She knew that the best way to do that would be through marriage to an American citizen. Clara could pay someone to marry her, which is a practice adopted by a few other women in her family, or she could combine convenience with pleasure, a marriage "for papers" and "for love."[2] Following the cultural and material logics of desire, Clara knew that the ideal man was an American citizen, preferably, according to her racial standards, white. She started going out with a thirty-two-year-old, blue-eyed man who had his own landscape company and who occasionally went to the bar with his friends after work. Robert was having problems with his wife—with whom he has a three-year-old son—and they had been separated for a few months. Clara saw real possibilities in constructing a relationship with him beyond the bar scene. Her relationship with Robert did not follow the path from customer to client, friend, or sponsor. Clara said that they immediately fell in love with each other. Soon after they met she became pregnant by him. Robert said he did not want a child with her and suggested that she have an abortion. Clara did not consider that an option. She is a very spiritual person, and grew up under different religious influences.[3] When she became pregnant, as in other decisive moments of her life, Clara called her spiritual adviser in Bahia and told her the dilemmas she was facing. The vision that her advisor had through reading the cards was clear: she saw a white man with blue eyes in Clara's life and she was on the right path. She should persist. Clara did not pressure Robert to accept the child at once; she knew from her advisor's vision that the time would come when he would want the child. Instead, she went on with her life, dancing until she was five months pregnant.

When Demetris learned about Clara's pregnancy and about Robert's refusal to accept it, he immediately offered to help her even more. When she became too big to be able to dance, he found her a part-time job in a friend's money transfer office. Then, after hearing her argument that the basement apartment where she was living was not suitable for a child, Demetris helped her to look for a bigger apartment in a more suburban area of Queens. He paid the brokers' fee, deposit, rent, and all the expenses of moving and furnishing the new two-bedroom apartment. He started to spend time there, while keeping his own office-apartment. Demetris assumed all the responsibility of a father in relation to the newborn child, Natalie. For a while Demetris dedicated all his free time to the care of Clara and Natalie. Nonetheless, romance was never part of Clara's vocabulary for describing their relationship. Clara knew that theirs was not the relationship that her adviser had envisioned.

Meanwhile, Clara registered Natalie under Robert's family name and sent him pictures of the baby. As a lawyer, she knew her and Natalie's rights and Robert's obligation as the biological father. Still, she decided not to use legal pressure. She waited. Meanwhile, Demetris helped her to pay for a marriage to an African American man from New Jersey in order to legalize her status in the United States. After Natalie's first birthday, Robert asked to see her. According to Clara, he just fell in love. Natalie, his only daughter, looked so much like him, and like Clara. "A perfect mixture," Clara remarked to me, invoking a Brazilian national narrative of betterment through racial miscegenation. Slowly Robert and Clara started going out again, first with baby Natalie, and then without her. Demetris started going to bars again, and little by little without major ruptures, he moved back to his apartment, while still helping Clara with the rent and with Natalie's care, along with Robert. In a big family baptism party for Natalie, Demetris assumed his new social role: he became Natalie's godfather and an official part of the family. Clara and Robert are planning on moving to a new place together. She dreams about a suburban house in Long Island with outdoor space where Natalie can play.

Teresa

Teresa now only sells outfits, but when she met Frank, she was still dancing. Frank is an Italian man in his sixties who moved to New York thirty-five years ago. He is separated from his Italian American wife, whom he still supports. He is the manager of an Italian restaurant in Manhattan and has been going to go-go bars for the last twenty-five years. From the beginning, Frank's relationship with Teresa, a mature woman in her forties, was more than that of a friend or a client. Soon after they met, Frank became Teresa's lover and sponsor. He began to support her financially and after six months, he asked her to stop dancing. Teresa did and, while keeping her own apartment, started staying at his apartment most of the time. She also traveled with him to Long Island where he had a second house, shared in alternate months with his estranged wife. Although Frank has been separated from his wife for more than six years, they had decided for financial reasons not to get divorced. Teresa told me that Frank said it would be too complicated to divide up his properties with his wife, and that an informal separation was better. Teresa was never really happy with this arrangement, and as the relationship did not evolve over the years, she grew more dissatisfied. According to Teresa, she had lost her freedom in return for much less than she was expecting. Teresa told me that, although for a while she enjoyed not having to work and the comfort of a house in Long Island, she felt that her life was becoming "stuck." She said she was unable to grow professionally because she became used to the money Frank gave her, and to the pretense of living the American dream. "It was just a dream," she reflected, "but the reality was that nothing of that was really mine. If he gets tired of me, or if he dies tomorrow, that's it, I have nothing. I stopped dancing because I saw the possibility of having a real relationship, a stable life, but that was a fake stability."

After two years of a relationship that, according to Teresa, "was going nowhere," she decided to go back to her own place and open her own business. She started making outfits for dancers in her own apartment to sell at the bars at night. To Teresa, financial and emotional independence came together. "Sometimes when I meet him today, he jokes with me, 'So did you get rich yet?' No, I haven't, but now I know that I can survive on my own. I don't sit back and think, so if he leaves me, what am I gonna do? I meet him in bars sometimes, we are still good friends, sometimes he gives me presents; if I need some money, he is very generous."

Ivana

This mix of friendship and sponsorship was also the case with the relationship between Ivana and Chris. Chris caught Ivana's attention by generously tipping her when she was onstage. While working the room, Ivana began to sit with Chris and in time started enjoying his company. Chris is a fifty-four-year-old Greek man who has been in the United States for more than thirty years. He has been married three times and now lives alone in a small apartment above his transfer money business in Astoria. After a few encounters in the bar, Chris gave Ivana his telephone number and invited her for coffee. From there they started going for dinner and soon enough they were going for a drink in Ivana's basement apartment. Chris became a friend and soon after, her sponsor. As a sponsor, Chris started waiting for Ivana in the bars until she finished work in order to take her home, and started paying some of her rent and personal expenses. He also paid for her English classes.

When I asked Ivana what attracted her in Chris, she said that it was his "experience." She told me that Chris was also "a father figure" to her, the father that she had lost when she was still a child, a person who could protect her and tell her what to do. With time, however, Ivana grew weary of the control Chris began to have over her movements. She did not quite comply. She started drinking a little too much and flirting with other men in Chris's presence. Gossip has it that one day somebody saw Chris holding Ivana's arm with more than acceptable force. Nana told me that Ivana told her about a nightmare she had about Chris. There are hints that the power balance in the relationship is not quite working. Chris changed from being a generous sponsor to being a possessive lover, and a demanding and not as generous client. Psychological and even physical abuse may very well arise in contexts like this. Nana, who lived with Ivana, calls her sometimes and does not hesitate to tell what she thinks about this relationship: "Not worth it, get out, no way." We think that Ivana is too young to be involved in a relationship with an older and controlling man, that she should stop working so much, reduce her expenses by getting a roommate, go to school, and get her life together. But at twenty-two, Ivana does not know how to balance all this in her daily life. How can she go to school if she is always so tired from working at night? How is she going to meet new friends outside the bar if she does not go to school? Without enough emotional and material help from family or friends, Ivana clings to a relationship with a man that would give her some of both, but at a price.

Identities and Distinctions

The ways through which each woman moved to the United States and the ways through which they entered the bar scene significantly affect both their relationships to bar customers and their lives outside the bar scene. Clara came to this country, as we saw, with the help and support of her extended family and friends, mainly women who already worked as dancers. From the beginning she was closely informed and assisted by more experienced women about the bar scene and was well instructed about what to expect from the different kinds of bar customers. Some of the other women in her life, a generation her senior, had been living in New York for a while and were already involved in relationships with American and foreign men, particularly Greeks and Italians. When she started dancing at Blue Diamond, Clara knew that she must have her own clients in order to have a more stable financial source. It did not take her long to find a Greek man who would be willing to be one. When she got involved with Demetris, Clara was not expecting a love relationship and she never intended to marry him. She knew that Demetris could not help her advance in terms of either legal or cultural citizenship. For one thing, Demetris, although separated, was not legally divorced. Moreover, and equally important, Demetris did not carry the markers of class and racial distinction that Clara values as a middle-class Brazilian woman. Despite his income level, Demetris could still be considered marginal to the hegemonic model of white middle-class masculinity as the ideal of the American nation. Instead of marrying Demetris, Clara engaged in a paid marriage with a man of African American descent, which could give her legal citizenship without compromising her access to the cultural citizenship that only a white American could provide her. Meanwhile, Clara decided to invest in a relationship with Robert, a man she fell in love with and who, not coincidentally, could provide her better access to American whiteness.

The case of Teresa and Frank was slightly similar to that of Clara and Demetris. Teresa also met Frank in the bar scene and he, like Demetris, evolved from client to sponsor. Nevertheless, their relationship took a significantly different path. Teresa saw in Frank the possibility of a relationship that could give her a more stable life, emotionally and materially. According to Teresa's standards, Frank was the right kind of man, not an American by birth but an American citizen and, being Italian, white enough on the racial scale of nationality. However, due to Frank's marital situation, their relationship could not develop in a way that could help Teresa advance toward incorporation into the United States. Frustrated about ever having a real relationship with Frank, Teresa decided to break it off and to concentrate on creating a business. Selling outfits in New York's bar scene, Teresa had a guaranteed alternative financial source for herself, but that did not provide her with the access to legal and cultural citizenship that a marriage to a white enough man could, and already into her forties, Teresa knew that she would have to stop dancing soon. In New York, Teresa's social life is still mostly connected to the bar scene and the Queens dancers' scene.

Working at night, Ivana did not have the time or proper guidance to continue her schooling or to engage in activities that would lead her to a more fulfilling social life beyond the bar scene. "Experience" was the term used by Ivana to explain her attraction to Chris. She seemed to be seduced by the comfort of the relationship, the constant gifts and emotional support that her relationship with her sponsor brought. However, despite his middle-class income level, Chris, as other Greek men of his generation, continued to occupy a marginalized position in U.S. society. He was not, as Ivana seemed to believe, the kind of mentor that could function as a strategy of advancement for either her legal or her cultural incorporation into the United States. In her early twenties and without a support network of family and friends, Ivana was more vulnerable than either Clara or Teresa ever has been. Ivana's isolation only grew in the bar scene and beyond it as she became involved with Chris.

Half-Lies, Half-Truths

Married and Divorced

Barbara is now a single woman, but she knows what it is to be married to someone in the United States. She was married for two years to Davi, who was born in Dominican Republic and raised in New York City and is in his late thirties as Barbara is. Barbara met Davi in a bar in Jackson Heights, Queens, where she was working. He arrived by bicycle very late one night and immediately caught Barbara's attention. As Barbara says, she likes people who are a little off, different from most, and "he looked so lost, by himself, agitated from the bike ride." During her break, Barbara went to sit with Davi and they immediately hit it off. Barbara is not the type of woman who waits when she wants something. "Life is short," she always says. "We must enjoy ourselves in the moment." Davi thought exactly the same. They both love the nightlife, getting drunk, and forgetting time. Davi owned a framing store in Lower Manhattan that employed two other Dominicans and an American man. He lived near his business in a rent-controlled apartment in the same building where he grew up and can be considered a native Dominican New Yorker. Davi knows everyone in the neighborhood and everyone knows him—the older Dominicans and Puerto Ricans of the neighborhood and the new, whiter, European-looking residents that arrived with the gentrification of the neighborhood. His episodes of drunkenness, loud arguments with ex-girlfriends, and street fights made him particularly known in the area. Barbara, however, did not know any of this and admired his popularity in such a fashionable neighborhood.

After just three months of passionate love and intense nightlife, they got married just before Barbara's visa expired. Davi knew of her need to get married. Their wedding at City Hall was followed by a party Barbara organized and paid for above an Italian diner, also on the Lower East Side. Davi's family and friends were there and also everyone Barbara knew here: other dancers from her network from Bahia and their friends and boyfriends. Barbara and Davi went to Las Vegas for their honeymoon. They were very happy for the first six months of their marriage. But Davi's alcohol consumption did not diminish as the excitement of their first meetings and wedding waned. Barbara, who continued to work five nights a week, became tired and in her free nights she preferred to stay home or just have some calm time. Davi, after a day of a work that he considered gruesome, was again ready to party. On his way home he would start drinking. Although they met in a gentlemen's bar, Davi did not think it proper for him, as her husband, to visit Barbara at work. The thought of her seducing other men started obsessing him. When Barbara would get home from work at four in the morning, Davi would be drunk and jealous and accuse Barbara of not being dedicated enough to him. Barbara, exhausted from a night of hard work, just wanted to sleep. But she could not, and the arguments were followed by the abandonment of passionate sex. Their love had a tone of romantic tragedy—desperate, defying good sense and social rules. Davi's business started suffering from his neglect, and Barbara started paying more of the bills than she thought she should. And because of that she had to work harder.

When I met Barbara, she and Davi had been married for more than a year. They had gone to Brazil together, and he was trying to slowly cut down his drinking and go to therapy. But it did not take me long to notice that this was a very fragile balance, a rest from an inherently troublesome relationship. Every time Barbara talked about Davi, her voice would tremble. Barbara seemed to be constantly exhausted and had noticeable dark circles around her eyes. The women from her network, particularly Nana and Clara, knew she was suffering; there was no hiding it when her arguments with Davi became louder and more constant every time they went out with friends. Just short of the two years necessary for Barbara to get her green card, they had a decisive fight.

After this fight, Barbara called Nana's apartment, where I had spent the night. Barbara sounded terrible. She had not slept at all since the night before and said she could no longer bear the situation. She asked Nana if she could come over, and we told her to come immediately. I will not dwell on the details of what happened that night as told to us by Barbara, but the three of us agreed that she would stay either with me or with Nana until she could gather her things and get ready to leave for Brazil. Nana and I would cancel her cell phone contract, gym membership, and English classes. Barbara spent two months in her hometown in Bahia. I was away for vacation when she came back at the beginning of July, and when we met in August she had already place to stay with Nadja, whose roommate, another dancer, had ꞏack to Brazil. The negotiations toward a definite separation and ꞉ook another six months, with Barbara moving back and forth between Nadja's and Davi's apartment. Finally, she assumed her new identity in the city—a free, single woman, with a green card that allows her to go to Brazil and back to the United States as she wishes. She continued to dance in the same bars and has since been living with Nadja. During my research, Barbara spent much of her free time hanging out either with me or with Sara, who was also single and lived near Nadja's apartment in Queens.

Singles in the Scene

Barbara and Sara, divorced women in their late thirties and early forties, free in New York, agree that marrying again is out of the question. What for? they ask each other. Sara had been married for about ten years in Brazil before she left for New York and did not enjoy the lifestyle of a married woman. She likes her independence and her ability to support herself. This was a new experience for Barbara, though. She was afraid that she would not be able to pay the rent and all the other expenses and still send money to Brazil for her child and for future savings. Sara encouraged her: "Yes, you can do it. As a woman you have the power to do whatever you want, though perhaps you will have to work a little more and to strategize better your relationship to men." Sara has a certain style of feminist thinking that argues that given patriarchal societal mores, women should take advantage of their location as desirable objects. Men, she says, should pay for their inherent gender privileges. From her experience competing with men in the bureaucratic market in Brazil, Sara is much aware of gender inequality: by virtue of gender inequalities men have the best paid and the most prestigious jobs. Men are the ones whose voices are heard and who have the money and freedom to have adventures outside the home, while their wives are at home taking care of the children. Sara had almost been trapped in such an unequal relationship when she first married. She had resisted; she despises this gender hierarchy, but seeks to take advantage of it as much as she can: "Do men want to exercise their masculine power over women? Good, but they have to pay for it."

Sara's expenses are relatively high for a migrant woman. Her needs and the needs of her son in Brazil are the needs of Brazilian middle-class members with reference to Brazilian values. Among other things, her expenses consist of paying for school and gym for her son in Bahia, fancy dinners and clothes, trips, and modern cars for her here and her son back home. Sara's basic expenses are at least $4,000 a month. Besides working five days a week, Sara also counts on the help of her male friends, clients, and lovers. The roles that the men assume in her life are at times interchangeable. It is not part of her feminist agenda to get involved with any man who is not able or generous enough to cover some of her expenses when her money falls short or when she desires some luxury items. Sara's boyfriend, Glaucus, and her lover, Fred, are both very generous men, and also assume at different moments the role of client, friend, and sponsor. She met both of them while dancing in Queens gentlemen's clubs.

Glaucus is a handsome Greek man of about Sara's age (forties) with tanned skin and a long Greek nose. He moved to the United States as a child in the 1970s. With ties to the older Greek immigrant community established in Astoria subsequent to World War II, Glaucus married a Greek American woman, worked his way up within the Greek immigrant business community, and is now a construction subcontractor. Fred is an Italian man in his fifties, the manager of an Italian restaurant in Manhattan. He moved to the United States with his family right after World War II. He stayed within the reach of his ethnic community of Italian immigrants in Queens and married an Italian American woman. It seems that the marriages of both men had the purpose of maintaining the cohesion of their ethnic communities and with time just wore out. Neither of them is divorced. They keep a friendly connection with their wives and their families but prefer to live in separate houses and to have independent lives from their estranged wives. Fred gives Sara expensive presents almost every time they go out, and also helps her by sending money for her son's expenses in Brazil and in paying off Sara's apartment there. They never get too close to each other. Sara has never gone to Fred's apartment because it is located in an area where his relatives and his wife's relatives live. Fred has never gone to Sara's apartment because that is an area that is reserved for her relationship with Glaucus. Sara tells Fred that she has an agreement with me, a very studious roommate who needs peace, silence, and no interference with domestic dynamics.

Sara and Fred go out for adventures in hotels in areas surrounding the city, which they both love and which became one of the main attractions in their relationship—its clandestine nature. Glaucus, who has two adolescent children in school, cannot afford expensive dinners or presents. Instead, he helps Sara with whatever she needs in terms of logistics. Before Sara bought her own car, Glaucus used to drive her home after work. When she decided to buy a car, he helped her make the deal and go through all the paperwork. At times, Glaucus goes shopping or goes to the bank when Sara cannot make it. He cooks delicious Greek food and fixes whatever is necessary in the house. Glaucus also fulfills the social role of her official handsome young Greek boyfriend at family events.

Having Fun

Barbara told me that she met Karl at a bar where she was working and they immediately became friends. Karl started going back to the same bar on the nights when he knew Barbara would be there. They went for dinner a couple of times and Karl invited her to see his place. Why not? I am not sure how the relationship has developed from there, and the information I have about their relationship, as is common throughout my work, comes from fragments of conversation gathered in a number of encounters with Barbara. As Barbara revealed to me, she was not looking for another passionate relationship like the one she had with Davi when she met Karl. From the beginning she developed an affection for him that was rather gentle. She says it is *"uma coisa de pele,"* a skin thing—that is, the chemistry in the relationship is not passionate. Karl seems to feel the same about her, and since they have met, he has come to care for her profoundly. Karl has called Barbara at least once every other day since they met. He has helped her find information about taking photography classes and given her books, newspaper clippings on subjects that he thinks are of interest to her, presents, and financial help. At first Barbara did not seem to know what to think of the relationship. But it was settled that they would see each other once a week, always on Wednesday. I was invited to one of those private party nights.

I got to Barbara's early on a summer evening so I could rest before we went out. The night starts late. Barbara usually arrives at Karl's place around midnight. We took a car service from Barbara's house with a Hispanic driver. We called Karl on our way, so he could come downstairs and pay for the ride, as is expected in encounters such as this. Karl lives in a three-story house on the fringes of Queens that he inherited from his family. He seems to live off his family money and refuses to talk about his personal or financial life. With his compulsion to buy books and intellectual curiosity about odd subjects, Karl's place is entirely covered with titles that to an outside observer seem unrelated. Karl's personality is close to that of the collector evoked by Walter Benjamin, for whom objects fall together in defiance of any systematic classification.

As much as I love books, it took me a while to get used to his collection. But we soon started talking about Barbara's new computer, wireless connection, and trivia in the form of disconnected information and jokes. Karl took me on a tour of the house and showed me his collections. He made comments about how the house would look after Barbara moved in with him. The tone of his voice revealed that he was just playing with the idea, not serious. He always seems to talk as if he does not really mean what he says. After a while, Karl called another car service to take us to a restaurant in Williamsburg, Brooklyn, where he grew up in a Jewish family from Eastern Europe. As we walked into a Thai restaurant people looked at us askance—in that area of Williamsburg people dress more casually than we had. We ordered immediately since the kitchen was about to close. Barbara did not even look at the menu and asked Karl to choose for her. She looked at me and said: "Men like that." Karl ordered appetizers and I ordered an entrée. We all had beers. We sat there a little awkwardly while waiting for the food. Barbara and I spoke in Portuguese, and Karl found it quite entertaining that while we were talking we were both touching our hair in a very languid way. Barbara then said in English, "I miss my country," and that felt only like something to say, without any meaning behind it. Karl said that she should get as much as she could from the States and back with her: "What about having a Thai restaurant there, e? Look at the decorations." And the conversation went on a like this until the food arrived and we devoured it.

aid the bill and we walked down the street and then jumped into another taxi and went to a lounge, this time in Astoria, a nice place and very laid back. We ordered a round of *caipirinhas*, Brazilian cocktails found in most bars in New York nowadays. Soon I perceived a wave of "let's have fun" coming from Karl, an attitude Barbara accepted; this was, I understood, a crucial part of their relationship. I listened to the music until they calmed down a little bit and asked them if we could leave. I knew we still had to go to Karl's house so we could get the "goodies," as he calls the fair compensation for Barbara's company and care. Besides gifts, this would include Barbara's cash for the night. So we jumped into another cab and this time Barbara said that he should sit on the middle; facing me she said: "Don't worry, let him touch you; he doesn't do more than that." I laughed. He sat with one hand on my leg and another on Barbara's, a display of heterosexuality, while instructing the cabdriver in Spanish.

Back in Karl's house, I was extremely tired and lay down, looking at a magazine, *Latina*. Karl got a Brazilian flag and put on some Brazilian music that Barbara had given to him. Barbara started performing, yelling and being jealous. "It is all a game," she said to me and laughed. When I decided to relax on the couch, expecting the scene to last for a long time, they suddenly called a cab. Karl gave Barbara the expected money for the night and for the taxi ride back to Queens. In the car, we laughed at the crazy night. "It was fun," I said, "although he gets very intense and demanding after a while." "That's part of the relationship, you see," Barbara said. "One has to be between a babysitter, a mother, and a therapist, and keep him very busy, giving him constant attention." "I see," I said, "but in the beginning the night was fun; just the last part got a little tiring." Barbara continued: "He helps me with my English, and he knows a lot about New York. Besides, I like him; he is a very unusual person, and you know I like people who are unusual, original." "I know," I said, "but that's nice too, that you go out with him; he is nice. Does Karl have a girlfriend?" "I don't even want to know," she said. "It is better if he has—for sure he has other women, but I don't know if in a relationship, or if it's just like me. He goes to bars, he gives money to the girls, and I think that this is his pleasure."

From what Barbara tells me, this was a typical night with Karl. They have been meeting for about three years on a regular basis. In the beginning, Barbara used to meet Karl once a week, but about one year after the night described here, they started meeting more often. At first, Barbara had a hard time understanding and coming to terms with the form that their relationship was taking. She was not sure whether Karl saw her as his girlfriend and if so, what kind of commitment she would have to him. However, what Karl seems to expect from Barbara's company is less a passionate girlfriend than a female friend who would add to his performance of masculinity, as embedded in the practice of conspicuous consumption and fun. This agreed with Barbara's present personal needs, that is, that passionate love was not necessarily part of the relationship, and that her role was close to that of a companion in outings, as manifested in Karl's waves of "having fun." This is, although Barbara does not articulate it as such, emotional labor—partly work, partly affection. The nights that Barbara spends with Karl are long and, at times, tiresome. Regardless of her mood, Barbara has to be willing to enjoy Karl's manifestations of fun. In addition, because emotional labor is not easily defined, the boundaries of their relationship are sometimes blurred in ways that make Barbara uncomfortable. An example of this is when Karl calls Barbara on her cell phone day and night. Notwithstanding, with time, Barbara, who seems to be increasingly weary of the bar scene, is becoming used to Karl's unique way of relating to her, and to his generous emotional and material support.

Misunderstandings

The relationship between Barbara and Davi constituted a series of misunderstandings about the role of class and race as embedded in ideas of gender, love, and romance. What Barbara had seen as hip about Davi was in part a misunderstanding of Davi's class and ethnoracial location within New York social structure. Davi was not, as Barbara had thought, so "integrated" into the Lower East Side trendiness, and she felt isolated from the neighborhood. His episodes of drunkenness and his fits of jealousy and aggression toward Barbara increased as their views of the correct balance between passionate love and financial responsibility grew apart. Their arguments betrayed an even deeper clash between their social positions and between Barbara's Brazilian middle-class expectations and Davi's Hispanic marginalized status in the U.S. racial and class hierarchies. After two years of an increasingly abusive marriage, and when she had gained a green card and legalized her status in the United States, Barbara left Davi and applied for a divorce. Barbara had gained, in her own words, the "freedom" to go back and forth from Brazil.

Sara, after being married and divorced in Brazil, was enjoying her status as a single woman. For years now, she has continued her relationships with Glaucus and Fred, both of whom she met while dancing. Fred, older and with grown children, has access to a larger disposable income and is content about being alone after so many years of marriage. Glaucus, who is younger, believes in love and longs for a fulfilling and stable relationship with a woman. None of them—Fred, Glaucus, or Sara—seems to want, or to be able to have, a marriage "for real." In her constant half-truths and the blatant lies that she has to constantly create in order to keep her relationship with both men, Sara creates a complex web of misapprehensions, misinterpretations, and mistakes about the roles of class, gender, race and morality. Her understanding of Glaucus and Fred seems to be rather incomplete in regard to their social location. Although her relationships with the men may provide financial and emotional support and excitement for her in the present, their somewhat marginal social positions do not help her advance toward social stability either in the United States or in Brazil.

Barbara's relationship with Karl seems to represent this same attempt to deal with situations as they come up while postponing a much-needed resolution that would lead to a career path beyond the role of a dancer and a more stable financial life. Although Barbara's encounters with Karl no longer happen in gentlemen's bars, the monetary mediation persists, although now the relationship between them has become more intimate. Nevertheless, their long nights of drinking and fun do not help Barbara find alternative venues in order to leave the bar scene in a more definite way. Karl's age and ethnic-racial background (he is in his early forties and of Jewish descent) makes him an acceptable prospect for a "real" relationship, which could help Barbara to move on and to find new forms of incorporation into the United States. However, with U.S. permanent resident status through her marriage to Davi, Barbara sees no reason to marry again. Barbara must, as she says to me, follow her own desires. Yet she needs Karl's financial help and became emotionally involved with him.

The ambivalence of the relationships that Sara and Barbara engage in results from this mix of a specific gender ideology that defines men as instrumental and the manipulation of desire as a legitimate means to achieve an end. As time passes, however, Sara's and Barbara's incorporation into either the United States or Brazil becomes more precarious because of their dim prospects for social mobility, even though Barbara has achieved her legal status and Sara is on her way out of illegality.

The Seduction of Whiteness

Suburban Dreams

Renata had been dancing for just two months when she first saw Brandon in the bar. He came with one of his friends, another firefighter. They like hanging out in twos or threes for a beer after work. Brandon is thirty-four years old and is of Irish descent. He has been working as a firefighter for the last ten years and owns a two-story house in a working-class area of Long Island. One of the few men his age at his firehouse who was still single, Brandon was looking for someone to date, and eventually to marry. As is common among men who prefer to have relationships with foreign women (Constable 2003), Brandon mentioned to me over dinner once how he resents American women as too aggressive and too uncompromising in relationships. Going to bars represented for Brandon an occasion to socialize with his male friends and a chance to meet women. Renata told me she had noticed Brandon from the stage when she was dancing and had found him attractive. "I will go talk to him in my break," she said to herself. Renata spoke very little English and, as is common in the bar scene, their communication was probably based more on body language when they first met.

Renata was working at Fringes, a bar that offers lap dances, and Renata offered Brandon a lap dance. Brandon tipped her generously that night and the nights that followed. He started going to the bar just to see her. One night Brandon invited Renata for dinner and said that he officially wanted to be her boyfriend. Renata told me that she was startled. This seemed really old-fashioned to her, but she was impressed that he was a gentleman. A very honest, straightforward man, *"um homem de família,"* a family man, Renata observed to me. She accepted his proposal, with just one condition: Brandon had to wait until she "resolved" the situation with her longtime boyfriend from Brazil, Sérgio. Coming to the United States, as we may remember, was a decision that Renata and her partner made as a couple with the objective of improving their economic life. Their business had been robbed and that had worsened their already precarious financial situation. It was the couple's decision that Renata would come first, since she could count on the help of her female cousins who were already here.

A little while after Renata met Brandon in the bar, the cousin with whom she was living decided to go back to Brazil with her husband. Living by herself was difficult for Renata; she could barely pay the rent and felt extremely lonely. Brandon started helping her materially and giving her the much needed emotional support and attention. He bought some essentials for Renata's new apartment and started spending time with her there. Meanwhile, Renata's Brazilian boyfriend arrived in the United States and took a job in a cable installment company in Chicago. Renata had to make a decision to continue her relationship with Sérgio or to get more serious with Brandon. We talked about the kinds of calculations she should consider in making her decision: as a Brazilian migrant woman, what could her Brazilian boyfriend do for her? Sérgio had a temporary job, did not speak English, and was living with two roommates in a small apartment in Chicago. He had asked her to join him, but what would she do there? "To be stuck in that struggle to make ends meet in a dreary immigrant quotidian, sharing a place with others?" Renata remarked to me. It would take years to make the kind of money they needed to go back to Brazil and make a life there. Plus, what guarantee did she have with him? Her expectation of having a family with him had been frustrated in the past, and for a long time their relationship had been shaky. Renata decided to make a major change in her life. She took a plane to Chicago soon after Brandon proposed to date her. She knew that with Brandon she could have a better and more fulfilling life, and perhaps, "God willing"—as Renata always says—even have the family for which she longed.

In Chicago, Renata explained her situation to Sérgio and said that, although she loved him, it would be best if they separated. "He suffered," she told me, "but he accepted it. It was the best we both could do, to free ourselves for other experiences." Renata said they parted on good terms and continued to be friends.[4] Back in New York, Brandon's roommate was leaving the Long Island house and Brandon invited Renata to live with him. She hesitated—this was too fast. She did not want to have another experience of living with a man without the security of being officially married, particularly when she was about to become illegal in the United States. Brandon promised Renata that if after a few months their living together worked out, he would marry her. Less than two months after they had met, she moved in with him. The negotiations toward marriage, however, took another six months. At his request Renata stopped dancing. He offered to support her financially while she went to school and adapted to her new suburban life. There was much to do at home, a garden that she had always dreamed of, long walks in the green paradise of front lawns. "If it weren't for the isolation and solitude," she complains. But Brandon tried to compensate for the strains of suburban isolation. He would call her from work every other hour and come home right after work, bring her food, go for drives with her, and pay for her English classes. Renata would happily accept it all if he were willing to marry her and to legalize her situation in the country.

Brandon did not want a marriage of convenience. He wanted to make sure that Renata was the right woman and that she would be dedicated to him. He introduced her to his friends and family, after which they became officially engaged. His education and morals dictated that they wait a few months between the engagement and the wedding, which should be a conventional ceremony in Long Island. Brandon's parents came from Atlanta for the wedding, and all his firefighter friends were there. Renata's dancer cousin and a few of her other friends, also dancers, came. Renata was heartbroken that her family from Brazil could not come, but the couple planned to have another wedding in Brazil. Brandon and Renata have been married for a year now, and she is living her suburban dream while working as a housecleaner for a wealthy older American woman on Long Island. They are trying to have a child. She still complains of isolation to Nana, one of her few friends here.

Nana and Jimmy

On the trip to a Long Island beach with Renata, Brandon, and Jimmy that I describe at the beginning of this chapter, Nana made sure that she was properly protected against the sun and that we would be out of that suburban boredom as quickly as possible. Jimmy just smiled, not caring one way or another. He seems to be an easygoing guy, sweet, and good-looking. Jimmy is cool, Nana and I agreed. He was born in Pennsylvania in a working-class family. His father worked in the car sales business and his mother worked as a secretary. Jimmy and his brothers grew up in a suburban house and went to college for a few years. During his college years, Jimmy grew weary of suburban life and dreamed of coming to New York. Even before graduating, he moved to Queens, at a time when Astoria was becoming attractive to adventurous suburban American youth bored with suburban isolation. Jimmy enjoys the edgy ethnic mix and the affordable rents in what one might view as a new style of U.S. working-class neighborhood: international, messy, with Greek cafés and Czech beer gardens, the smell of Arab tobacco, and the sound of Brazilian music. An aspiring artist, Jimmy also enjoys the proximity of the Museum of Modern Art PS1, and the sculpture garden by the East River.

Jimmy did not meet Nana in the bar scene but at a Greek café on a summer afternoon in 2004, just three months after she had moved to New York. They talked by the café counter while sipping their iced coffee and exchanged telephone numbers. Nana, like him, likes the excitement of urban life: the mix, the music, the nightlife, and above all, the glamour of just being in New York. Although she lives in an area in Queens with a high concentration of Brazilian migrants, her reference point in New York is Manhattan or more precisely, Fifth Avenue. Extremely aware of fashion, Nana has a thing about Fifth Avenue. She very often calls me and other people from there. When one asks her where she is she answers: "Fifth Ave, dear!" I finally told her that this did not tell me much to identify her location in the city: "Fifth Ave is huge, you know." (Fortunately for her, Jimmy works in Manhattan very near Fifth.)

In our encounters in the city we would walk downtown from Fifth Avenue between Thirty-Fourth and Thirty-Fifth Streets, where the Graduate Center where I was pursuing my PhD is located. Sometimes we would sit comfortably in the lounge of the Anthropology Department talking about our condition in this country and transnationally, between Brazil and the United States. It was in these encounters that Nana and I analyzed the various facets of her relationship with Jimmy vis-à-vis her legal situation and her desire to stay more permanently in the United States. We felt that going back to Brazil was not even an option for her. We agreed that Nana needed a break from that dreary everyday struggle to make ends meet and that there were no desirable men at all in Brazil, particularly in Bahia. Nana is a fierce critic of Brazil's gender hierarchy. I remember that since early in her life, her relationships with men, like mine, were troubled. We were both considered too opinionated, too free, too out of control, and too loud when we first met in our college days. We were not part of the same group of people, but we had common friends and when we met each other we would recognize some common traits. We also drank a bit too much, smoked, and betrayed our boyfriends from good families. People talked about us, and we were considered outcasts.

While I moved to New York, Nana continued to date Brazilian middle-class men with the hope of finding a partner in an egalitarian relationship. Her hopes were frustrated and she started having only brief sexual encounters with both white and black Brazilians and foreigners, and for the real bad nights, "you just pretend it didn't happen." Nana felt vulnerable as a relatively successful, although struggling, middle-class woman and thought that men, particularly Brazilian men, saw her as an easy target for clinging on to, but she saw little chance of having the kind of relationship that she longed for. She did not have high hopes of finding an ideal person in New York either. When Nana first met Jimmy, she mostly had a green card in mind. That did not mean, however, that she would marry just anyone or that she did not like him. Quite the opposite—she was attracted to him. She was also exploring the possibility of reentering the country with a student visa and did not discount the possibility of a paid marriage. We examined her options carefully and it seemed that she did not have anything to lose in investing in a relationship with Jimmy.

After a month of dating, Jimmy took Nana to visit his family in Pennsylvania, and she liked them. Jimmy's family, despite all the differences, felt familiarly provincial and homey to her. They also approved of her. To Nana, everything with Jimmy felt right and easy. They had the same taste in music, liked fashion, and knew the names of films and artists. They went out to museums, plays, and concerts, and he was very organized in his home, she said, when commenting on his apartment. Soon after they met, Nana told Jimmy about her legal condition and made it clear to him that only a marriage would keep her in this country in a way she considered acceptable. Nana absolutely did not want to lose her legal status and even considered leaving the country.

Jimmy, based on the willingness with which he became involved with Nana, seemed to be also longing for a more serious relationship. At his age and coming from a middle-class educational and professional background, Nana embodied the necessary markers to be a successful wife and citizen of the United States: exotic, beautiful, sexy, intelligent, knowledgeable, fashionable, and professional. As I imagine Nana through Jimmy's eyes, she was the right age and had the right body, the right color, and an exquisite accent that would fit just right for him. Jimmy would not let her leave. He told her not to worry and in less than two months, before her six-month visa expired, they got married in City Hall with Ivana, Brandon, and Renata as witnesses. I was in Brazil for winter vacation and was a little shocked with the pace at which it all happened. "That is what happens to immigrants in the U.S.," Jimmy's mother explained to me over lunch once. Jimmy and his family have a positive view of a country that is willing to integrate those who work hard enough and do the right thing. Nana was doing the right thing by marrying a U.S. citizen, and this was a legitimate form of immigrant adaptation, from their point of view. They had cases like this in the family and all agreed that they were on the right path to becoming a modern transnational couple. His family paid for a generous wedding and celebration in a party house in the suburbs of Pittsburgh for about five hundred guests. Renata, Brandon, and I were Nana's only guests.

Jimmy even liked the fact that Nana worked as a dancer, although they had agreed that this would be temporary. She would stop after she had regularized her legal situation here and learnt enough English. She was also planning to go to graduate school. After the wedding, Nana danced for another five months. But she was resolved to stop dancing as soon as possible. She applied for secretarial jobs but knew that, because of the language barrier, she had little chance of getting anything. She started studying English with a discipline that impressed me, and Jimmy helped her when they had extra free time together. Their schedules did not really coincide since he would come home just when Nana was leaving for work at night and he was already gone when she would wake up next day at one or two in the afternoon. Nana always complained about dancing, with me and with everybody she talked to, outside and inside the bar scene. She hated to be up all night long and commented on how missing nights of sleep makes one look older and stressed out. It is also terrible for the skin and keeps women from having a rich social life outside the bar in "normal" daytime. With very few exceptions, she also hated the men who go to bars—sleazy, low-life men. She said that she hated Greeks, including Greek restaurants in Astoria. She crosses the street so she does not have to smell Greek food.

Nana went to Brazil for a month with Jimmy and decided that she would not dance again upon her return. In Brazil, she bought a stock of underwear and G-strings to resell here, so she could survive for a few months until she found a decent job. Jimmy totally supported her decision. A loving husband, he assumed the responsibility of paying rent and other house expenses. Jimmy took Nana on trips to the Southwest and to concerts with his friends. Jimmy's friends' girlfriends became Nana's girlfriends, and except for Renata and me, she stopped hanging out with Brazilians. Remember that Nana cut her long beautiful black hair because she did not want to look like a Hispanic woman. She also started forgetting Portuguese words. Once while window-shopping together, she told me that there were too many foreigners in the United States, that this was a real problem. Nana, like Jimmy, was also against the antiwar protests during the Republican convention, arguing that the protestors "went too far." I told her, ironically, that she was on a good path to integration and yelled that she was becoming a good mainstream American. I finished with, "Good luck!" and did not see her for a while. With her new looks, manners, and opinions it did not take her too long to find a job in a nice gallery in Soho that belonged to a friend of one of Jimmy's friends. Nana called only a few dancer friends after getting the job; she thought that if she told them while she was still in the process, their evil eyes could bring bad luck and she would not be able to get anything she wanted. Nana told them that this was the way that people advance in life, not by dancing and being alienated in the low nightlife of New York. She said one must struggle and strategize, be clever, like her. Barbara particularly did not appreciate Nana's comments.

Marrying into the American Nation

What Renata and Nana had in common from the first time they met in La Casa was their aversion to the bar scene. Nana told me that when she saw Renata in the bar she immediately perceived her discomfort and the disjuncture between Renata's present situation and her background. That was how Nana saw her own experience as a dancer. Nana and Renata immediately clicked, and consistently used between themselves a language of class and respectability to differentiate them from other dancers. They also used economics to justify their presence in sexual labor. Nana and Renata saw their work in a gentlemen's bar as a way to get financial resources to invest in their careers. They both wanted to get out of the bar scene as soon as possible. They both knew, from observing other dancers, that a relationship with a sponsor would not lead to their goal. They both used a language of morality to justify their refusal to engage with Greek or Italian older men as sponsors, but saw "real possibilities" and no serious moral constraints in going out with white men of their own age.

Both Brandon and Jimmy can be considered to possess American whiteness. In her study of the construction of whiteness in the United States, Sacks (1994) examines how Euro-Americans from the southern and eastern parts of Europe became incorporated into whiteness. Sacks argues that this shift in racial identity paralleled the expansion of the American middle class after World War II, spurred by what she defines as "affirmative action." She points out the roles of the GI ⅃ the Federal Housing Authority, and the Veterans Administration promoting college education, home ownership, and suburban living fᴄ . Euro-Americans, to the detriment of African American men. In this process, American whiteness became inclusive of Euro-Americans who were able to ascend to the middle class. Brandon and Jimmy's parents were beneficiaries of the expansion of the American middle class and of the inclusiveness of whiteness.

However, racialization is an ongoing process. To be white assumes that one performs the values and behaviors that are associated with positions of privilege in a hierarchical social structure. To be a white American male is to display a kind of masculinity that is relationally positioned to other masculinities and femininities. In the U.S. post/ neocolonial order and as manifest in the context of gentlemen's bars, to be a white American male is to have access to, and to be the subject of desire for, migrant women. As Kelsky (2001) argues in the case of Japanese women in their relationship to Western men, white men become eroticized as the embodiment of wealth and as representing the opportunity to access American institutions. As white men, both Brandon and Jimmy become icons of American values, and so symbolize not only help (as Greek and Italian sponsors do) but also the rescue of Renata and Nana, as Third World women. By using a language of class and respectability, and by foregrounding their educational and professional background, both Nana and Renata distinguished themselves from other dancers and became legitimate prospects for incorporation into the United States as wives and mothers. Their suburban weddings symbolized their entrance into the American national body and into the national family values of whiteness.

Distinctions

The encounters that take place in gentlemen's bars have an effect on dancers' lives far beyond the bar scene. Unlike theatrical performance, dancers' work extends in time and space and decisively affects their personal lives. I have argued that the relationship between Brazilian dancers and clients is different from that of dancers who are U.S. citizens. While U.S. dancers tend to have relationships that are more bounded by the bar scene and the more commodified aspects of interactions with clients, migrant dancers' relationships with clients might extend beyond the bar scene. Relationships between Brazilian women and clients tend to blur the boundaries between work and romance and to become "strategies for advancement" (Brennan 2002) and a means to access U.S. institutions. This does not mean that emotion and other more subjective considerations are absent from these relationships. What this does mean is that those considerations and preferences are bounded by what Constable (2003) has defined as "cultural logics of desire," as manifest in hierarchies of race, gender, class, and nation within the bar scene and beyond it.

In the case of sponsors, as in the relationship established between Clara and Demetris, Teresa and Frank, and Ivana and Chris, a mix of feelings and interests, desire and deceit, are mediated by an ideology of help. For older Italian and Greek men with disposable income, masculinity seems to be embodied in their ability to provide for their favorite dancers financially and yet maintain some strategic distance. Most of these men are married, or separated but not yet divorced, and cannot help dancers become citizens by marrying them. In addition, Italian and particularly Greek men are desirable as clients or sponsors but not as husbands or boyfriends because of their less desirable ethnic-racial and class location both within the United States and in the hierarchy of nations.

From the perspective of most dancers, white Americans are the most desirable men who frequent the bars. They present migrant women with the possibility not only of becoming legal U.S. citizens but also, as Ong (1996) suggests, of achieving "cultural citizenship" through immersion in the cultural and social institutions of privilege that whiteness entails. On the other end of the spectrum of desirable masculinities, most Brazilian dancers, as in the case of a number of women in Clara's family, consider a relationship with men of African descent only as a means for achieving legality through paid marriage in a pure instrumental way, with no affect or intimacy involved. The fact that I did not give any account of encounters between dancers and the men with whom they engaged in paid marriages is itself revealing of the secrecy and stigma that surround these relationships. On no occasion was I invited to meet either Clara's or Sara's husband, nor have I ever met them at family events. The racism that is embedded in Brazilian dancers' preferences and attitudes toward black men reveals how racial attitudes cross borders of nation-states and are reconfigured as new forms of relationships develop in different contexts.

The various relationships that dancers engage in with men beyond the bar scene reflect the complex material and subjective considerations that face dancers in their trajectories of desire. Although it might seem, at times, that the women are being overly manipulative in their relationship to them, this is only partly true. They have to make resolute and life-changing choices that will affect important aspects of their lives, particularly in regard to their legal status in this country. In addition, Sara and Barbara (and we can say the same for the other women, but to a lesser extent), as modern and mature women, are fierce critics of gender inequalities and see their relationships with men as a way of taking advantage of an order they consider unjust. Nevertheless, the choices these women make involve diverse affections and feelings, such as fear, loss, frustration, anxiety, desire, and hope.

The ways in which Brazilian women are incorporated into the United States are the result of a long history of colonialism and post- and neocolonialism. In New York, Brazilian women who work as dancers are located in a position in which economic need intersects with a language of sensuality, as racially defined. To some extent, the women who move to New York are able to manipulate these symbols and to use them in their favor. The consequences of such manipulation, however, are beyond their control and may define their fate in their new country in ways they are not able to predict.

Chapter 7

Transnational Ties

All the relationships in which the nine women involved in this project engage are affected by and have an effect on their material and emotional lives, both in the United States and in Brazil. Of these women, only two, Justine and Nadja, have gone back to Brazil to live on a more permanent basis, although the rest keep close ties to their family and friends in Brazil. The ones who have papers—documented legal immigrant status in the United States—travel home at least once a year, and the ones who do not entertain a trip home as a goal and sometimes an obsession. None of them are free from the social references, obligations, hopes, and dreams that span the two countries. They are often caught in the ambivalent spaces between them. One place is projected onto another, sometimes in unexpected ways. Real and imagined, the images we carry with us are filtered through constant comparisons and parallels between multiple spaces—spaces of wealth and poverty, material spaces, and subjective spaces between worlds.

How do the politics of sexuality, gender, and nationality that these nine Brazilian women live in the United States find their reflection in the body politic back in Brazil? How is what they are and what they acquire in the United States translated into a Brazilian reality that they may no longer recognize as their own? Divided in their belonging between two nations, as is common to a transnational condition, the women project into one place what they are in the other. Their future is uncertain, and dancing does not guarantee an identity in terms of a desirable class or racial location in the United States. As we will see, even the women who got married "for real" and are immersed in the network provided by their husbands' families and friends do not have their expectations in terms of social class mobility in the United

States entirely fulfilled. What defines middle-class identity in Brazil is their prior location in a system of values that is not immediately translatable in the local/global context of New York. With the exception of Nana and Renata, their relationships are most likely to be with other migrants. Moreover, the men they meet are more likely to be from the working class and not to have the same values as the middle class back in Brazil, such as, for example, believing in the importance of a college education. The comfort Brazilian women from the middle class have among their kin in Brazil, in a familiar atmosphere and with the racial and class privilege that they enjoy, is of crucial importance in the construction of their subjectivity and expectations.

If the initial goal of these women's migration was to maintain their middle-class identity in Brazil and the lifestyles that were associated with it, have they been able to achieve this? Are they in fact able to return to Brazil and reclaim the location that they work so hard to sustain from the United States? Does the material capital that they accumulate in migrating and working as dancers in New York add to their symbolic prestige back home? Or do the mystery and silence that surround their lives overseas compromise their social location there?[1] As time passes, which of these women are able to manage a position that is "flexible" (Ong 1999) enough to maintain a middle-class position in both countries, and which are more uncomfortably caught in between?

Volatile Incorporations

Clara

Remember that the critical reason Clara decided to come to the United States was her inability to make the kind of living that would be compatible with her class expectations as a young lawyer. One of the main reasons she moved to New York was to save enough money to reinvest in her career and life in Brazil, including paying off an office space and a car. However, once in New York, instead of saving money Clara began to enjoy the lifestyle that the fast flow of cash allowed her. She rented a basement apartment on her own (a place that she would intermittently share with Barbara and Nana, and that ended up being rented by Ivana). Clara did pay off her office in Brazil, but there was no guarantee that she would have enough wealthy law clients to sustain the lifestyle that she was finally able to experience in New York. In New York, Clara bought the much-wanted new clothes and shoes. She also furnished her apartment and was free to meet people from other cultures and other nationalities, and to "have fun," in the hedonistic words with which she describes her initial experience in New York. She went back to Brazil after her six-month tourist visa expired and in the three months she spent in Bahia, it became clear that her next stay in New York would be more permanent. She remarked to me on various occasions that there was no way she would go back to the kind of struggle she experienced before her move. Clara enjoyed seeing her family and friends, but even the parties in Bahia paled in comparison with the kind of excitement she had in New York. She rented out the office that she had paid off and packed her suitcases to return to the United States.

At this time, Clara had no intention of going back to Brazil, at least for the next few years and perhaps, as she came to perceive, never permanently. Clara continued dancing and started entertaining the idea of marrying in the United States, crucial to guarantee her legalization in the country when her visa expired. She could opt, like some of her aunts and cousins did, for a paid marriage, but young and with good prospects, she preferred to chance a marriage that could combine papers, love, and desire. By then, it was clear to Clara that she should invest her money, time, energy, and emotional life primarily in the United States. Brazil became a place where she would go for vacation or for more extended periods, but an unlikely place for her to be able to make a living again. The relationships that Clara developed with the various men in her life can be seen as strategies to make viable her stay in this country and maintain the kind of lifestyle that accorded with the standards of middle-class Brazilians. A car, a laptop computer, a very expensive couch, and a two-bedroom apartment in the suburbs overlooking a grove of trees was, for Clara, a dream that would take many years to be realized in Brazil. But that was not enough to guarantee the necessary flexibility and mobility of her transnational condition. Once her attempt to marry Robert failed, even when she became pregnant by him, Clara, with the financial help of her sponsor, Demetris, married an African American man for papers. This was a path that other of her kinswomen had chosen in order to be able to move freely between the United States and Brazil, enjoying, as some say, "the best of both worlds." But what that does that mean, and for whom is that possible?

A regional plague and the fall in the prices of Brazilian cocoa in the international market ruined cocoa farms in the area of Bahia where Clara is from and where her family had attained their wealth.[2] Large farms were abandoned; workers were dismissed without land of their own and left to search for whatever rare day jobs they could find. A considerable number of unemployed in the countryside congregated around the landless movement, which is now politically significant in that area. Clara is now completely alienated from this reality, and she has visited her family country house only once since she has been in the United States. "There is nothing to do there," she said to me. Clara goes mainly to Salvador when she goes to Brazil for vacation. She did buy an office there, where she had initially planned to establish herself as lawyer. However, she had it rented out, not finding it feasible a return to her career in Brazil. Now, Clara seems to concentrate her efforts only toward incorporation into the United States, mainly through her relationships with men. As we have seen, Robert returned to her and they established a semi-suburban lifestyle in the outskirts of Queens. However, as a woman who once believed in investing in her career and in being independent, Clara does not seem to comfortably fit in the housewife role. She goes back to work as a dancer at times and when need arises, and, from our conversations and from what both Sara and Barbara tell me, she does not seem sure that her relationship with Robert is as solid as she wants it to be, for her own sake and that of her daughter's future.

Sara

Although Sara and Clara are from the same family and socioeconomic context, the generational difference makes their experience in the United States substantially different. Sara moved here when she was in her forties and divorced, and had an adolescent son for whom she is the main provider. She had temporarily quit her job in a government agency. Her plan was, if all went well, to stay in the United States for the three years for which she had unpaid leave from her job. From the beginning, she planned to overstay her U.S. visa and try to legalize her immigrant status later on by engaging in a paid marriage. Coming out of an unsuccessful marriage and having little hope for an equal gender relationship, Sara did not look forward to getting too involved with another man or to living with one as a couple. More than anything, Sara appreciated her freedom. Moreover, she had to concentrate on making money not only for herself but also to sustain a comfortable middle- to upper-middle-class lifestyle for her son in Brazil: an apartment in a semi-luxurious condo, a car, private school, and national and international trips.

Although Sara married for papers within the first year that she arrived in New York, 2002, by the end of my research in 2005 she had not yet received her green card. Her lawyer said the delay was due to changes in the administration following 9/11. It was also a long time without going to Brazil. Yet it was in Brazil and in the education of her son that Sara invested most of her efforts. Her expenses in the United States were restricted to maintaining her household, while her social life centered on the bar scene. She mainly related to women who worked as dancers (particularly the ones tied to her extended family network) and to men who were clients whom she met in gentlemen's bars. Two of these men have become to her a mix of boyfriend, lover, and sponsor. When Sara is not working, talking on the phone to Brazil, or caring for her body, she alternates spending time with the two of them. She seems to be postponing any significant life changes, which I see as inevitable as she grows older and her time in the bar scene seems to be expiring. Sara, though, avoids talking about the future.

It is not clear to me how Sara will benefit from her investment in her son in Brazil. What has she constructed for herself besides reproducing a middle-class lifestyle for her family back home? How will this lifestyle be maintained when the inflow of cash stops when she stops dancing? Is it, perhaps, too late for her to reinvest in her professional life in Brazil? Will she go back to a government position that cannot sustain the kind of life to which she has become accustomed? Just recently, after four years of waiting, Sara received her green card and was allowed to go back to Brazil without the risk of not being able to reenter the United States legally. She now is able to travel freely between the two countries. What will come of her transnational moves will likely constitute a series of calculations, confusions, and misinterpretations about how one place translates into another, in material and symbolic terms. Meanwhile time is passing.

Sara, like the other women in her generation, has become obsessed with her face and her body transformations with aging. Her body, more than ever, has become what she is. Sara began to depend even more on a careful manipulation of her appearance and performance in order to be able to continue working as a dancer. Aging is seen as something to be disguised with outfits and makeup, or fixed with Botox, silicone implants, or plastic surgery. Sara has done it all. As she ages, however, and as the money she makes from dancing starts slowly to dwindle, Sara has become more dependent on her personal relationships with Glaucus and Fred as sources of material and emotional security. But when she will be capable of making a situation that was meant to be temporary into a seemingly permanent condition is not clear.

Different Whitenesses, Still Whiteness

Renata's Unsuccessful Return

Issues of class and social mobility are also crucial to Renata's life both in Brazil and in the United States. Most of the information that I have about Renata's transnational material and emotional investments and about her return trip to Brazil came from Nana. Even after Renata stopped dancing, Nana continued to be her closest friend in New York. Right after Renata married Brandon in a suburban wedding party here, the couple decided to travel to Renata's hometown in Brazil and to have another wedding party there, so her family and friends could also participate in this important moment in her life. Nana and Jimmy were in Brazil at the same time and Brandon and Renata visited them as their honeymoon trip to the Northeast. The description that Nana gave me of this trip came both from facts and from imagined "scenes of arrival" that she projected onto Renata, as she compares herself with her and measures the degree of success of her own choices.

Nana describes in detail the scene of Renata arriving at Belo Horizonte's airport wearing a fake-fur coat on a January morning, in the middle of the Brazilian summer, when the temperature was 100 degrees

Fahrenheit. Even if Nana did not know what coat Renata was wearing when she left New York, she could imagine from her own observations of other people what she judged to be Renata's lack of sensibility to Brazil's climate and social expectations in relation to the foreign. People in Brazil, according to Nana, are no longer naïve and uncritically willing to accept what comes from other countries as representing comfort and modernity. As Nana told me, Renata's father and sister were more embarrassed than happy to see Renata arrive with all the symbols of North American wealth so ostensibly displayed on her body and in her gestures. "Ridiculous," was what Nana remarked, referring to Renata's attitude toward her family.

Before her arrival, Renata arranged for her family to rent a fairly comfortable upper-middle-class beach house, and made arrangements for a somewhat ostentatious wedding party to take place there. She counted on the generosity of Brandon, who worked extra shifts during the months before the trip. It is not that money came easily for him, but he could afford to satisfy some of his transnational wife's desire because of the differences in currency between Brazil and the United States. Renata's family was happy to have that kind of cash flow coming in, but they were also very critical about how it was spent. From my own nomadic subject position, and projecting from my observations of similar behaviors, I can conclude that her family could probably think of two or three other more productive ways for using this cash. And I can see the conflict in the relationship between Renata and her sister in defining what is the most appropriate way to live life and to spend money. Renata's sister wanted to open a hair salon and her son needed to be in a much better school if he were to go the university later on. Their father's house needed repairs.

Renata, still with Brandon's help, financially supported the salon and the house's repair but thought that her nephew's education was a problem for her sister to deal with; she could eventually pay for it with the money from the salon. Still, these extra expenses added to the cost of the wedding reception and the beach house, plus generous lunches and dinners for everybody. Brandon became uneasy, and Renata's family did not approve of his manners. From what Nana described to me of her own experience when traveling with Renata and Brandon to

a beach in Bahia, and from what I can observe from other Am
can picture Brandon being uncomfortable with the heat and w,
is at time perceived as the excessive closeness of Brazilians' b
and being unwilling to deal with street kids or to eat exotic food

The trip, as Renata described it to Nana, was a nightmare. Renata
came back to the United States, as she said, "traumatized" and estranged from her family and friends. Her incorporation into the United
States through her marriage with Brandon, an American citizen, and
the legal and financial gains that she acquired with it did not translate
either into social prestige or into her family's appreciation for her deeds
and for what she had become. From the United States, Renata continues to help her family financially, sending a monthly stipend to her father and helping with extra expenses. However, she refused to continue
helping with her sister's salon, which finally had to be closed down. Renata and her sister no longer speak on international calls. Renata no
longer has any desire to go back to Brazil, not even for a vacation. She
now dedicates all her efforts to integrating into the United States and
having a family with Brandon.

Recovering Gender and Class Status: Nana's Marriage

Nana has also dedicated much effort and time into integrating into
U.S. society. Single, highly critical of Brazilian gender and class hierarchies, and relatively successful in her career path in Brazil, Nana came
to New York to try a new way of life and to save money to invest in
Brazil. However, she did not dismiss the possibility of staying in the
United States for a more indefinite period of time, if things worked out
well. Coming into the country after September 11, and being very conscious of the political climate in the United States, Nana knew that if
she wanted to have a full life and career here, she could not stay in the
country illegally. As we have seen, before her six-month visa expired,
Nana began to look for strategies to make sure she maintained her legal status. Together, Nana and I visited schools' international students'
offices and shopped for universities where she could enroll. But Nana,
although a sociologist, was never an academic; the student's path did
not appeal to her. She wanted something more immediate, more prac-

tical. What that would be exactly we did not know, and she needed time to think things through. It was while dwelling on this dilemma and also considering a paid marriage that Nana met Jimmy. As we saw earlier, although Nana did not have too many expectations for a real loving marriage, she knew of girlfriends whose marriages to foreigners had worked out. After pondering for a few weeks, and given that at this point she had already decided that she was not going back to Brazil—"at least," as she said once, "for the next five years or so"—Nana decided to explain her legal situation to Jimmy and to propose a marriage.

A few trips to Pennsylvania in order to meet Jimmy's family and friends, the wedding, the honeymoon—all that happened much faster than Nana was expecting and it was with astonishment and a certain disbelief that Nana saw herself jumping into some kind of American dream. "I can't even believe that this is me here," was the phrase that she kept repeating to me at her American-style wedding celebration in the suburbs of Pittsburgh. Through marriage she became integrated into a way of life reminiscent of working-class America and into what can be defined as American whiteness. Although Jimmy's father had lost his unionized job and his siblings were following uncertain career paths, they had a beautiful and comfortable house in the suburbs with all the facilities that in Brazil would be considered typical of an upper-middle-class household, including three cars in the garage. Nana sent home to Brazil a film of her wedding party along with an album of pictures portraying her newly acquired family's lifestyle: the dream house with the green lawn with smiling blond people in front.

Nana continued to dance and with the money that she could save by moving in with Jimmy, she could send enough money to her mother in Brazil to pay for a repair to their house. Happy pictures of her marriage and the cash flow into her mother's household helped to change the stigma that Nana had suffered back in Brazil as a single and independent woman with a history of troubled relationships with men. By marrying into mainstream white America, Nana recovered her gender and class status back in Brazil and proceeded along a path toward further integration into U.S. society. Nana now works as a personal assistant to a fashion designer and plans to spend her vacations in Europe, a place that is associated with sophistication and class for most Brazilian from the middle class.

Local Men, Global Lovers

Nadja: Shaky Upward Mobility and Local Men

During the three years that she lived in New York, Nadja worked six days a week on a regular basis. She lived quite a restricted life in terms of spending time alone, keeping her housing, food, and entertainment expenses to a minimum. Most of what she earned while dancing (more than $10,000 a month), she sent back to Brazil. Her efforts enabled her family to survive the financial crisis that had lasted decades. Her father, who had worked for a transportation company nearly all his working life, had been unemployed for five years prior to her move, and her mother tried to make ends meet by working as a nurse assistant. Her brother, who owned a small bakery, helped, but it was never enough and the family debt increased. In her second year in the United States, Nadja bought a truck for her father and helped her brother build a house in a semi-periphery neighborhood. She also started payments on a four-bedroom apartment in a new upper-middle-class section of Salvador for herself. In the third year, she opened a fashion store in Brazil, with her cousin as the main partner and manager.

During the four years that Nadja lived in New York, she went to Brazil only once. She would have gone more often if it were not for her legal status. She entered the United States with a tourist visa and had overstayed the expiration date. She did not want to take any chances, for particularly since the second year after 9/11, more and more people had been stopped by customs at the airport and sent immediately back to Brazil. She changed her tourist visa to a student visa with documentation provided by an English school in New York, but we doubted this would guarantee a safe and free return to the United States, since entrance to this country with student visas had also been under stricter surveillance.

The only way that Nadja could attain full legal status in this country was through marrying a U.S. citizen. That was what all her friends advised her to do. But Nadja always had ideals of romantic love.[3] She likes a passion that defies convenience, and the idea of marrying just for papers never appealed to her. Moreover, she had in mind a life that had more reference to Brazil than to the United States. Nadja always considered her stay in the United States temporary. She never invested in anything in the United States—she never really dedicated much time or effort to learning English, did not have any American friends or boyfriends, and kept her living situation somewhat transient. While Barbara, with whom she shared an apartment, painted and decorated her room and kept the common kitchen and dining room neatly furnished, Nadja's room was piled with boxes packed with things to send to Brazil: a microwave, a toaster, a mini-oven, a printer, and all sorts of smaller things and decorations. She tried to choose the expensive clothes that her clients gave her with the Brazilian climate in mind—tops and light pants and shoes.

Although Nadja and Barbara live together, they very rarely socialize because Nadja spends a great deal of time with Daniel. She very often stays in the apartment that Daniel shares with another Brazilian on the Upper East Side of Manhattan, around Seventieth Street between First and Second Avenues.[4] Daniel is from an upper-middle-class family from Rio de Janeiro. His father had a managerial position in a Brazilian bank and his mother is a housewife. His older brother, following in his father's footsteps, is also a manager at a bank. One of his sisters is a dentist and the other, younger, is still in college. Daniel never liked school. He went to a private expensive university where upper-middle-class kids go, normally headed for administrative and managerial disciplines, when they are not accepted into public, and better, universities. Daniel spent most of his college days playing volleyball on the fashionable Leblon beach and surfing at Barra da Tijuca beach, upper-middle-class neighborhoods in Rio de Janeiro. As he approached his thirties, Daniel and his parents realized that without a good education, Daniel had very few choices in the labor market that would support a middle-class status and lifestyle in Brazil. With no source of income, he could not get married and move out on his own or with his own family. The move to New York, where two cousins and a few of his friends were already living, became an option. In New York, he works for a limousine company managed by one of his cousins. The work is flexible and pays well enough for him to share a two-bedroom apartment in Manhattan and to go back and forth between Brazil and New York, reactualizing his middle-class status, lifestyle, and perceptions of a good life.

Nadja and Daniel have days of passion and abandon when Nadja very rarely returns to her apartment. Then they have days of withdrawal from each other. Nadja spends these days going to work and staying home mostly watching Brazilian TV and not talking to any of us. Nadja wants to marry Daniel and have kids and a nice life, but she knows that this is impossible in his current situation. One part of her love for him is the projection of a reality that could be lived only in Brazil, and only under different circumstances. Nadja's middle-class fantasy life with Daniel is predicated upon his middle-class lifestyle in Brazil, a lifestyle that Daniel's family has but that without a proper education he cannot afford. His present life status as middle class is precarious and depends on the fragile balance between staying in New York and in Brazil. He has a tourist visa that he is careful not to overstay. Every six months he goes back to Brazil for one or two weeks and renews his visa. Because he has family possessions in his name, and given the status of his middle-class family, U.S. embassy officials overlook his repeated entrances into the country.

Daniel does not want to meet Nadja's friends, much less her dancer girlfriends. But he likes her money and independence. Nadja, who as a dancer in Manhattan earns many times more than Daniel, has proposed to him that if they married, she could be the breadwinner in the household. He should not be concerned about money, she said to him. But that is not the only concern that Daniel has and that Nadja does not seem to be able to articulate. In the same way that Nadja's desire for a life with Daniel spans two nations, Daniel's assessment of what it would mean to be married to Nadja must account for what their lives would be like both in the United States and in Brazil. Despite the fact that in New York Nadja has a much larger income than he does, her life and lower-middle-class family background in Brazil are not compatible with Daniel's own background and family expectations. By marrying Nadja, Daniel would lose the much-valued lifestyle of a middle-class Brazilian who lives between nations. Although he does not make much money and lives a somewhat modest life in New York, in his frequent visits to Brazil he has increased his social capital and is considered successful by his family and friends. If he marries Nadja, Daniel has much to lose, pragmatically and symbolically speaking.

To begin with, Nadja's skin is a little darker than Daniel's, not acquired mainly by sun exposure on middle-class beaches. She is from northeastern Brazil, a region that is admired for its folklore and Af-

·al inheritance. It is a region whose general population is
ᴥed, if not always in reality, in the ways it is represented in
·y of the southern part of Brazil. It is also a region from
⸻ ᴀ ᴌarge number of impoverished migrants arrive in Rio de Janeiro
in search of a better life in lower-status jobs in the service industry. If
in New York, Nadja and Daniel can be clustered together as Brazilians
or Latin Americans of almost undistinguishable brown colors, this is
not the way they are seen by Brazilians knowledgeable about the nuances of race and its association with social and geographical locations.
Such Brazilian distinctions are often reproduced among Brazilians in
New York with transnational references and implications. Classifications of race and class, as defined transnationally, interfere with Nadja's
and Daniel's relationship. By marrying Nadja, Daniel would not only
lose his freedom to go back and forth between Brazil and the United
States as he pleases but also curtail his chances of finding a more suitable woman who could fulfill his and his family's class- and race-based
expectations. A desirable woman may not make as much money as
Nadja does, but she certainly would not be an erotic dancer. Preferably, she would have a paler skin color and dress more modestly, come
from a good middle-class family, and be enrolled in a university or be on
her way to a more professional career in an office environment. Nadja
does not articulate all these nuances in the negotiations that affect their
troubled relationship.

Nadja has many reasons to desire a man like Daniel. She is thirty-
six years old and the only one of her friends who has never been married. Her subject location as both a desirable and a respectable woman
has not been achieved in her own eyes or in the eyes of her family and
social network, particularly in Brazil. Daniel, as an idealized man, becomes, at times, an obsession to Nadja. "If he just weren't this stub-
born, idiotic, Brazilian macho [that] he is"—Nadja articulates Daniel's
refusal to marry her mainly in terms of gender, but never in terms of
class or race. She becomes frustrated with his resistance to accepting
what seems to her to be a very reasonable proposal: to marry her and to
occupy a secondary financial position in their future happy household
with the children of her dreams that exists suspended in an undefined
space between the United States and Brazil, not quite viable either here
or there. If in the United States, their class and racial differences were

masked by an imaginary unity of Brazilians in New York, after Nadja moved back to Brazil, it became clear that their differences were insurmountable. They broke up shortly after she moved back.

According to what Barbara told me, Nadja's apartment in Salvador is as unsettled as her bedroom in New York. In both places, Nadja's life, housing conditions, and eating habits feel temporary. One place is constantly projected onto the other and neither is complete in itself. Nadja still longs for a stable marriage that could give her the much-valued status of a respectable woman. In Bahia, Nadja's fashion store is impeccably stocked with expensive brands. Yes Brazil, Sartore, Rosa Chá, Tropical Chaos, and Traffic are brand names known nationally and worldwide, thanks to a relatively recent explosion in the Brazilian fashion industry.[5] Through the clothes she sells and wears and the relationships in which she engages, Nadja mixes very global and very local references. To appeal to North American tastes now imported by Brazil in the form of breast size, she had silicone implants. To appeal to world mainstream parameters here and there, she had liposuction on her stomach first and, just recently in Brazil, on her buttocks. She put Botox in her forehead and in her cheeks. "Really?" I said when Barbara told me the latest news. "And how does she look now?" "She is looking good but feeling a little sad," Barbara continued, her tone changing from gossip to concern. "She says that she wants to come back to New York, at least for a while, maybe dance a little more, make a little money. You know how Brazil is, right?" We worry about Nadja's juggling to maintain her middle-class position in Brazil if she cannot come to New York for a renewed inflow of fast cash to sustain her lifestyle and expenses with her store, her body, and herself, and still be able to help her family.

Justine's Cosmopolitanism

While working as a dancer, Justine rarely had relationships with men from the bars where she worked. Like Nadja, working in Manhattan where relationships between dancers and clients are more limited to the bar scene, Justine liked to keep the diverse spheres and relationships in her life separate. The sexuality of men in a bar, she thought, should be explored within the bar's confines. Dancing for her was, above all else, experimentation. Because of her family class location, Justine did not have any particular urge to make money. Her father gave her a generous monthly allowance. Upon her arrival in New York City, she lived in a comfortable penthouse belonging to a friend in Lower Manhattan. "But anyhow," she said to me, "it wouldn't hurt to have some extra money, and working, one gets to know the city and its movements better." Being part of a network of artists, Justine soon found work as an artist's model. Someone knew a Brazilian model that could introduce her to the scene. The market at that time was flooded with Brazilians who had recently moved to New York, mostly middle-class women and gay men from alternative lifestyles in Brazil. They believed that modeling was, besides being a way of making money, a way of experiencing New York. It was also as a way of experiencing the city as well as making money that Justine started dancing.

Justine likes to think about her social roles as performances. In the bar, Justine performed a role; outside, she performed others—and the different roles should not clash, for existential and aesthetic reasons. She loved the performance of dancing and being desired on the stage, but she thought that such desire would not be sustained outside the bar. Justine told me that, in the few times that she went out with bar patrons—once with a math professor and another time with a lawyer—she was terribly disappointed. The teasing and the fantasies that played out in the bar disappeared completely, and her glamorous self was hurt. Never again, she said to herself.

Besides dancing, she continued modeling and wandering through the city in search of adventures. It was then that Justine preferred to have relationships with both men and women. She met quite a number of them and did not worry if they overlapped. Just before she moved to New York, she ended her long-term relationship with an Italian filmmaker fifteen years her senior. She had started seeing a Brazilian man her own age, from a similar family and social background. Cesar lived in the same neighborhood in Rio de Janeiro, went to the same movies and gatherings, and had finished his MA in fine arts. They both decided to leave Brazil in 1994 and, while Justine came to New York, he preferred Paris. After the move, they visited each other either in Paris or New York on a monthly basis for about a year, until Justine broke off the relationship. "I lost patience with negotiating with boyfriends when I started dancing," she said. "All of a sudden I had all those men at my feet and it did not make sense to me that I still had to deal with a boyfriend asking me about my life." And she moved on. She started her sexual encounters throughout the city. The first man that she had a relationship with in New York was an Austrian Brazilian American photographer.[6] Her second lover was an Algerian cabdriver who, in a confusion of languages, mistook one address for another. He took her to eat at restaurants frequented by Arab taxi drivers and to his basement apartment in Astoria, which she found later to be a neighborhood where Brazilians different from her in terms of class lived. The third was an African American radio show host, the friend of a Brazilian actress girlfriend. He had long dreadlocks and liked poetry, dancing, and S&M.

Around this time, Justine met a Scandinavian student of philosophy from New York University. He was deeply concerned about the meaning of life and death, and they argued about the relationship between existence and aesthetics. They went to hear jazz in the East and West Village clubs and spent many hours in his apartment in Park Slope, Brooklyn. The balance between the Scandinavian and the African American men worked for about a year. Then Justine met a jazz bassist and had a passionate and troubled relationship with him for about a year. Luca was from an Italian American family who lived in Long Island but had ties to the Lower East Side. He had decided to return there looking for music and an artistic lifestyle in the 1980s. He lived on Stanton Street, where he and Justine spent much time between fits of jealousy and an intense sex life. When the cycle of sex and jealousy started involving physical aggression, Justine panicked. She took a vacation to Central America for a month, where she visited friends from school. When she came back to New York, she was cured of her passion for the hot-blooded jazz musician.

Just before she left, Justine had met a Jewish lawyer and intellectual at a Starbucks. They exchanged telephone numbers and she called him when she came back from her trip. Michael represented the equilibrium she thought was lacking in her life. He had a job and a large rent-controlled apartment, and saw the world through rational eyes. Never was he indelicate with her and he never asked any personal questions about her life. When he invited her to occupy an extra-large beautiful room in his place, Justine did not hesitate and soon became accustomed to the comfort and the gentle life. Plus, he never asked her about where she spent her free afternoons or nights. Michael liked that Justine worked as a dancer and a model and did not mind that she had lovers. They eventually married for documentation, tax, and legal status, and Justine continued her experimentations, sexual and otherwise, in New York City and across continents.

In six years of marriage, Justine had also traveled to India, the Caribbean, Africa, and Asia, and had spent time in various countries of Europe, where she cultivates friends and lovers, some of whom she met initially in New York. In her trips to more exotic places, she met both native men and other travelers. In her annual trip to Brazil, she met a woman DJ and journalist, with whom she fell in love. For five years Justine's gender and sexual identity changed every time she went back to Brazil. In Brazil, Justine became immersed in a network of gays, lesbians, bisexuals, transsexuals, and a variety of sympathizers, people who, in one way or another, did not fit into the pattern of a heterosexual monogamous couple with children. For Justine, although the model of the monogamous straight couple was a failed institution, it was a contract that she needed for legal and social status.

With the emotional, material, and logistic support of her husband, she went back to school. She stopped working as a model but kept dancing at least once a week. Her marriage was fine and she found more lovers. Between 2000 and 2005, Justine fell in love a number of times: with an Italian artist, a Caribbean intellectual, an older Englishman, a young Spanish architect, an Indian jeweler, a Jamaican vegetarian restaurant owner, and a Brazilian who enchanted her with the story that he had illegally crossed the U.S.-Mexican border through the desert. Justine also had more brief encounters with a few women: a Russian psychologist, a Dominican filmmaker, and an American photographer. In 2006, Justine, to my surprise and that of all who knew her, decided to move back to Brazil.

In Brazil, Justine has kept an ambivalent gender and sexual identity. As is becoming more common for women of her age and social status, Justine is not looking forward to sharing a life with anybody. With a good job as a university professor, she enjoys her friends and an alternative lifestyle while having occasional sexual encounters with foreign men and women, and with local men of African descent. Traditionally, places like Brazil and some islands in the Caribbean have been known for encounters between foreign men and local women. More recently the gender pattern has changed, and a number of foreign European and American women come to these places in search of local men, usually of darker skin colors. Assuming the role traditionally associated with imperial subjects (men and women), Justine realizes her cosmopolitan identity through her intimate encounters with men and women from different parts of the world. Justine once jokingly said to me that she likes to "know the world in its intimacy." As a traveling cosmopolitan, Justine moves freely and with comfort between places in the United States and Brazil, in addition to visiting Europe, Asia, and Africa as a global trekker in search of adventures, including sexual ones.

Transnational Incorporations

Flexible citizenship is a concept that Ong (1999) has developed to define the quality needed for the successful transnational mobility of contemporary subjects. As a response to the compression of time and space and to corporate strategies and expansion worldwide, flexibility became the modus operandi of modern individuals who must now be able to transit between two or more nation-states. However, transnational mobility does not take place in a vacuum in order to fulfill capital and labor demands. Rather, transnational processes are constrained by state and cultural institutions that both delineate and are delineated by everyday practices of particular individuals. For the women in this study, the factors that influence successful mobility between two countries, two nation-states, depend on the social, material, and professional net available to them both in Brazil and in the United States.

Both Sara and Clara acquired their legal status through paid marriages with African American men, from who they keep a social and emotional distance. This is a practice that is not considered desirable or legitimate in either Brazil or the United States. Although they achieved legal U.S. citizenship and can now cross the physical borders between the two countries, they have not achieved the necessary conditions to be fully incorporated into U.S. cultural citizenship. In New York, they somewhat marginal lives, constrained as they are to the bar scene.

Brazil, the deterioration of the economy in the region where they are from makes their return unlikely. For Sara, it is as if her investment in the future was directed almost entirely toward her son and her son's career. However, a career as a lawyer might not guarantee a successful location in the middle class for her son either, even after he passes the bar exam. Clara, as we have seen, left the country after finding that as a young lawyer, she was not able to fulfill her life expectations, and now she sees no way of returning to Brazil in order to reinvest in her career. On the other hand, she seems uneasy with the role of housewife and her financial dependency on Robert does not make her comfortable. Clara's return to Brazil is very unlikely, except for vacations, while the career ambitions she had as a modern women growing up in Brazil have had to be put on hold.

Nana and Renata, by marrying white American citizens, became what Constable (2003) calls ideal "colonized nationals," prospective wives and mothers of the American nation. After their marriage, it did not take them long to have their green cards come through, in contrast to the three years that it took Sara to get hers after marrying an African American man. The ways in which the bureaucratic apparatus functioned in regard to the two different marriage processes may illustrate the ways in which the state influences the legitimacy of personal relationships based on perception of race and class. In doing so, state institutions also determine who will be able to cross the material borders of nation-states with more or less flexibility. Nonetheless, it is necessary to look at cultural institutions and values such as family and gender ideologies in order to account for the ways in which people are or not able to cross not only material but also more symbolic borders. The miscalculations that Renata made of her family's expectations, for example, made her return to Brazil awkward, to say the least. The alienation from her father and sister that resulted from her unsuccessful trip led to her concentrated efforts to fit into U.S. family values. Although suffering from isolation, Renata is resigned to the conservative lifestyle of white suburban Long Island, and as she told me recently, she has decided to listen to Brandon's suggestions to forget about Brazil. Nana's eagerness to incorporate into U.S. whiteness and national values has also affected her flexibility to live between borders. In her life prior to moving to the United States, Nana was politically critical and critical of gender inequalities such as those expressed in the monogamous heterosexual couple. However, legal and material considerations led not only to her marriage to Jimmy but also to her buying into an ideology of incorporation in the body of the American nation. This was expressed in her distancing herself from other dancers, and from other Brazilians for that matter, and in her cutting her hair not just for aesthetic reasons but not to look Hispanic. As she plunges into U.S. legal and cultural citizenship, Brazil seems to be fading from her horizon.

Both Nadja and Justine worked in Manhattan bars and they both made considerable amounts of money. Yet the difference between the two is illustrative of the different possibilities of reproducing class and racial privileges as defined transnationally. Most of what Nadja earned here was sent back to Brazil, while she maintained a somewhat restricted life in New York. Coming from the lower-middle class, Nadja used to work almost every day of the week in order to help her family to recover from a continuous economic crisis. By dating a Brazilian man from an upper-middle-class family from Rio de Janeiro, Nadja kept her hopes for the future in Brazil and never invested in her stay in the United States. Her return to Brazil, though, is proving to be more difficult than Nadja had expected, and her family's material life has started to deteriorate again since the cash inflow from her dancing has stopped. Nadja's situation becomes even more complicated since she overstayed her U.S. visa, which makes her transit between the two countries uncertain, to say the least. Justine, in contrast, a member of the middle upper class, never had financial problems. Her coming to the United States was a purely individual project, and the stability afforded by her class location allowed her to venture across borders at ease. It was Justine who first came to me with the concept of "nomadic subject" to describe how she felt about her condition in the world. Although living in Brazil, she does not see this move as a "return," but rather as another temporary "base," fitting for her cosmopolitan lifestyle, enabling her to cross the symbolic and material borders of nation-states with ease and flexibility.

Chapter 8

Expanding Networks

The relationships between erotic dancers and their clients, friends, lovers, husbands, or boyfriends in New York have consequences that reach far beyond the confines of the bar or of any specific geographic location. Rather, these relationships have unexpected outcomes as they expand these men's expectations to realize their fantasies of adventure, love, and desire. Meeting a Brazilian woman in New York becomes, indeed, a stepping-stone toward a series of interconnected relationships that span nation-states and have an effect on a number of women and men in other countries. The language of help, at times, is how some men justify their traveling to search for women from peripheral locations. At other times, a longing for the exotic and for other venues of desire and satisfaction are in play. Never just one thing or the other. As much as Brazilian dancers confuse affection and monetary exchange, the men they meet are torn between worlds, between seemingly contradictory ways of living their lives and experiencing their bodies, of defining a trajectory that would fit with an ambiguously defined desire for the other.

Nana's Best Friend: Having Fun and Helping Out

Nana's influence in the creation of transnational ties does not stop with her relationship with her husband. Soon after she started working as a dancer, she met Tommy, who became one of her best male friends in New York. Tommy does not like to think of himself as a regular client in gentlemen's bars, but as someone who just passes by once in a while to have a beer and talk to the girls, a friend. Tommy likes the girls. "Some of them are really smart, like Nana; too bad they have to work in a place like this," he sometimes says, reflecting his ambivalent thinking about sex-related commerce. Tommy is a handsome white male with a strong, if a little overweight, body, short hair, and blue eyes. He has a job as a unionized electrician, which allows him to go for days or even weeks without working. He listens to Air America and is politically liberal. For three years before he met Nana, Tommy had a girlfriend who was a young Haitian American corporate accountant. But he says she wanted a very conventional life with children and a house on Long Island, on which they would pay the mortgage for a lifetime. Tommy is twenty-eight years old and thinks that this is not the life he wants just now.

Before Nana got married, Tommy used to come to her place and hang out in the afternoons. Sometimes he would cook or invite her and Ivana for dinner, drive them to the shopping mall, or just go out for a beer. As a friend, Tommy helped them both with their English and did little jobs in the house. Nana dispelled the boredom of his life. She liked to tell him about what it is like to be Brazilian, what it is like in Brazil. Nana gave him Brazilian music and showed him pictures. "You should go there, it's beautiful and a nice place to visit," she told him, and mentioned as an aside how difficult it is to live and to make money there, the poverty. After a while, Tommy started entertaining the idea of a trip to Brazil to check it all out: the women, the beauty, and the poverty. For Tommy all these come together.

Tommy bought a Brazilian Portuguese phrase book and with Nana's help started learning the language. He had taken Spanish lessons in high school and picked up Portuguese words fairly easy. He started researching websites that promoted encounters between Brazilian women and foreign men. To Tommy one thing was clear: he wanted to know the country through the body of its women. And he was not quite looking for romance. Among all the sites he searched, he chose the site of a German man who had been living in Rio de Janeiro for ten years. This site, like other similar sites, emphasizes the natural beauty of Brazilian women. "Besides being beautiful, Brazilian women enjoy having sex," Tommy said to me, sharing a belief common among sex tourists (Brennan 2002). Although Tommy never identified himself as such in his conversations with me, he could easily fit into the category of sex tourist as defined in the discourses created to describe encounters between foreign men and native women from peripheral locations. Tommy showed me the site he had chosen: it had pictures of women, most of them of darker skin color, wearing either thongs or nothing. The women's butts were exposed, meant to symbolize the result of a very Brazilian racial mixture, as Tommy himself told me later. He said: "Nana thinks I like blackies, but you see, I don't. I don't like when they have flat noses and their skin is too dark. I like them mixed, with fine noses but with big buttocks. I like them mixed."

On his arrival in Rio de Janeiro with his best buddy from childhood (a man who has traveled to Thailand and had an Indonesian girlfriend), Tommy checked into a hotel in Copacabana. Next day, they met the German guy from the website he had joined, Hans, and sat over Brazilian beers in a bar on the wide Copacabana strip. Observing the girls, Hans showed them some pictures of the girls who were associated with his agency, just like the ones walking up and down the streets. They would meet them at Help later on at night. Help is a nightclub well known in the sex tourism global circuit for encounters between foreign men and Brazilian women.[1] From our interview, it was not clear how the transactions between agents, women, and clients exactly happen. Hans probably gets a cut from offering his mediation services, either from the men or from the women, or from both. Tommy told me that he did not give any money directly to Hans but paid for joining the website, and soon after their arrival, he and his friend rented from Hans a small penthouse apartment in the neighborhood. They paid all the expenses from then on with the apartment, food, drinks, and parties. Each day, beginning in the afternoon, they had women coming over. In the video that Tommy showed me, there were five dark-skinned women in their late teens and early twenties splashing water with sexy movements. The camera stopped systematically at their buttocks. At night, he had filmed two dark-skinned cousins kissing each other. Next day, relaxation in the famous Rio de Janeiro saunas: "you pick the woman, for massage and sex." Tommy told me that he would not have been able to manage, even at twenty-eight years old, without Viagra. His first trip lasted ten days.

Hans wanted to make sure that his white male comrades had a good time. It was not only a matter of money, but also of sharing a way of being in the world and celebrating the brotherhood of the white men from

the Northern Hemisphere. Hans always had fun watching ⎯
enjoying themselves and "helping out these poor women." The .
of help came up again and again in my conversations with To⎯
is as if the sexual appeal of these women and his sexual access to
were justified by the inherent position of inequality between them ⎯
such inequality is seen in a positive way. According to Tommy, by virtue of their racial mixture and the hot and festive climate, Brazilian
women, particularly the ones of dark skin who also happen to be the
poorer, like sex. For them it is not such a big deal to sell sex for money
and enjoy it too. Indeed, as we have seen before, the belief that in Brazil, people, particularly Brazilian women, have a playful attitude toward
sexuality is not only expressed by sex tourists, but by most Brazilians,
who view this as a national characteristic.

And, for much less than he would pay in the United States for a
professional sex worker, Tommy can have fun with a number of women,
and help them too. In his second visit to Brazil, somewhere in between
sex for money, sex for fun, and sex for help, Tommy started going more
steadily with a dark-skinned twenty-one-year-old woman from a poor
suburb of Rio de Janeiro—Cidade de Deus, City of God, which lent its
name to the celebrated movie by Brazilian director Fernando Meire-
lles. Tommy met Fátima at Help. He did not distinguish Fátima from
the others in the beginning. She in fact appeared in the amateur porno
video he showed me. I vaguely remember her face among the others at
a moment when the camera stops at her soaping her body. But on his
second visit, Fátima started calling him, being more available than the
others, spending the night in his apartment. "She lived so far and sometimes could not go back home, so she stayed with me," Tommy told
me. Fátima told him about her family and of a cousin who needed a leg
operation. She invited him to her house. Tommy said he had never been
in such a poor place. As in most shantytowns in Brazil, the sewage system is precarious and the houses are somewhere, as musician Caetano
Veloso expresses, between being under construction and being in ru-
ins. Seven family members shared a small two-bedroom house, with a
kitchen-living room and an open space in the back. They served Tommy
feijoada, Brazil's national dish made of beans and meat. "It was so human," Tommy remarked as he tried to explain to me his feelings toward
another dimension of reality, totally new to him. Fátima's cousin could

hardly walk and the house needed repair badly. It would not need much money to have it fixed. Tommy gave Fátima $500 back at his place in Copacabana. He began feeling responsible for her. Back in the United States, he began sending her money regularly and going to Brazil to see her and her friends whenever he could.

After a Saturday afternoon summer party at Queens PS1, I sat with Tommy in a corner of an Irish pub over two pints of beer. I asked him about Fátima. He told me about her, the precarious condition of her house and her cousin's leg. He said he had never really done anything for anyone in his life and this was the first time he felt as if he could make a difference in someone's life. Tommy wants to help Fátima and was even considering bringing her to New York. He had recently paid $3,000 to a mediator who could arrange to get a visa for her to enter the country. "The only real problem," Tommy told me, "is that I don't want to get married. I don't believe in love, you know, but she thinks that she loves me. She is young, she doesn't really know about things. How can I say that to her? That she doesn't love me, she loves what she thinks I am, an American with money. But I can't say that to her. I can't say that I want to help you but it is not about love. And how can I say that? We can hardly understand each other. She speaks no English and my Portuguese, you see, is not enough to explain these things." "Maybe you can try to explain that to her," was the only thing I could say. "I don't know," he replied. "If I say this to her she will still want to come here, if she will accept my help." "Maybe she would," I said, "but she will need you there for her in the beginning, you know." And I continued, uncertain of what to say: "Maybe she loves you. You know, love is never just one thing or another. It comes with what each person is and has. I don't know. What is love, anyway?"

"I don't know," he says, "if love is like caring if she is well or not, if she lives or dies, I think I love her, but I don't want to be married, although I would like her to live with me and would try to make things nice for her. But she should know she can have a richer guy. She is young and beautiful and she can have whatever guy she wants. But I could put up [with] living with her. Yes, I wouldn't mind that. Maybe I love her. Yes, what is love?" Me: "Love is a flexible thing, I guess. It can be one thing or another." "Yes," he said, "but I don't want to get married, like I want go down to live in Brazil later in my life, when I retire, and

I don't want go there married. It is like going to Las Vegas and not being able to gamble. In Brazil I can have any woman, and you imagine if I go there married." "Yes, but there is a lot of time for that. I understand you, I guess." "Yes, maybe I love her, I don't know. I want to bring her here." Since his first visit to Brazil, two years ago, Tommy has returned eight times, and with the money he has been sending to Fátima, she has fixed her house a little and paid for her cousin's operation. Tommy also has bought Fátima brand-name clothes and authentic Puma sneakers.

Wishful Buddhism: Expat Dreams

Sam is a tall black man in his early sixties with gentlemanly manners and a laugh that resonates in your ear long after you leave him. I was looking for an African American man who had engaged in a marriage of convenience or a paid marriage with a Brazilian erotic dancer, when Nana mentioned him. Since neither Clara nor Sara ever introduced me to their arranged husbands and since it was a strategy of my work not to force upon people any issue that they did not want to talk about, I decided that I would find another man who fit the profile I was looking for. Nana knew Sam from the ESL school where she had taken classes and told him about my research. Sam was an English teacher there and immediately agreed to be part of my research. I called him up and we met at Nana's place on a bitter cold February day. I explained to him about my research and he did not hesitate to tell me about his life and how he got involved with the woman who is now his legal wife.

Sam was born in the southern United States, experienced the thrill of the Greenwich Village artistic community in the 1970s and 1980s, and then struggled to make a living as an actor in New York and Los Angeles for thirteen years. Tired of the United States, he decided to go to Rome and then to Paris, where he taught English and restarted his career as an actor in a classical theater company. The company traveled around Europe for about a year, after which he went back to his teaching job in Paris. He said he liked his life there and would have stayed forever if it had been possible to stay legally. But he did not have a permit to work and in 2004, during a period when the European economy was already showing signs of weakness and the French government had begun cracking down on illegal immigrants, Sam had to leave his job. He worked for an agency that catered to liberal professionals and his boss told him he could have his job back any time, after he had sorted out the legal documentation in the United States. Sam returned to New York but was unsuccessful in obtaining the necessary work visa to teach English in France, since there were many qualified professionals there that could do the same job.

In New York, Sam started working as an English teacher at Queens College while searching for other options to fulfill his dreams to be an expat. It was then clear to him that he no longer wanted to live in the United States. According to him, having lived in a foreign country for nearly four years, he could no longer readapt to the American lifestyle. "You see," he said, "after you've been an expat for years, discovering a calmness and relaxation that had never been my experience before, I realized that in terms of my values and priorities, America wasn't the best country in the world." Comparing Europe with the United States, Sam points out: "In Europe, the average person does not have as much in terms of materialism, but they all seem to have a better quality of life. When I was living there, I used to see people all the time. Here everybody works all the time; there is very little time for socializing with family and friends. Everybody here works until ten o'clock at night, and at that time you don't go out. Their values are different, their priorities are very different. People in America—both natives and assimilated immigrants—are pursuing the American Dream. They have to have the big car, the big house. They work because they have to compete if their colleagues are working and if they want to produce on the same level."

Certain that he did not want to stay in this country, Sam started searching the Internet for relationships that could work as a stepping-stone to fulfill his dreams to live again as an expat. He found a website called Immigrant Mate, later shut down, that promoted encounters between people who were mainly interested in a marriage of convenience, that is, marriage to gain legal status in different parts of the world. Through the site he met a French woman and a Brazilian woman, both living as undocumented immigrants in New York. The French woman, he told me, was much younger than he, and he had the impression that she was looking for a real marriage. The age issue, according to Sam, seemed to be a true drawback for her. The Brazilian woman was about his age, and they went out a few times to get to know each other. But she seemed to be too desperate, and he perceived it as a sign of instability when she revealed that she had been living illegally in this country for over twenty years—a sign that was confirmed when she left a long, ranting message on his cell phone about what she expected and did not expect from him. Sam said that by then he had had enough of the Internet experience, never having been a technophile in the first place.

Instead, Sam started, jokingly, putting the word out that he was looking for a foreign woman to marry so he could live in another country. Sure enough, it didn't take long for one of his ESL students to suggest that he seriously consider going to Brazil to find a suitable candidate there. He went to Rio de Janeiro for a summer vacation, but it was not there that he met his wife-to-be. Back teaching in New York, one of his students came to him after class and asked if he was still interested in marrying a foreign woman for papers. The woman was a young Brazilian who was searching for a mate not for herself but for her mother. She told him that her mother was forty-seven years old and was currently involved in a long-term romantic relationship with an American man, but that this man was very noncommittal in regard to matrimony. Now that she had overstayed her visa, she needed to get married in order to regain her legal status. Sam got her mother's telephone number and after a week he called to invite her for coffee. The first time they met they had a great conversation and she told him about her life and, although her daughter had advised her not to, said that she worked as an erotic dancer in a strip club. "Really?" he said, laughing. "You know, I am a pretty open guy; of course, I had no problem with that at all." Sam liked Diana for being so straightforward and honest with him in their first meeting, and he also liked her warm and worldly demeanor.

They decided to meet again and after a few weeks he said to her: "So I guarantee you that I will be 100 percent cooperative in assisting you in this process. And I also guarantee you that with my consummate acting skills that we will be successful in obtaining this goal, but I want you to guarantee me that you will be equally cooperative in helping me getting papers to immigrate to Brazil." Sam did not want any money for the arrangement, for he saw it as a fair exchange since he was as interested as she was in getting a free pass to another world. Plus, Sam really liked Diana; she was obviously from a good family of middle-upper-class background, which he could infer from her education, fine manners, and the way she decorated her apartment. Diana had been a housewife married to an engineer in Brazil and had decided to try out a new life after the marriage ended. She came to New York with her daughter, who worked as a bartender in a strip club and studied fashion design during the day. "We would look like a great couple," Sam figured, and they soon started making plans for the wedding. All was done with great taste, according to Sam. Diana had a beautiful, very classy wedding dress, brought in excellent Brazilian food, and hired a professional photographer to register both the official wedding in City Hall and the party she gave at her apartment afterward. "I had a wonderful time," Sam said. "It was really easy, and that came out in all of the pictures. Some of my friends came, all her friends."

It was at this point that I asked Sam, without wanting to be intrusive, about his personal life. Sam, being a very discreet man, was quite reticent. "What about your personal relationships?" I asked. "What do the other people in your life think about your getting married this way?" "Oh, my friends know me. This was not at all out of character for me. I have traveled a lot, and I am very open. It's Sam, it's who I am. They were very supportive." "Yes," I persisted, "but what about your more intimate relationships? Have you been involved in a more romantic relationship during this process?" Sam replied: "You see, I don't like Americans. When I lived abroad I always found it so much easier. It's not just because you are a foreigner and considered somewhat exotic. It's because it's much more relaxed. I always felt easier and I have always done better. When I came back to the States, I wasn't looking for a relationship. I was and am basically on my own."

After a pause, he continued, in a tone that revealed something between the disclosure of a secret and a statement of matter-of-fact information: "You see, I am gay," he said, "and I would say that having a relationship is not a priority at this stage of my life. It's a double standard, if you are gay or straight. At my age . . . I think when you are young it's a big part of your life. You think about building a life together with someone. The love of my life I had at my university. If I could turn back the clock, I would have chosen that relationship, because nothing that came along since equaled that intensity. I think a lot of people think it's always around the next corner; my experience is that one's true soul mate only happens once or twice in your lifetime . . . do you know what I am saying? If you miss it, you've missed it."

Sam then started telling me how Buddhism has influenced his way of seeing life and accepting the choices one must make throughout one's lives. For Sam, life is composed of sufferings and of overcoming sufferings through the teachings of the Soka Gakkai. Among other things, the Soka Gakkai's Buddhist practice consists of the daily chanting of the "Nam-myoho-renge-kyo," a mantra-like phrase that literally means, "I devote myself to the Lotus Sutra" but that also contains in itself the principles and ideals of the Soka Gakkai organization and school of thought.[2] As Sam explained to me and from what I could learn from one of the meetings at the New York Soka Gakkai center that I went to with him, this was a different kind of Buddhism from the more Zen-oriented one I was more familiar with. The chanting of "Nam-myoho-renge-kyo" is intended to help concentration and illumination, a path out of the mundane events that agitate the mind, leading to peace and harmony of body and soul. But the chanting with one's own will and faith does not just lead to acceptance of worldly and otherworldly matters; for if one concentrates enough, if one chants and believes enough, the Soka Gakkai teachings contend, one's wishes and dreams will eventually come true. That was a significant departure from a more passive way of understanding and practicing Buddhism that I knew of before meeting Sam, and that might explain both his resilience in accepting his fate and his drive to fulfill his dreams to be an expat, overcoming the obstacle that his sexual preference and racial positioning might present to him in his transnational moves.

Sam and Diana got married in the beginning of 2009, and right after that they started the application process for Diana's permit to work, and then for her green card. In November of that same year, Sam went to Brazil again, this time to register with the federal police for his permanent visa. He spent another month there, and said he just loved it—the beach, the sand, the warm weather. It all reminded him of his childhood years in the South. "Yes, but Brazil has also a lot of problems," I mentioned to him, and provocatively asked, since the subject never came up in our conversations: "What do you think about racism in Brazil? What do you think about racism in the U.S.?" He promptly and articulately responded: "It's my understanding that racism is alive and well in

Brazil and in the U.S. Obviously I am a very black man." "But you are an American black man," I interjected. "Yes," he said, "but you are going to see that I am black before you get to the American part. I have certainly in my lifetime encountered racism in many different places, and I have dealt with it as a young person, a middle-aged person. I think it exists everywhere, and I think you have to have a very, very thick skin in life to deal with issues like racism. I don't think it will be an ideal place, but it depends on who you are. I have gone around the world, and there is no place where I didn't make friends."

Yes, Sam is well aware of racism in Brazil and in the United States, but it does not seem, given his personality and his Buddhist thinking, that this will discourage him from realizing his dreams. Sam has done a little research on the job and real estate markets in Brazil and, with the support of the friends he made through contacts with his students and his legal wife, he is constructing a social net that can support him in his transnational move. He sees his moving to Brazil as permanent. He sees Brazil as a place with real possibilities for the future. "There," he says, "you don't have the feeling as you have in Europe that you are stealing someone else's job. The economy in Brazil is booming." Here he was echoing the widespread perception about Brazil in international arenas. Although it was already late at night, we finished this conversation over two cappuccinos that Nana gently offered us while watching a YouTube video of a CBS *60 Minutes* special entitled "Brazil's Rising Star," aired on December 12, 2010. To be an expat in Brazil, given the prospects of economic development in Brazil and in the United States, might not be a bad idea after all. We will see, and wish, by chanting "Nam-myoho-renge-kyo" somewhere in our unconscious, that all goes well.

Scandinavian Anguish

Another relationship that began in the United States and had as a consequence the expansion of transnational networks was that between Justine and her friend Mattheus. Anguished about life and existence while going to New York University, Mattheus fell in love with the sense of bodily reality that he saw in Justine. I met him and Justine at jazz concerts in the Village a few times. Aware of the workings of the unconscious, Mattheus did not deny the associations between race and fantasy. He liked dark women and was not attracted to Scandinavian women. His lack of desire was coupled with his lack of desirability as a too anguished and too existential young man, unlikely to develop a more linear project of life and career. Mattheus dated Justine for a few months, but the relationship ended when he finished his MA and had to move back to Sweden. He proposed to Justine that she come with him, but she did not even consider that a possibility. She kept his bike and his bookcase and moved in with the jazz musician she was already dating. Mattheus kept dreaming that they would be together some day. For a few years, he wrote to Justine telling her he was sure she was the perfect woman for him. Sweden was not quite a real place in Justine's geography, though. There was not a doubt in her mind that New York was the place to be. Mattheus came every year for three years to see her and to hear jazz and go to cafés. Then he decided that he would rather be visiting other places. His adjunct teaching position at Stockholm University, although providing no security or benefits, still allowed him to travel in Europe and overseas. For the first time, Mattheus traveled outside the Northern Hemisphere, Europe and the United States. Coming from an inheritance of Scandinavian condescension for the Third World and with a certain attraction for exotic types, Mattheus decided to go first to Cuba.

In Havana it did not take him more than a few days to fall in love with a waitress in a bar where he enjoyed sipping his afternoon beer, although Mattheus would have preferred to have wine. Although she was not a prostitute, Cynthia took him to her place at night to avoid the prostitution raids that are common in Havana because of the Cuban policy that seeks to restrict and control what is perceived as prostitution on the island. She had a daughter and an elderly mother with whom she shared a rundown apartment not far from downtown Havana. Older and more experienced, Cynthia, at age thirty, did not expect to fall in love with Mattheus and did not expect him to fall in love with her. Prostitution and casual encounters with foreign men in Cuba are not new. They were common before the revolution and have become common again since the country was reopened to foreign tourism and investment in the 1980s. Cynthia probably knew that she had little chance of being happy forever with a white man with blue eyes.

As Brennan (2002) found in the case of Dominican women in their relationship with foreign men, an initial passion or intense desire fades, and a woman must strategize to transform the relationship into much-needed financial help for herself and her family. Mattheus sent Cynthia money from Sweden a few times after their encounter, then stopped when the prospect of maintaining the relationship fell through, particularly, as he said, because she had a child.

Still, I asked Mattheus, why Cynthia? Why not just any other woman? "I saw a real possibility there," Mattheus told me over glasses of wine in the East Village, where we continued to meet every time he visited New York, even after Justine went back to Brazil. "Possibility of what?" I asked. Mattheus paused to reflect and moved slightly in his seat. Then he began a long monologue about the nature of desire. I will not reproduce our rather convoluted conversation; suffice it to say that we ended up agreeing with the basic Hegelian idea of the self that is only completed through the other. But where he saw this alterity in relation to his mother and the Oedipus complex, I saw it in colonial relations and white privilege. Mattheus said that I was being insensitive, and I accused him of being an idiot. No middle ground was achieved on this visit. Another year passed before I met Mattheus again in the East Village. Again, over glasses of wine, we talked about the nature of desire and difference.

This time, he told me he was deeply in love with another Brazilian woman. Mattheus met Martha on a website for encounters between Brazilian women and foreign, particularly European, men. Martha is from the very north of Brazil, with a mix of indigenous ancestry. Different from the women in popular destinations for sex tourists, such as Havana and Rio de Janeiro, women from the north of Brazil are reputedly more family oriented, more modest, and purer, in a cultural and racial sense (Piscitelli 2007). Mattheus was not quite expecting, however, to find a very Catholic woman who was rather modest and sexually inexperienced. It was difficult for him to reconcile his sexual fantasies with what he found when he first met Martha in a restaurant by the river in Belém, the capital of Pará, the northern part of the country in the Amazon area.

Martha is twenty-five years old and is the daughter of a military officer. She lives with her family in a traditional home in a middle-class neighborhood, while she goes to college for a degree in business administration. Martha's dream, Mattheus told me, is to have her own business exporting local products to southern Brazil or overseas and to buy a house for her parents in one of the new gated communities spreading around the city. She is tired of the poverty all around her, and she dreams of having a house where her parents can put their chairs on the front porch and talk, as in the old days, without iron bars and fear. According to Mattheus, Martha is beautiful and educated in her conversation and manners. Martha and Mattheus went for beers and dinners by the river, and to the cinema, museums, and galleries. Martha showed him the University of Pará and the exuberant Emílio Goeldi Botanic Gardens. When they had sex, Martha told Mattheus that it was her first time, although, as he mentioned to me, she never said she loved him. She said, however, that according to her family values, she expected the first man she slept with to be the one she married. Mattheus was unsure what to think about all that. Yes, he was looking for someone to have a serious relationship with that could lead to marriage, but they did not know each other well enough, and despite her being reasonably well educated, she spoke very little English. His Portuguese and Spanish were not much better. Nevertheless, they parted with a promise to meet again and to continue their relationship.

Four months after Mattheus's trip and after numerous e-mail messages back and forth, Martha traveled to Stockholm to meet him. She arrived in May and stayed for a month. Despite the gentle late-spring weather, Martha was always cold and avoided going out on her own in the afternoons when Mattheus went to the university. She read books and magazines she brought with her and tried to improve her English by watching English-language TV. Martha was afraid of getting lost in the city and felt conspicuous in the presence of the very white Swedish people. She waited for Mattheus to come home, which he did, sometimes late, and often with a bottle of wine to accompany dinner, a Scandinavian family habit. Mattheus is afraid that she interpreted his drinking as excessive and as a sign of his dissatisfaction with their relationship. She grew unhappy, and their sex was not very good. Mattheus expressed his confusion to me by telling me that she slept fully dressed in pajamas. He did not know if she was avoiding him or just feeling cold. I consoled him by saying that I very often sleep in my pajamas in the United States and, with a body made for the tropics, often feel colder than most natives from northern lands. Lack of communication was the main reason Mattheus gave for the failure of their encounter and for the difficulty of any possible future relationship.

After a month, they parted, confused. Mattheus was no longer so sure that the woman he was dreaming of would be able to adapt to the Scandinavian weather, temperament, and lifestyle. Plus, his present financial situation was not very encouraging. Immigration laws are very strict in Sweden, and to be able to marry and bring a woman from overseas one has to have an income higher than Mattheus earns as an adjunct professor. His family background, educational history, and apartment in a much-valued area of Stockholm helped him in applying for government permission to bring an overseas wife. But that would not be enough to prove he could be the sole financial and social provider in a middle-class lifestyle. Mattheus likes spending generously, drinking, eating well, and traveling, which he would have to give up if he establishes a relationship with a woman who probably would not be able to make a living in Stockholm unless she took a low-status job as a domestic or sex worker. This would, of course, be incompatible with Mattheus's class and intellectual status. He kept the relationship in suspension while still corresponding with her and expressing his love and his willingness to work things out. Martha was the first to give clear signs that the relationship was not going to work. She started writing less often, though still keeping open the possibility of marriage, until she ran into a former boyfriend.

Not knowing Martha or this other man, I could rely only on Mattheus's psychoanalytical interpretation. According to Mattheus, Martha's ex-boyfriend came back to her only after learning that she was about to be engaged to a Scandinavian man. That happens, Mattheus said, because desire follows a triangular structure—a person only desires that which is desired by a third person. Thus, Martha's ex-boyfriend would desire her only so long as Mattheus was still in the picture. Otherwise, continued Mattheus, he would lose interest in the monotony of certainty. "I see," I said and pushed him further. "And where does your desire for her come from?"

We started disagreeing again when he made the third party in his relationship to other women his mother, evoking the Oedipus complex and his repulsion for anyone that resembles his mother. That would explain his desire for a woman from the tropics, the furthest model from his own mother. Then he started telling me all about his early relationship with his mother and father and how that made his relationships with women so problematic. He also mentioned his sense of abandonment, rejection, and so on. This was when I told him I had had it with his psychoanalysis, and that the model of desire of a white man for a woman from the tropics reflects colonial and postcolonial relationships of power. While he saw difference as embedded in one's individual experience, I saw difference in terms of social and historically given structures of fantasy and inequality.

But our discussion this time did not end so disagreeably, and we retained what we thought to be a few important elements of that which we call desire: again the Hegelian formation of the self in relation to the other, the fluidity of a desire that goes from one level of experience to another (in this case individual and sociohistorical), and its malleability and embedment in all relationships in our lives, alongside power. We did not discuss much about power, and briefly referred to Foucault. The Foucauldian language of desire is more seductive and better fit, we thought, to understand our relationships with other people and our own relationship. Caught in the middle of these multiple transnational triangular relationships, my own relationship with Mattheus oscillates between desire and distancing. In our last encounter, desire was clearly in the air: our legs touched, glasses were caressed while our gaze stopped on each other's hand. He casually touched my breast when we parted hurriedly, for some reason, at the Union Square subway station. In our e-mail exchanges we continue our discussion of desire and our game of seduction.

Mattheus asked me to translate into Portuguese the e-mail he wanted to send to Martha on her birthday. I asked him for permission to reproduce it, and here it is:

Dear Martha,
I fully understand and respect your decision and I wish you the best of luck in your life. You are a wonderful person and I feel sure you will have a good life. The experience I had living with you shook my existence, and it has affected my life profoundly.

Thank you very much. I have now been admitted to the PhD program in Stockholm, and I am very happy about that. I am of course sad that things didn't turn out differently between us, I am sad we didn't spend more time together, and I am sad we had such a hard time understanding each other. In July I will go to Brazil; first I will fly to Fortaleza and from there I will take a bus to Belém and from there a boat to Manaus. I will only stay shortly in Belém and I hope very much to see you. I really need to say goodbye to you in a proper way, you have been very important to me, so please give me a chance to say goodbye to you in a proper way. I only ask you that we go to that restaurant, by the river in the botanic garden with the birds and the high tower that we went to last time. I have no intention of changing your life, I just need to see you this one last time to say goodbye.

Conclusion

Spaces of Betweenness

Like many of the women in my research project, I live in the suspended space between the United States and Brazil. And, as for many of these women, to me, one place becomes the specter of the other, its shadow, and its distorted mirror image. I write these concluding thoughts in Brazil. The decision to do so was as much deliberate as it was a consequence of my semi-nomadic, transnational position. After living in New York for nearly twelve years, and following my own desires, projections, and trajectory of life, I decided to return to Brazil. It is not yet a definitive return. This I insist on postponing, trying to create minimum conditions to maintain my now ontological condition of transnationality. *O Brasil me espanta.* How to translate *"espanta"*? An awkward adjective for an astonishment that one usually has for the unknown. When one says, *"Você, às vezes, me espanta"*—You, at times, astonish me—one wants to convey surprise at an unexpected aspect of that person. This is not quite what happens to me, to us who no longer belong in just one place permanently. We know, by experience or from the news, about most aspects of Brazilian society and its structure of inequality.

Yes, Brazil now occupies a different location in the world's geopolitical cartography. Worldwide, in the Lula years (2003–2010), Brazil was celebrated as a rising star in diplomatic encounters, and Lula's voice could be heard on issues from Iran to Venezuela, as the middle man between corporate and U.S. and European-centered interests and the interests of the world's underdog and emerging nations in the international arena. Lula finished his eight years, two consecutive turns as the president of the country, with a nearly 80 percent approval rating. With the expansion of the economy and the implementation of welfare programs, there was a progression of the lower class out of poverty and a growth of what has been called the new middle class.[1] However, quality of life did not improve much and in some cases worsened. Environmental depletion is notable not only in rain forest areas, but also in cities. Urban greenery and forests have been destroyed as Brazilian cities experience a construction boom of apartment buildings or the more precarious urban occupation in *favelas*, or shantytowns. As consumer power rises, the number of cars rapidly increases without necessary improvements in the road and transportation systems. In Salvador, a small subway system has been under construction for nearly fifteen years, stalled by accusations of corruption at various levels of government. Urban expansion occurs without the necessary parallel growth of the sewage system.

Inequality, although somewhat better, is still a hallmark of Brazilian society. The chaos, the open sewers, the fear of violence, and the street kids knocking on car windows saying how hungry they are: these kids are all black or almost black. Inside the cars we are almost all white, or almost white, since we have more money and status. Off-white, if we take into account global and postcolonial racial configurations. We know of this reality; we are part of it too. It is different from just visiting a foreign country. In a foreign country one might understand, lament, or celebrate a certain reality. To us who are from Brazil but no longer of Brazil, this foreignness is in us, in our psyche and in our material life. We are integral parts of this reality, and we need not only a discourse about it but also a daily practice of survival and coping, and for better or for worse, a means of intervening in it too.

The middle class in Brazil is different from the much larger middle classes in the wealthier countries of what has been defined as the Western part of the Northern Hemisphere. Despite the improvement in Brazilian economic conditions over the past few years, and the growth of the middle class, we continue to constitute a somewhat small elite. The majority of the population is below the poverty level. Salvador, the capital of the state of Bahia, is a city of nearly three million inhabitants, and double that if one counts the greater metropolitan area (Carvalho and Pereira 2006). The third city in the country in terms of population size, Salvador is also one of the most unequal. One can see *favelas* from nearly any point in the city. As in Rio de Janeiro, the rich and the poor live side by side, geographically speaking, with shantytowns and luxury buildings occupying neighboring strips of land. One of the first cities in

Brazil and one of the most important ports for sugar cane commerce, Salvador was established during the colonial regime of slavery, which led to its present social and racial makeup—a large and mostly poor black population, a small mixed-race middle class, and an even smaller off-white elite.

The visual contrast amazes me every time the plane that brings me home reveals the shadows of high-rises against the brown bricks of the sea of shantytowns. People from the middle class very rarely visit the shantytowns. To them, the inhabitants of *favelas* are just part of the vast mass of dark poor, without much distinction. I drive with my parents mainly to my brothers' apartments and to shopping malls along the large valley avenues, through which open channels of sewage run like postmodern rivers; the margins of these rivers are covered with green grass and exuberant red and yellow flowers. On the hills on each side of these valleys are the *favelas*, a multitude of mostly brick houses. They fascinate me, but to my parents they seem to be nonexistent, invisible from the comfort of their rolled-up windows and air-conditioned cars. They are used to it; that's the way it is—the sewage, the flowers, the slums. The comfort of the car pains me as the ultimate alienation. I want to open the windows, but I am told it is too hot outside and the noise of the wind disturbs conversation. They want to hide their fear from me and from themselves that a street kid with a piece of glass as a weapon will threaten them by demanding money, no longer humbly begging.

I am taken by a profound melancholy, a kind of melancholy defined as *tristesse* by Orhan Pamuk (2005), trying to understand his own melancholy in relation to Istanbul as he reads Lévi-Strauss's *Tristes Tropiques. Tristesse* is a concept used to express a kind of melancholy that refers not only to the individual or a general human condition but toward the other, the unknown once-colonized space that reveals itself with a mix of attraction and repulsion as one faces the stark contradictions of beauty and chaos—the precariousness of life in the tropics. Although according to Pamuk this *tristesse* is just a reaction of Western eyes when confronted with tropical chaos, I find this concept apt for expressing the profound, sharp melancholy I feel when I face the familiar and yet already unknown place from which I came. It rains nonstop if one comes in the winter months from June to August. Then, the city is particularly impossible. The beautiful and inviting beaches of the summer, the main spaces of entertainment and socialization in the city, are all off limits. The water from the rain drains down the streets and, mixed with the sewage, is discharged untreated directly into the ocean. As I drive with my family and friends, it is as if the ocean itself becomes almost invisible. Local people do not usually go to the beach in the winter months because of the cold breeze off the ocean. But the darker water of mud and polluted runoff adds an extra melancholy to the scene, a *tristesse*. It rains nonstop. It is June, and I cried for the first three days after arriving from the United States, not having been here in this month for nearly a decade. What became of the happiness of summer vacations when, as the stereotype goes, one parties all the time? Our maid, a black woman, said that it took her two and half hours to get to the center of the city from the urban sprawl of high-rises, nearly gated communities, where my family lives now and from which it would take thirty minutes on a clear day.

On the third night after my arrival, my father, sensing my distress, came to talk to me. In silence he entered the room where, caught in melancholy, I stared into nothingness, my mind whirling with comparisons, estrangement, and contradictions. In his humble way of talking— my father is a shy man of few words—he said: "It must be very different from there. You see, here it is all very messy, things are different from there; there you have no walls in front of the houses. Here it is different." My father, following a family tradition that goes back to Middle Eastern merchants who settled in the hinterlands of the northeast of Brazil, is a self-made man who mixes a North-South buying and selling business and the ownership of middle-sized *fazendas* (farmlands).

Locally my father can be considered middle to upper-middle class. In the 1990s he passed through a continuous economic crisis, which he has somewhat recovered from recently. Like most Brazilians, my father must struggle to maintain his and his family's status. He knows well the hardships of economic instability and political chaos. During the time I was absent, the social-economic conditions neither of the country nor of my family got much better. Because of successive economic crises my family lost our home in a central middle-class neighborhood in Salvador, moving successively to smaller rented places until the time came to buy a new home. Our new apartment is no longer located in an established urban neighborhood with urban facilities, stores, churches, and street vendors. We used to see people walking and in the distance the sea, central to my geographical existence. My father's accustomed silence grew more stern as his social status became more precarious. My mother, a woman given to parties, charity, and social effervescence, withdrew into one after another of the evangelical churches that have spread through the country as traditional social institutions of support and sociability have disappeared.

Now, in the bedroom where he came to talk to me, my father did not try to hide or to make invisible what is on everyone's face: the poverty, the sewage, the contradiction. As a good member of the middle class, as usual at different points in history, my father blames our problems mainly on corruption—present corruption, past corruption, corruption on the federal, state, and city levels. He started by mentioning the current PT (the ruling Workers Party) scandals, but perceiving my lack of support for his argument, he changed his tone. In this time of reconciliation, political disagreement is not welcome. Father mentions, then, the decaying train-track structure. Because of accusations of corruption, the structure has been abandoned for nearly fifteen years while still under construction and now looks like a monstrous ruin cutting across the valleys. My father, like most Brazilians I know, is aware of the social structure of the country. Despite the belief that middle-class people are alienated, my father is deeply aware of the structure of inequality of Brazilian society, but like most Brazilians, he does not see himself as having an active part in perpetuating this system. I didn't remind him of that in this conversation. It was also a time of reconciliation for me, and I spoke nothing of my controversial positions.

As O'Dougherty (2002) argues, the Brazilian middle class has developed a discourse of victimization to cope with economic and political crisis. What happens in the country is usually blamed on corruption and at times on global forces. The silence about daily inequalities, the relationship to one's subordinates, the silence about the open sewers, the *favelas*, and the kids in the street—this silence is exasperating to a newcomer. Many times in conversation with other Brazilians living overseas we comment on the shock, the impossibility of living daily life with such social tension here after experiencing being away for an extended period of time. Many come back to Brazil to find that a real return has become extremely painful, materially and psychologically. However, if one has to come back, if one has to live here on a more permanent basis, one has to deal with all that. This was what my father told me at the end of our short conversation.

In addition to the discourse of "we are victims of the system, the corrupt politics," people must develop strategies for coping with the harsh reality of corruption, extreme inequality, and violence. These are perceived as the main sources of Brazilian problems by most Brazilian middle- to upper-middle-class people who are part of my family network in Bahia—resignation and pessimism for some, for others a sense of absurdity coupled with humor and a festive lifestyle that tries to compensate for social chaos with forgetful happiness and a playful sensuality. These constitute points of release of social tensions and strategies, which help to deal with a reality that feels beyond one's control and will. It is when they are immersed in such social contradictions and through the construction of such discourses about the Brazilian self and sexuality that Brazilian women imagine their migration.

Redefining the Nation in Transnational Spaces: Gender, Class, and Race

In writing this book, I had in mind to dispel what I believed to be one-dimensional images of Brazilian women as they cross borders of nation-states and as they work as erotic dancers. I was uncomfortable with the representation of these women as immigrants, and further, as immigrant sex workers. I thought that neither of those terms accounted for the complexity of their experiences and the transformations in their social identities as they moved between Brazil and the United States. It was my impression that the ways in which immigrants have been depicted in most literature reduce them to a sphere of work, survival, and loss, and do not account for their desires, ambiguities, and dilemmas. Likewise, much of the academic, popular, and activist literature about sex workers associates immigrant sex workers with human trafficking and sees women in the sex industry as mere victims of global structures of inequality. Without neglecting the complex socioeconomic context in which they navigate, my goal in this book was to construct a different picture of the women I encountered in New York gentlemen's bars. As noted, although there were women from different social backgrounds working as erotic dancers, from the beginning, I was struck by the number of women from the Brazilian middle class. They did not correspond to images of poor immigrants fleeing poverty or of women coming into the U.S. sex industry without knowing what to expect. The dancers I encountered in New York were educated women who came to this country with the support of a transnational network constituted mainly of other women, friends and family members, who also worked as erotic dancers and who informed them about what erotic dancing entailed. Although economic considerations were of foremost importance in their decision to come to the United States and to work in New York's sex industry, they were not the only ones. These women's motivations must also be seen in relation to a much deeper history of colonialism and post- and neocolonialism that has delineated imaginations, fantasies, and desires as constructed transnationally.

Throughout this book, I have adopted a transnational frame of mind as I inhabited the spaces and followed networks and social processes that cross nation-states. Although my research cannot be considered multisited, at all times I was concerned about how the nine women in my research constructed their lives between Brazil and the United States. It has been my argument that this process began while they were still in Brazil. As part of the Brazilian middle class, they grew up in the 1970s, 1980s, and 1990s imagining themselves part of a global modernity with common aspirations of a consumer lifestyle as it emanated from centers of symbolic and economic power. But by the mid-1980s, signs had begun to appear that these aspirations could not be realized in Brazil. As the public university system started to crumble and strikes abounded, as salaries shrank and inflation reached four digits, middle-class Brazilians started rethinking their life trajectories, desires, and plans for the future. Political and economic transformations also rearrange the ways one relates to one's body and self and how one relates to others. In the case of Brazilian women, political economic transformations have intersected with nationalist representations of the Brazilian body. Although it has been argued that with globalization the role of the nation and the borders of nation-states would increasingly disappear, this has hardly been the case. Borders of nation-states are enforced more strictly than ever, while nationalist ideologies remain crucial in the formation of people's collective and individual identities. Historically constructed as the symbol of the nation, Brazilian middle-class women developed a particular discourse about their bodies as embedded in the category "*morena*."

For most of the women in my research, to be a *morena* from the middle class means to have an instrumental view of their bodies and a playful way of dealing with sexual display. Throughout history, the body of the Brazilian woman, particularly of the *mulata* as a national symbol, came to signify the capacity to mix and to incorporate foreign bodies into the body of the nation. It is my argument that it is through the articulation of this distinct racial category that Brazilian middle-class women begin to forge their transnational practices and imaginations. On the one hand, "*morena*" refers to a more modern self, body, and sexuality that corresponds not quite to the mix of races, as in the case of the category "mulata," but to a capacity to blend the local with the global. On the other hand, this category articulates a distancing from a reality of chaos and poverty that these women feel they do not deserve, avoiding questioning the system of inequality in Brazil. Ultimately, these women's decision to migrate can be seen, in the Brazilian context, as yet another middle-class privilege.

Yet once they are in New York City, the social identity of such women becomes even more complicated. Although they occupy a privileged class and racial position in Brazil, they enter the United States in a position of subalternity. As exhaustively argued in studies of race, racialization is an ongoing process of subject making that happens in conjunction with one's position in the labor market and in terms of one's gender and sexuality. The process of racialization and class repositioning of these women began when they arrived in the city. Moving to the neighborhood of Queens, a working-class neighborhood occupied mainly by migrants from peripheral countries, already represented a major change in their social identity. In Queens, and particularly in gentlemen's bars, Brazilian women tend to be clustered with other Hispanic minorities. However, from the point of view of Brazilian dancers, Hispanics do not fit their criteria of class position. Being from the middle class, the nine women in my research—like Brazilians in the United States at large—actively try to distance themselves from

Hispanics. In gentlemen's bars, Brazilian women do that by developing complex discourses that involve ideas of race and class while using a language of morality and sexual propriety. As we have seen from my ethnographic observation in the bar scene, bars constitute scenarios where race and class are reconfigured through performances of gender and sexuality. Through a language of morality, identifications and differentiations take place, and new hierarchies are constructed. Differences in how one dresses or undresses one's body, how one smiles or wears one's hair, how one accepts tips and spends money—all are markers that define who belongs to what cliques and networks formed in the bar.

Another significant source of differentiation concerns dancers' relationships with clients both within and beyond the bar scene. As we have seen, dancers' work consists of not only performing onstage but also socializing with clients when on the floor. When talking to clients, dancers must encourage them to buy them drinks. Talking to clients is a performance of seduction in which a dancer must sell her personal appeal. In the postcolonial context of New York gentlemen's bars, a dancer's nationality serves as a prop to incite men's fantasy and desire. The nation appears both through dancers' bodily performance and through a constructed, albeit fragmented, spoken narrative. The Brazilian nation appears as a source of both beauty and chaos, and dancers must combine a discourse of economic need and fun in a way that is consistent with their own social location and sensibilities. In the interactions that take place in the bars, it is not only clients who choose their favorite dancers. Dancers also choose clients whom they judge suitable to them. In Queens bars, through the observation of clients' performances of masculinity, dancers must decide what kinds of relationships they want to have with different clients; in doing so, dancers also create or reinforce hierarchies of class and race as reconfigured in transnational spaces. Sponsors, amigos, and psychopaths are categories that dancers use to classify clients and the relationships they have with them within the bar scene.

Unlike dancers who are U.S. natives, however, whose relationships to clients tend to be bounded by the bar scene, migrant women experience bars not just as a workplace. Rather, bars also constitute their main space of socialization. It is in gentlemen's bars that most dancers meet men who become important relationships, and who represent their linkage to society at large. The kinds of relationships dancers have with clients are hierarchically organized within the structure of U.S. society in terms of race and class, and represent different access to U.S. legal and cultural citizenship. Dancers' relationships to bar customers beyond the bar are a crucial arena through which dancers become incorporated into U.S. racial and class configurations. Marriage to an American citizen is for most migrant dancers the only way to achieve or maintain their legal status in the United States. For only if they are legal can they think of moving to other job markets, or, equally important, move freely between Brazil and the United States. Depending on the conditions under which the women enter the country and the bar scene, their chances to meet people will be more or less restricted to gentlemen's bars and to people associated with them. Clara's aunts and nieces, for example, have ended up constructing a tight family of women in New York. If, on the one hand, this is helpful in guiding individual women to navigate within the dynamics of the bar, on the other, this tight net represents a drawback. It hinders these women's ability to have encounters with people from other circles, thus limiting their integration into U.S. society at large. Clara's family members socialize mainly among themselves or with other dancers and bar clients. Even their intimate relationships are associated with the bar scene, when clients become their boyfriends, lovers, sponsors, or husbands.

The same can be said of Barbara, Ivana, and Sara. The three of them had encountered men who were bar clients, and they all had hopes that those relationships could help them in their social mobility in the United States. But that did not quite happen. The men they became involved with were immigrants themselves and had a somewhat marginalized position in the United States. Although Barbara was able to legalize her situation, she was not able to have the kind of incorporation into U.S. society that she expected, as illustrated by the alienation she felt living in the fashionable neighborhood of the Lower East Side. When the social misunderstandings between her and her Hispanic husband grew, divorce became inevitable. She moved back to live with another dancer from her Bahian network in Queens. Ivana's relationship with an older Greek man not only did not help her to move outside the bar scene, but also threatened the freedom she needed to be able to meet more suitable men. Sara's relationships with both Glaucus and Fred seemed to be an endless tale of fabrications and deceit, as neither man could offer her a way out of a lifestyle limited to the bar, nor could they help her gain legal status. Instead, Sara, as other women in her network have done, engaged in a paid marriage to a man of African descent. I never met this man and she hardly talked about their relationship. The silence with which Sara protects her marriage reveals not only her attempt to keep the semi-legality of the relationship hidden but also her discomfort in having such a close commitment with someone who could be considered a subordinate in light of both Brazilian and U.S. racist values. The association with people of African descent in the United States could in fact function as a reminder of her ambivalent social status and indicate the risks of downward mobility that she faces with her transnational move. The racism characteristic of the social structure of Brazilian society and the middle class are, in this way, reconfigured within a new and different context.

From the perspective of most of these women, white U.S. men are the most desirable. In the U.S. and global hierarchy of race, class, and cultural values, whiteness signifies social status and occupies a privileged position vis-à-vis other racial-ethnic and national variants. White American men represent to Brazilian women not only access to legality, but also entrance into an imagined American middle class that they envisioned when still in Brazil. In my research, only two of the nine women were able to find the right kind of men—white—but their process of incorporating into American whiteness is not as straightforward as one would expect. Both Renata and Nana married men of Italian and Irish descent whose parents took part in the expansion of American middle class through labor unionization and the creation of a strong welfare system. However, neither of these men carries the markers of class as defined by the Brazilian middle class, and particularly represented by college education. Although in the global hierarchy of nations the women can be said to have married up, from the perspective of Brazilian middle-class values, this is not necessarily the case. It is true that both women live now more economically secure lives, but those gains are not easily translatable into an equivalent Brazilian reality.

Renata's awkward return to Brazil reveals her unease with living across borders. Alienation from her family in Brazil and the isolation of a Long Island suburban lifestyle remind her of her transnational losses.

The picture for Nana seems a little brighter, but not free of problems. By marrying the right kind of man, Nana was able to recover her gender status in Brazil, damaged by her purportedly bad sexual behavior as a single woman with multiple partners prior to her migration. In addition, Nana's money remittance to her mother in Bahia in order to fix their house functioned as a marker of her social upward mobility. But in accordance with her and her friends' feminist and class ideals of independence and self-reliance in Brazil, Nana's marriage is an uneasy compromise. For in Brazil, much has been said recently in the media and literature about Brazilian women's reliance on marriage to U.S. and European men in order to move up the social ladder. Nana's eagerness to fit into the United States, illustrated by her distancing herself from other dancers (including her onetime best friend, Barbara), shows that she does not want to be associated with what she perceives as the marginal life of immigrants. Nana cut her hair short; she forgot Portuguese words; and the last time I spoke to her on the phone she said she no longer wants to go to Brazil, not even for vacation. I cannot help but perceive her curtailing her ties with Brazil as she strives to incorporate into the United States as profound losses in her life and psyche.

Nadja's trajectory also illustrates how life conditions, as defined transnationally, affect people's mobility and their capacity to incorporate themselves into different national settings. With her male family members unemployed or underemployed, Nadja's flow of cash from dancing became crucial to her family's return to, and maintenance of, a middle-class lifestyle in Bahia. Her family's social condition has become to a large extent dependent on her, a fact that tied her even more to Brazil and made her perceive her life in the United States as transitory. Her relationship with Daniel, a Brazilian man from an upper-middle-class family from Rio de Janeiro, reveals her preoccupation with establishing new ties with Brazil, even as she moved transnationally. As Nadja refused to invest in the United States, and as (following her romantic inclinations) she refused to see marriage to an American citizen as an option to gain her citizenship, her return to Brazil seemed inevitable. In addition to sending money to her family, Nadja opened a fashion store in Bahia and bought an apartment in an upper-middle-class neighborhood there. She had high hopes for the future. However, reality fell short of her expectations. The last time I heard about Nadja from Barbara, I learned of the end of her relationship with Daniel and the difficulties in keeping her business. Nadja now thinks about returning to the United States and going back to dancing, the only way she can guarantee her incorporation back into the Brazilian middle class, while living her life in a rather marginal social location in the United States.

Throughout the making of this book, Justine's difference from the other women has become increasingly more defined to me. While the other women's social positioning vacillated between the middle and the lower-middle classes, Justine always occupied a comfortable location in the upper-middle class. The security that her family financial situation allowed her was manifest in all spheres of her life and the choices she has made along the way. Dancing was for her a chance to explore her gender and sexual identity rather than a source of income and a way to maintain a class identity back in Brazil, as it was for the other women. Investing in her education and circulating in more middle-class circles in the United States, Justine has constructed herself as what might be best defined as a cosmopolitan. Among all these women, only Justine, who pursues an entirely individualistic life project, appears to embody the ideal contemporary transnational persona. She not only can cross freely and with ease the borders of nation-states, but also can formulate her own informed critique of the provincialism of the center. Most of these women, however, have to cope with their own lives and dilemmas as well as with the lives of their family members and significant others, both in Brazil and in the United States. For them, the spaces of betweenness are more difficult to inhabit, and the symbolic and material borders of nation-states not much easier to cross.

Notes

Introduction

1. "Go-go dancer" is the preferred expression among Brazilians to refer to what is commonly labeled an "erotic dancer" in U.S. popular culture and academic literature. I use the terms interchangeably throughout the book.
2. I choose the word "migrant" instead of "immigrant" to emphasize the transnational condition characteristic of most people who today cross the borders of nation-states. Although not all of them can afford to travel back and forth to their home countries, they define themselves as belonging to two or more different locales and do not fit the image of immigrants who have cut their ties with their home country. I use the word "immigrants" only in association with immigration laws or to convey mainstream representations of those who cross borders. For an extensive list of studies on Brazilian emigration, see the bibliography organized by Maxine Margolis, at *www.brasa.org/news.html*.
3. Both prostitution and erotic dancing, in addition to a variety of activities such as phone sex, escorts, massages, sex shops, and peep shows, can be considered modalities of sex work. However, it is important to note that each of these varieties of sex work represents different services offered, different negotiations between workers and clients, and different social meanings, and each is governed by different kinds of social and state control.
4. For a discussion of the complex roles and identities of "native" anthropologists, see Narayan 1993.
5. For a discussion on alternative models of modernities, see Knauft 2002 and Rofel 1999.
6. For a discussion of sexuality and agency, see Wardlow 2006 on Huli women in New Guinea and the effects of modernity. See also Alexander 2005 on erotic autonomy and the politics of decolonization in the Bahamas.
7. As Constable (2006) argues, although there is a tendency in academic and activist literature to blur the experiences of domestic workers, brides, and sex workers, it is necessary to look at the differences among these categories of gendered migration.
8. Influential organizations such as NOW (National Organization for

Women) and CATW (Coalition against the Trafficking in Women) emphasize the dangers and perils of sex work and associate these perils particularly with women immigrants. A number of liberal organizations such as COYOTE (Call Off Your Old Tired Ethics) or Sex Workers Alliance are examples of attempts to demarginalize sex work.

Chapter 1

1. The epigraph quotation is from Jacques Derrida, *The Postcard* (Chicago: University of Chicago Press, 1987), 23.

2. Throughout this book I use the concept of a Global South to convey a political-economic rather than a purely geographic divide between more developed countries and those considered underdeveloped countries or emerging economies, as in the case of Brazil. Likewise, I use the concepts First World and Third World interchangeably with concepts such as centers of economic and political power and peripheral locations. While I recognize such distinctions beyond a clear-cut definition, I want to emphasize the inequalities that exist between nation-states that have experienced different processes of colonization, and that have occupied specific geopolitical locations within neo- and postcolonial contexts.

3. In a suggestive book entitled *Seductive Imperialism* (2000), Brazilian historian Tota demonstrates the role of state-financed cultural propaganda behind the U.S. government's expansionist efforts since World War II.

4. In his study of the Brazilian educational system, David Plank (1996) shows how the promise that education would put Brazil among the world's "developed countries" was disrupted with the deinvestment in public higher education, one of the measures used to cut state expenditures. Plank points out that the promise of development through education was one of the main cornerstones in the construction of a utopian view of Brazil as a modern country, present in nationalist discourses since Getúlio Vargas's years (1930–1945). As in other social spheres, however, the education system revealed the ambivalence toward democratic projects of a country fractured by social inequality. In Brazil, primary and secondary public education is at state and city levels, and usually of a low standard. Middle-class children typically go to private high schools, which better prepare them to take the entrance exams for universities, the *vestibular*. In the 1980s there were two main university systems in the country: federal universities, subsidized by the federal government and with free tuition for students, and private Catholic universities. Children from the working class would typically go to public primary and secondary schools that would channel them into technical schools and more recently into private colleges with lower standards. Only recently, with the governance of the Workers' Party (PT) presidents Lula and Dilma Rousseff, has the public university system begun

to expand again and more people, particularly blacks from the working class, a number of them through affirmative action programs, started to have access to it. See Guimarães 2003 for discussion about racial and social inequality and affirmative action in public universities.

5. They wanted to take part in what had been promised to them: an exciting and financially viable life. However, as De Kooning (2005) found for middle-class graduates in Cairo, they were unable to move away from their parents' homes and to realize the independent life that they so much desired.

6. Sara had maids and a wealthy extended family to help with her child and the household; she cites her ex-husband's "weak personality" as the motive for her divorce. His "weak personality" surely has to do with his inferior social position, as we can infer from the fact that Sara was probably one of the most wealthy and desirable women in her town.

7. See Caldeira (2000) for a thoroughly study of the effect of fear and violence on Brazilian cities.

8. "A Novidade," by Gilberto Gil, Bi Ribeiro, Herbert Vianna, and João Barone, 1986.

9. Despite the proliferation of musical styles in Brazil, particularly in the 1990s (see Dunn and Perrone 2002), I concentrate on Brazilian rock, a style that expresses more fully the ambiguities and dilemmas of the middle-class youth growing up in the 1980s.

10. The asphalt represents a space occupied by the middle class in places like Rio de Janeiro and Salvador, as opposed to the *morros* or hills occupied by shantytowns (see Norvell 2001).

11. "Brasil," by Cazuza, George Israel, and Nilo Romero, 1988. See Hamburger 1999 on Brazilian soap operas as a political arena.

Chapter 2

1. Following Foucault, Stoler (1995) points out that, situated within a colonial and imperial context, discourses on sexuality do more than define distinctions of a European bourgeoisie. They map the moral parameters of European nations and identify marginal members of the body politic by defining property rights and citizenship in the colonies as well. Stoler looks at discourses on sexuality in terms of their linkage to nationalist projects and the wider politics of exclusion, which are based on ideas about cultural competences and sexual proclivities, and produce racial distinctions. According to Stoler, the idea of racial degeneration itself constituted the theoretical and legislative edifice of colonial regimes and secured the relationship between racism and sexuality (31). To her, both race and sexuality are ordering mechanisms, formative features of modernity, deeply embedded in bourgeois liberalism and its images of racial purity and sexual virtue. Citizenship itself is defined by the bourgeois discourse, peopled with

surreptitious invaders in the body politic. Sexual prescriptions function to delineate first-class citizens, meaning white Europeans, and to exclude those who do not fit the racial ideal of a nation.

2. Women could vote in Brazil beginning in 1932.

3. The first Brazilian beauty pageant took place in 1921, just one year after the first U.S. national beauty pageant in Atlantic City.

4. In her work on race and gender in Brazil, Simpson (1995) examines how this ambivalence is embedded in Xuxa, a blond model from southern Brazil who became a TV megastar in the 1980s. Central to Xuxa's success, according to Simpson, was the appeal of her whiteness as a signifier of modernity. In the most famous children's show in the country ever, Xuxa's performances promoted a consumerist lifestyle in tune with First World values and goods. Despite the fact that her "helpers" in the show were all blonds like her, and the music as well as the general scenario of her show was more in tune with the United States than with Brazil, Xuxa came to represent the Brazilian nation. To Simpson, Xuxa achieved that status not just through cinematic devices, such as arriving at the show each day in a spaceship that viewed images of the country from above. Rather, according to Simpson, Xuxa came to embody the nation by playing out Brazilian racial anxieties through her relationship with a worldwide celebrity—Brazilian soccer player Pelé. Representing the extremes of whiteness and blackness in Brazil, the couple Pelé/Xuxa, Simpson argues, corroborated the ideology of "racial democracy" in Brazil, while giving Xuxa license to promote whiteness as the hegemonic ideal in her show.

5. According to Hasenbalg and Silva (1990), studies of race in Brazil have moved from an emphasis on racial classification to a concern with the mechanisms through which racism and discrimination are perpetuated in daily life. Recent scholarship on race in Brazil, however, focusing on the perspective of the working class, particularly those of domestic servants, seems to lack a more nuanced understanding of racial identity within the Brazilian middle class, which at times scholars refer to interchangeably as the "elite." Twine (1998), for example, an anthropologist, adopts her own North American racial classificatory system and throughout her book defines the middle-class/elite population of Vassália, the locus of her research, as Euro-Brazilian. Besides the fact that this term is rarely, if ever, used in Brazil, the definition assumes an unproblematic Brazilian middle-class racial identity that ignores native understandings. Likewise, Sheriff (2001) points out that "*moreno*" is the most common term for nonwhites in Brazil; I would say that "*moreno*" is also the most common term for nonblacks there.

6. Sheriff (2001) also found this aversion to talking about race common among middle-class Brazilians of lighter color in her research.

7. Norvell (2001) found references to actual *mulatas* rare, revealing a fear of conveying a sexual message, since prostitutes and transvestites in Copacabana are self-fashioned as *mulatas*. According to Norvell: "Since

skin tone is continuous and Brazilians seem not to like discrete categories, *moreno* is perfect in this regard" (195). As the author reveals, in Brazilian society the origin of the *moreno's* brownness does not have to be defined as coming from exposure to the sun in the leisure hours or from racial mixing, increasing the ambiguity and flexibility of the category.

8. In contrast to the *mulata's* samba, a better way of picturing a *morena's* style might be the world-famous bossa nova song "The Girl from Ipanema," which describes a suntanned woman who strolls on the beach promenade of a middle-class neighborhood to a white man's contained admiration. The intersection between race, music, and class is also analyzed in relation to other music styles that have appeared in the past decades. See Dunn and Perrone 2002; and see Sovik 2009 regarding the role of pop star Daniela Mercury and "axé music" in the creation of newer hegemonic ideologies of mixing.

Chapter 3

1. See Smith 1996 for a thorough examination of New York City's gentrification process and Papayanis 2000 for an analysis of how gentrification has affected the city's sex industry.

2. In accord with Zoning Amendment 12-10, adult establishments are so classified when they "regularly feature" or devote a "substantial portion" of their business to displays that contain either live performances characterized by an emphasis on "specific anatomical areas" or "specified sexual activities," or employees who, as part of their employment, regularly expose to patrons "specific anatomical areas" in a venue not customarily open to the general public during such features because it excludes minors.

3. See Delany 1999 and Friedman 1986 for descriptions of the Times Square sex scene in the 1980s, just before the gentrification of that area began.

4. In 1990, Brooklyn and Queens accounted for 60 percent of the population of New York City and housed two-thirds of migrants. By the 2000 U.S. Census, Queens, where most Brazilian erotic dancers live and work, had experienced the largest absolute population increase, 277,781 people, a growth rate of 14.2 percent. White non-Hispanics made up 32 percent of the borough's population, while Hispanics accounted for 25 percent, black non-Hispanics 19 percent, and Asian non-Hispanics 17.5 percent. For an excellent analysis of neighborhood politics in Queens, see Sanjek 1998.

5. Although there are agencies that mediate the relationship between dancer and bar, all the women I interviewed had a friend who made the arrangement for them. Most erotic dancers in both Manhattan and Queens bars are considered independent contractors, and as such they are not required by most employers to have work permits or legal status in the United States.

6. Despite the fact that this is not the way dancers make most of their money,

on a slow night, this small amount guarantees that the dancer can at least cover her transportation and food expenses. Since the beginning of the night is usually quite slow, dancers can choose to arrive late and forgo the payment.

7. When uncompliant clients tip dancers, they may throw the money on the floor so the dancers have to pick it up, a situation that is considered humiliating. Such actions may be isolated minor incidents or may turn more serious, as when a client gets upset and tries to get back at the dancer by throwing a drink at her, or even physically attacking her.

8. Besides serving the new Manhattan affluent classes, the migrants in these neighborhoods create a type of subeconomy. According to Sassen, local services, goods, and activities offered at lower prices than in the larger economy developed to meet community demand, leading to a "re-circulation of wages" that in turn stabilizes low-income areas (Sassen 1988, 296).

9. See Lewis 2000 for discussion of the legal implications of lap dancing and its ambivalent moral positioning between the definitions of stripping and prostitution in the case of Canadian laws.

10. See Gilman 1985 for a discussion of race markers on the body, particularly buttocks, and its associations with the Black Venus's buttocks.

11. Some upscale bars specialize in black bodies or dedicate one night a week to bodies of a particular race or country.

Chapter 4

1. It is likely that women from these different places also form their own cliques based on nationality, or even on specific regions within their country of origin. Here, however, I am concerned with unraveling how processes of identification and differentiation happen from the perspective of Brazilian dancers.

2. In the Brazilian soap opera *América* (2003), which depicted Brazilian immigrants in the United States and was broadcast by TV Globo simultaneously in Brazil and on U.S. Brazilian cable TV, a Brazilian dancer is presented as a bartender who at times dances on the bar counter.

3. *Vedete*, from the French *vedette*, refers to a movie or TV star; it became mostly used in Brazil to describe women dancers who appeared on the TV show hosted by Chacrinha, *Cassino do Chacrinha*, very popular in the 1980s. Teresa associates it here with Sargentelli "*mulatas*," although the social and racial contexts of the two shows were different.

4. See also Giacomini (2006) for more on *mulatas* as a professional category.

5. See Norvell 2001 and Farias 2002 for analyses of how beach areas in Brazil are well demarcated by class, race, gender, and sexuality.

6. A municipal law requires that during the performance clients are not allowed to touch dancers by any means and that dancers' touch is restricted

to some body parts. For example, while performing a lap dance, dancers should only touch clients either on their shoulder or on legs in order to balance themselves. However, the work of the dancers while on the floor talking to clients is not officially considered part of their performance and thus is subject not to regulation but to the personal negotiations between a dancer and a client.

Chapter 5

1. Recent works on masculinity (Cornell 2005; Whitehead and Barrett 2001) have replaced an emphasis on a duality between men and women with an emphasis on a multiplicity of masculinities hierarchically organized on material and symbolic structures.
2. Customers may go to the same bar for days, months, or years in a row, and then one day they may stop going—they may start to frequent another bar, or they may stop going to bars altogether.
3. See Frank (2002) for an examination of men's visits to the club scene as a tourist practice.
4. I have heard comments from customers that Brazilian dancers are different because "they enjoy dancing." Brazilian dancers, much like sex workers in tourist destinations in poorer countries, are believed to be able to blur the lines between professionalism and fun, as opposed to dancers of other nationalities who are believed to be either too aggressive or too cold.
5. As Savigliano put it so well: "Exotic places, persons, and things often display the amicable side of the other: plants, perfumes, clothing, jewelry, foods and spices, art, courtship, songs, and dances. The threatening side, equally exoticized, remains in the background, a haunting violence: dictators, volcanoes, diseases, polygamy, poverty. The femaleness of the exotic is identified precisely in this ambivalence" (Savigliano 1995, 81).
6. For example, when interviewing dancers, managers usually say that going out with clients is frowned upon. Many times I heard my dancer friends say that a relationship with a "man from bars" should be kept within the limits of the bar. However, other times I have been invited by the same women to go out with them and a client for dinner.
7. Despite the laws forbidding smoking in bars in New York, smoking is allowed in Greek bars and clubs after a certain hour of the night, and this practice seems to heighten the atmosphere of transgression.
8. Because she has a son in Brazil, Sheila divides her time between New York and Rio de Janeiro. Since she never let her entrance visa for the United States expire, she has not yet had problems with reentering the country. Sheila seems to manage this transnational arrangement by staying with a boyfriend while in New York and at her family's house in Brazil, thus not having to pay rent in either country.

9. See Frankenberg 1997 for an analysis of the construction of whiteness and its association with class formation in the United States.

10. Money showers are a potlatch-like practice in which a client changes a fifty- or hundred-dollar bill for singles and either he or the bartender at his request "showers" a dancer with them. Money showers are quite common in Queens bars, particularly among the Greek and Albanian clientele.

11. This view was corroborated when some of the Albanian patrons of Blue Diamond were arrested on charges of killing members of a rival Italian Mafia.

12. Although I have heard of physical violence against dancers, I choose not to focus on it in this book in order to dispel what I believe to be an exaggerated perception of the risks that dancing entails. None of the women I encountered ever suffered physical violence from their clients, although they have experienced verbal abuse such as described here.

Chapter 6

1. U.S. women are likely to invest in their education or other social projects in this country (see Frank 2002), while most Brazilian women prefer to invest the bulk of their income in Brazil. Out of the nine women in my project, only Nana and Justine made concentrated efforts to invest in their education in the United States and they were the only ones who, not coincidentally, met their partners outside the bar scene.

2. A few women in Clara's family are married to African American men from a single family in New Jersey. Paid marriages cost about $10,000 and a number of dancers engage in this practice.

3. Clara's family is Catholic, but in Brazil, Catholicism can be mixed with beliefs from other traditions without major contradictions. She believes in the Catholic God and saints, but she also believes in the Karma of Kardecism, a religious tradition based on the thinking of the French philosopher Allan Kardec. She also frequents a psychic card reader who mixes Kardecism and the African Brazilian religious tradition of Candomblé.

4. This seemed to be a very positive view of Sérgio's acceptance of the situation; from my observations of other Brazilian couples in the United States, I have seen Brazilian men react in a quite opposite way to similar situations. Usually Brazilian men resent Brazilian women for "selling themselves out" to American men and the lifestyle they can offer.

Chapter 7

1. Although the women do not tell most of their family and friends in Brazil what they do for work in New York, the comments, or rather the silences, I

have heard in my trips to Brazil indicate that people are intrigued about the lives that women have overseas, particularly if they do not marry.

2. This is an area described in the well-known novel by Brazilian author Jorge Amado, *Gabriela, cravo e canela* (1959), adapted for the screen in 1983 by film director Bruno Barreto, with Sonia Braga as the protagonist.

3. To Nadja, in order to be in a relationship with a man, she has to feel something: "it is a skin thing," she said to me once while we were window-shopping in Soho. "Like there is this guy, an older Italian man, he gives me tons of money, but the thing is that I don't really like him—*é uma coisa de pele*—it is a skin thing, doesn't happen even if I try." Nadja makes a strict distinction between business and love relationships. She accepts gifts or money for company, inside and outside the bar, but she keeps her distance and does not transform these encounters into personal relationships.

4. Living in Manhattan, rather than in Astoria, Queens, is associated with a more middle-class status, and there is a concentration of Brazilians who live in this area of the city.

5. Besides exporting Brazilian models to the world's catwalks (a phenomenon epitomized by Brazil's most famous supermodel, Gisele Bundchen), Brazil also exports designs and textiles, and a style of dressing and body that appeals to internationally inclined consumers. Brazilian's famous flip-flops, Havaianas, and bikinis can be found in most casual fashion stores in New York and in Paris airports; Brazilian green and yellow colors are perhaps among the most popular in the fad for foreign flag T-shirts that has taken over world cities since the turn of the twenty-first century. Brazil has a definite appeal not only in the international sex scene but also in the fashion arena, and Nadja wants to be part of it too.

6. His paternal grandparents, supporters of the Nazi expansion in Europe, flew to Brazil after World War II, and his parents pursued their graduate studies in the United States during the Brazilian dictatorship.

Chapter 8

1. Help was closed down in the beginning of 2010 in the middle of much public uproar and debate about the role and morals of the sex industry. In the process of gentrification of parts of Copacabana, it will be replaced with a new Museum of Image and Sound.

2. For more information, see the website *www.sgi.org*.

Conclusion

1. See IPEA (Instituto de Pesquisa Econômica Aplicada, *www.ipea.gov.br/portal*) for an analysis of the new class configuration of Brazilian society.

Bibliography

Abu-Lughod, Lila. 1993. *Writing Women's Worlds: Bedouin Stories*. Berkeley: University of California Press.

Alexander, Jacqui. 2005. *Pedagogies of Crossing: Meditations on Feminism, Sexual Politics, Memory, and the Sacred*. Durham, NC: Duke University Press.

Alexandre, Ricardo. 2002. *Dias de luta: O rock e o Brasil dos anos 80* [Days of struggle: Rock 'n' roll in Brazil in the 1980s]. São Paulo: Editora DBA.

Allison, Anne. 1994. *Nightwork: Sexuality, Pleasure, and Corporate Masculinity in a Tokyo Hostess Club*. Chicago: University of Chicago Press.

Altman, Dennis. 2001. *Global Sex*. Chicago: University of Chicago Press.

Alvarez, Sonia. 1990. *Engendering Democracy in Brazil: Women's Movements in Transition Politics*. Princeton, NJ: Princeton University Press.

Appadurai, Arjun. 1990. "Disjuncture and Difference in the Global Political Economy." *Public Culture* 2(2): 1–24.

———. 1991. "Global Ethnoscapes: Notes and Queries for a Transnational Anthropology." In *Recapturing Anthropology*, ed. Richard Fox, 191–209. Santa Fe: New School of American Research Press.

Assis, Gláucia. 1999. "Estar aqui, estar lá: Uma cartografia da imigração Valadarense para os EUA" [To be here, to be there: A cartography of immigration from Governador Valadares to the U.S.]. In *Cenas de um Brasil migrante* [Scenes of a migrant Brazil], ed. Rosana Reis and Teresa Sales, 125–66. São Paulo: Boitempo Editorial.

Augustin, Laura. 2003. "A Migrant World of Services." *Social Politics: International Studies in Gender, State, and Society* 10(3): 377–96.

———. 2005. "Migrants in the Mistress's House: Other Voices in the Trafficking Debate." *Social Politics, International Studies in Gender, State, and Society* 12(1): 96–117.

Balibar, Etienne, and Emmanuel Wallerstein. 1991. *Race, Nation, Class: Ambiguous Identities*. New York: Verso.

Barton, Bernadette. 2006. *Stripped: Inside the Lives of Exotic Dancers*. New York: New York University Press.

Basch, Linda, Nina Glick-Schiller, and Christina Szanton Blanc. 1994. *Nations Unbound: Transnational Projects, Postcolonial Predicaments, and Deterritorialized Nation-States*. Langhorne, PA: Gordon and Breach.

Bell, David, and Gill Valentine. 1995. *Mapping Desire: Geographies of Sexualities.* London: Routledge.

Berger, Joseph, and Fernanda Santos. 2005. "Trading Status for a Raise." *New York Times,* December 26. proquest.umi.com/pqdweb?did=1173787492&sid=2&Fmt=10&clientId=78910&RQT=309&VName=HNP.

Bernstein, Elizabeth. 2001. "The Meaning of the Purchase: Desire, Demand, and the Commerce of Sex." *Ethnography* 2(3): 389–420.

Bernstein, Elizabeth, and Laurie Shaffner, eds. 2005. *Regulating Sex: The Politics of Intimacy and Identity.* London: Routledge.

Beserra, Bernadete. 2003. *Brazilian Immigrants in the US: Cultural Imperialism and Social Class.* New York: LFB Scholarly Publishing.

Besse, Susan. 1996. *Restructuring Patriarchy: The Modernization of Gender Inequality in Brazil, 1914–1940.* Chapel Hill: University of North Carolina Press.

———. 2005. "Defining a National Type: Brazilian Beauty Contests in the 1920s." *Estudios Interdisciplinarios de America Latina y el Caribe* 16(1).

Bhabha, Homi. 1994. *The Location of Culture.* London: Routledge.

Bourdieu, Pierre. 1984. *Distinction: A Social Critique of the Judgment of Taste.* Cambridge, MA: Harvard University Press.

Braidotti, Rosa. 1994. *Nomadic Subjects: Embodiment and Sexual Difference in Contemporary Feminist Theory.* New York: Columbia University Press.

Brennan, Denise. 2002. "Sex Tourism as a Stepping-Stone to International Migration." In *Global Woman: Nannies, Maids, and Sex Workers in the New Economy,* ed. Barbara Ehrenreich and Arlie R. Hochschild, 154–68. New York: Owl Books.

Buarque de Holanda, Sérgio. 1983. *Raízes do Brasil* [The roots of Brazil]. Rio de Janeiro: Livraria Olympio. Originally published 1936.

Burana, Lily. 2001. *Strip City.* New York: Talk Miramax.

Burawoy, Michael. 2000. *Global Ethnography: Forces, Connections, and Imaginations in a Postmodern World.* Berkeley: University of California Press.

Burdick, John. 1998. *Blessed Anastacia: Women, Race, and Popular Christianity in Brazil.* London: Routledge.

Butler, Judith. 1997. "Performative Acts and Gender Constitution: An Essay in Phenomenology and Feminist Theory." In *Writing on the Body,* ed. Katie Conboy, Nadia Medina, and Sarah Stanbury, 401–18. New York: Columbia University Press.

Cabezas, A. 1999. "Women's Work Is Never Done: Sex Tourism in Sosua, Dominican Republic." In *Sun, Sex, and Gold: Tourism and Sex Work in the Caribbean,* ed. Kamala Kempadoo, 93–123. New York: Rowman and Littlefield.

Caldeira, Teresa Pires. 2000. *City of Walls: Crime, Segregation, and Citizenship in São Paulo.* Berkeley: University of California Press.

Caruth, Cathy. 1995. *Trauma: Explorations in Memory.* Baltimore: Johns Hopkins University Press.

Carvalho, Inaiá M., and Gilberto C. Pereira (orgs.). 2006. *Como anda Salvador* [How Salvador is doing]. Salvador: EDUFBA.

CHAME (Centro Humanitário de Apoio a Mulher). 2000. *Migração feminina internacional: Causas e conseqüências* [Women's international migration: Causes and consequences]. Salvador, Brazil: CHAME.

Chapkis, Wendy. 1997. *Live Sex Acts: Women Performing Erotic Labor.* New York: Routledge.

Chaterjee, Partha. 1993. *The Nation and Its Fragments: Colonial and Postcolonial Histories.* Princeton, NJ: Princeton University Press.

Clifford, James. 1988. *The Predicament of Culture.* Cambridge, MA: Harvard University Press.

Clifford, James, and George Marcus, eds. 1986. *Writing Culture: The Poetics and Politics of Ethnography.* Berkeley: University of California Press.

Collins, John. 2004. "'X Marks the Future of Brazil': Protestant Ethics and Bedeviling Mixtures in a Brazilian Cultural Heritage Center." In *Off Stage/On Display: Intimacy and Ethnography in the Age of Public Culture,* ed. Andrew Shryock. Stanford, CA: Stanford University Press.

Constable, Nicole. 2003. *Romance on a Global Stage: Pen Pals, Virtual Ethnography, and "Mail Order" Marriages.* Berkeley: University of California Press.

———, ed. 2005. *Cross-Border Marriages: Gender and Mobility in Transnational Asia.* Philadelphia: University of Pennsylvania Press.

———. 2006. "Brides, Maids, and Prostitutes: Reflections on the Study of 'Trafficked' Women." *Journal of Multidisciplinary International Studies* 3(2): 1–25.

Cornell, Raewyn. 2005. *Masculinities.* Berkeley: University of California Press.

Correa, Mariza. 1996. "Sobre a invenção da mulata" [About the invention of *mulata*]. *Cadernos Pagu* 6(7): 35–50.

Cowie, Elisabeth. 1993. "Pornography and Fantasy: Psychoanalytical Perspectives." In *Sex Exposed: Sexuality and the Pornography Debate,* ed. Lynne Segal and Mary McIntosh. New Brunswick, NJ: Rutgers University Press.

Crapanzano, Vincent. 1980. *Tuhami: Portrait of a Moroccan.* Chicago: University of Chicago Press.

———. 1986. *Waiting: The Whites in South Africa.* London: Paladin Grafton Books.

———. 2005. "A cena: Lançando sombra sobre o real" [The scene: Shadowing the real]. *MANA* 11(2): 357–83.

De Kooning, Anouk. 2005. "Global Dreams: Space, Class, and Gender in Middle Class Cairo." PhD diss., University of Amsterdam.

Delacoste, Frederique, and Priscilla Alexander, eds. 1987. *Sex Work: Writings by Women in the Sex Industry.* Pittsburgh: Cleis Press.

Delany, Samuel. 1999. *Times Square Red, Times Square Blue.* New York: New York University Press.

Derrida, Jacques. 1987. *The Postcard.* Chicago: University of Chicago Press.

Desmond, Jane. 1997. "Embodying Dance: Issues in Dance and Cultural Studies." In *Everynight Life: Culture and Dance in Latin/o America*, ed. Celeste Frazer Delgado and Jose E. Munoz, 33–64. Durham, NC: Duke University Press.

Dias Filho, Antonio J. 1999. "Fulôs, Ritas, Gabrielas, Gringólogas e garotas de programa" [Fulôs, Ritas, Gabrielas, experts on gringos, and sex workers]. Master's diss., Universidade Federal de Salvador.

Duggan, Lisa. 2006. "Introduction." In *Sex Wars: Sexual Dissent and Political Culture*, ed. Lisa Duggan and Nan Hunter, 1–14. New York: Routledge.

Dunn, Christopher. 2001. *Brutality Garden: Tropicália and the Emergence of a Brazilian Counterculture*. Chapel Hill: University of North Carolina Press.

Dunn, Christopher, and Charles Perrone, eds. 2002. *Brazilian Popular Music and Globalization*. New York: Routledge.

Enloe, Cynthia. 1983. *Bananas, Beaches, and Bases: Making Feminist Sense of International Politics*. Berkeley: University of California Press.

Escobar, Arturo, and Sonia Alvarez, eds. 1992. *The Making of Social Movements in Latin America*. Boulder, CO: Westview.

Fabian, Johannes. 1983. *Time and the Other: How Anthropology Makes Its Object*. New York: Columbia University Press.

Farias, Patrícia. 2002. "Corpo e classificação de cor numa praia Carioca" [Body and skin color classification on a Carioca beach]. In *Nu e vestido: Dez antropólogos revelam a cultura do corpo Carioca* [The naked and the dressed: Ten anthropologists reveal the culture of the Carioca's body], ed. Míriam Goldenberg, 263–302. Rio de Janeiro: Record.

Fernandes, Leela. 2000. "Restructuring the New Middle Class in Liberalizing India." *Comparative Studies of South Asia, Africa, and the Middle-East* 20(1): 88–104.

Fleischer, Soraya Resende. 2002. *Passando a América a Limpo: O trabalho de housecleaners brasileiras em Boston, Massachusetts* [Checking up on America: The work of Brazilian housecleaners in Boston, Massachusetts]. São Paulo: Anna Blume.

Foner, Nancy. 2000. *From Ellis Island to JFK: New York's Two Great Waves of Immigration*. New Haven, CT: Yale University Press.

Frank, Katherine. 2002. *G-String and Sympathy: Strip Club Regulars and Male Desire*. Durham, NC: Duke University.

Frankenberg, Ruth. 1997. "Local Whiteness, Localizing Whiteness." In *Displacing Whiteness*, ed. Ruth Frankenberg, 1–33. Durham, NC: Duke University Press.

Freeman, Carla. 2000. *High Tech in High Heels in the Global Economy: Women, Work, and Pink-Collar Identities in the Caribbean*. Durham, NC: Duke University Press.

Friedman, Josh Alan. 1986. *Tales of Times Square*. New York: Delacorte Press.

Freyre, Gilberto. 1963. *Casa grande e senzala* [The masters and the slaves]. Brasília: Editora Universidade de Brasília.

Giacomini, Sônia. 2006. "Mulatas profissionais: Raça, gênero e ocupação"

[Professional *mulatas*: race, gender, and labor]. *Estudos Feministas* 14(1): 85–101.

Giddens, Anthony. 1992. *The Transformation of Intimacy: Sexuality, Love, and Eroticism in Modern Societies*. Stanford, CA: Stanford University Press.

Gilman, Sander. 1985. "Black Bodies, White Bodies: Towards an Iconography of Female Sexuality in Late Nineteenth-Century Art, Medicine, and Literature." *Critical Inquiry* 12(1): 204–42.

Guano, Emanuela. 2002. "Spectacle of Modernity: Transnational Imagination and Local Hegemonies in Neo-Liberal Buenos Aires." *Cultural Anthropology* 17(2): 181–209.

Guerreiro, Goli. 1994. *Retratos de uma tribo urbana: Rock brasileiro* [Portraits of an urban tribe: Brazilian rock]. Salvador: EDUFBA.

Guimarães, Antonio S. 2002. *Classes, raças e democracia* [Classes, races, and democracy]. São Paulo: Editora 34.

———. 2003. "Acesso de negros às universidades públicas" [Access of blacks to public universities]. *Cadernos de Pesquisa* 118: 247–68.

Gupta, Akhil. 1992. "The Song of the Nonaligned World: Transnational Identities and the Reinscription of Space in Late Capitalism." *Cultural Anthropology* 7(1): 63–79.

Hamburger, Esther. 1999. "Politics and Intimacy in Brazilian Telenovelas." PhD diss., University of Chicago.

Hanchard, Michael, ed. 1999. *Racial Politics in Contemporary Brazil*. Durham, NC: Duke University Press.

Hasenbalg, Carlos, and Nelson do Valle Silva, eds. 1990. *Relações raciais no Brasil* [Racial relationships in Brazil]. Rio de Janeiro: Rio Fundo Editora.

Hochschild, Arlie Russell. 1983. *The Managed Heart: Commercialization of Human Feeling*. Berkeley: University of California Press.

———. 2000. "Global Care Chains and Emotional Surplus Value." In *On the Edge: Living with Global Capitalism*, ed. W. Hutton and A. Giddens, 130–46. London: Jonathan Cape.

Hofbauer, Andreas. 2006. *Uma história de branqueamento ou o negro em questão* [A history of whitening or blacks under scrutiny]. São Paulo: FAPESP, Ed. UNESP.

IPEA. Instituto de Pesquisa Econômica Aplicada [Institute for Applied Economic Research]. *www.ipea.gov.br/portal/*.

Johnson, Dale L., ed. 1985. *Middle Classes in Dependent Countries*. Beverly Hills, CA: Sage Publications.

Jolly, Margaret, and Lenore Manderson, eds. 1997. *Sites of Desire, Economies of Pleasure*. Chicago: University of Chicago Press.

Kelsky, Karen. 2001. *Women on the Verge: Japanese Women, Western Dreams*. Durham, NC: Duke University Press.

Kempadoo, Kamala. 1998. "Introduction: Globalizing Sex Workers Rights." In *Global Sex Workers*, ed. Kamala Kempadoo and Jo Doezema, 1–27. London: Routledge.

———. 1999. "Continuities and Change: Five Centuries of Prostitution in the

Caribbean." In *Sun, Sex, and Gold: Tourism and Sex Work in the Caribbean*, ed. Kamala Kempadoo, 3–35. New York: Rowman and Littlefield.

Knauft, Bruce. 2002. "Introduction." In *Critically Modern: Alternatives, Alterities, Anthropologies*, ed. Bruce Knauft, 1–55. Bloomington: Indiana University Press.

Landes, Ruth. 1947. *The City of Women*. New York: Macmillan.

Lesser, Jeffrey. 1999. *Negotiating National Identity: Immigrants, Minorities, and the Struggle for Ethnicity in Brazil*. Durham, NC: Duke University Press.

Lewin, Tamar. 2005. "Up from the Holler: Living in Two Worlds, at Home in Neither." In *Class Matters*, by correspondents of the *New York Times*. New York: Times Books.

Lewis, Jacqueline. 2000 "Controlling Lap Dance: Law, Morality, and Sex Work." In *Sex for Sale*, ed. Ronald Weitzer, 203–15. New York: Routledge.

Liepe-Levinson, Katherine. 2002. *Strip Show: Performances of Gender and Desire*. New York: Routledge.

MacKinnon, Catherine. 1987. *Feminism Unmodified: Discourse on Life and Law*. Cambridge, MA: Harvard University Press.

Mahler, Sarah. 1995. *American Dreaming: Immigrant Life on the Margins*. Princeton, NJ: Princeton University Press.

Maia, Suzana M. 2009a. "Intersections of the Transnational: Brazilian Erotic Dancers in New York City's Gentlemen's Bars." *Vibrant* 6(1): 37–64.

———. 2009b. "Sedução e identidade nacional" [Performing seduction and national identity]. *Estudos Feministas* 17(3): 769–97.

———. 2010. "Brazilian Women Crossing Borders." In *Gendering Border Studies*, ed. Jane Aaron, Henrice Altnick, and Chris Weedon, 63–82. Cardiff: University of Wales Press.

———. Forthcoming. "Performing Desire and National Identity: Brazilian Erotic Dancers in New York." In *Translocalites/Translocalidades: Feminist Politics of Translation in the Latin/a Américas*, ed. Sonia Alvarez, Claudia de Lima Costa, Verónica Feliu, Rebecca Hester, Norma Klahn, and Millie Thayer, with the assistance of Cruz C. Bueno. Durham, NC: Duke University Press.

Margolis, Maxine. 1994. *Little Brazil: An Ethnography of Brazilian Immigrants in New York City*. Princeton, NJ: Princeton University Press.

———. N.d. Bibliography of Brazilian Emigration. *www.brasa.org/news.html*.

Marmo, Herica, and Luiz Andre Alzer. 2002. *A vida até parece uma festa: Toda a história dos Titãs* [Life even looks like a party: The complete history of Titãs]. Rio de Janeiro: Record.

Martes, Ana Cristina B. 1999. *Brasileiros nos Estados Unidos: Um estudo sobre imigrantes em Massachusetts* [Brazilians in the United States: A study of immigrants in Massachusetts]. São Paulo: Paz e Terra.

Marx, Anthony. 1998. *Making Race and Nation: A Comparison of South Africa, the United States, and Brazil*. New York: Cambridge University Press.

Massey, Doreen. 1994. *Space, Place, and Gender*. Minneapolis: University of Minnesota Press.

McCallum, Cecilia. 2005. "Racialized Bodies, Naturalized Classes: Moving through the City of Salvador da Bahia." *American Ethnologist* 32(1): 100–117.

McClintock, Anne. 1995. *Imperial Leather: Race, Gender, and Sexuality in the Colonial Conquest.* New York: Routledge.

Mosse, George. 1985. *Nationalism and Sexuality: Respectability and Abnormal Sexuality in Modern Europe.* New York: Howard Fertig.

Nagel, Joane. 2003. *Race, Ethnicity, and Sexuality: Intimate Interactions, Forbidden Frontiers.* Oxford: Oxford University Press.

Narayan, Kirin. 1993, "How Native Is a 'Native' Anthropologist?" *American Anthropologist* 95(3): 671–86.

New York Planning Federation. 2008. "Everything You Ever Wanted to Know about Adult Entertainment Regulations." *www.nypf.org/adult_ entertainment.htm.*

Norvell, John Michael. 2001. "Race Mixture and the Meaning of Brazil: Race, Class, and Nation in the Zona Sul of Rio de Janeiro." PhD diss., Cornell University.

O'Dougherty, Maureen. 2002. *Consumption Intensified: The Politics of Middle-Class Daily Life in Brazil.* Durham, NC: Duke University Press.

Ong, Aihwa. 1996. "Cultural Citizenship as Subject-Making: Immigrants Negotiate Racial and Cultural Boundaries in the United States." *Current Anthropology* 37(5): 737–62.

———. 1999. *Flexible Citizenship: The Cultural Logics of Transnationality.* Durham, NC: Duke University Press.

Owensby, Brina P. 1999. *Intimate Ironies: Modernity and the Making of Middle-Class Lives in Brazil.* Stanford, CA: Stanford University Press.

Pamuk, Orhan. 2005. *Istanbul: Memories and the City.* New York: Knopf.

Papayanis, Marilyn Adler. 2000. "Sex and the Revanchist City: Zoning Out Pornography in New York." *Environment and Planning: Society and Space* 18(3): 341–54.

Parker, Richard. 1991. *Bodies, Pleasures, and Passions: Sexual Culture in Contemporary Brazil.* Boston: Beacon Press.

Parreñas, Rhacel. 2001. *Servants of Globalization: Women, Migration, and Domestic Work.* Stanford, CA: Stanford University Press.

Perrone, C., and C. Dunn, eds. 2001. *Brazilian Popular Music and Globalization.* Gainesville: University Press of Florida.

Pheterson, Gail, ed. 1989. *A Vindication of the Rights of Whores.* Seattle: Seal Press.

Pinho, Osmundo de Araujo. 2004. "O efeito do sexo: Políticas de raça, gênero e miscigenação" [The effect of sex: Race, gender, and miscegenation politics]. *Cadernos Pagu* 23:89–119.

Pinho, Patricia de Santana. 2009. "White but Not Quite: Tones and Overtones of Whiteness in Brazil." *Small Axe* 13(2): 39–56.

Piscitelli, Adriana. 2004. "Entre a Praia de Iracema e a União Europeia: Turismo sexual internacional e migração feminina" [Between Iracema Beach and the European Union: International sex tourism and women's migration]. In *Sexualidades e saberes, convenções e fronteiras* [Sexualities and knowledges, conventions and frontiers], ed. Adriana Piscitelli, Maria F. Gregory, and Sérgio Carrara, 283–318. Rio de Janeiro: Garamond.

———. 2007. "Shifting Boundaries: Sex and Money in the North-East of Brazil." *Sexualities* 10:489–500.

Plank, David N. 1996. *The Means of Our Salvation: Public Education in Brazil, 1930–1995.* Boulder, CO: Westview Press.

Povinelli, E., and G. Chauncey. 1999. "Thinking Sexuality Transnationally." *GLQ* 5(4): 439–50.

Price-Glynn, Kim. 2010. *Strip Club: Gender, Power, and Sex Work.* New York: New York University Press.

Rofel, Lisa. 1999. *Other Modernities: Gendered Yearnings in China after Socialism.* Berkeley: University of California Press.

Rohter, Larry. 2005. "Brazilians Streaming into U.S. through Mexican Borders." *New York Times,* June 30.

Sacks, Karen Brodkin. 1994. "How Did Jews Become White Folks?" In *Race,* ed. Steven Gregory and Roger Sanjek, 78–102. New Brunswick, NJ: Rutgers University Press.

Sales, Teresa. 2003. *Brazilians away from Home.* New York: Center for Migration Studies.

Sanjek, Roger. 1998. *The Future of Us All: Race and Neighborhood Politics in New York City.* Ithaca, NY: Cornell University Press.

Santos, Augusto Salles. 2002. "Historical Roots of the Whitening of Brazil." *Latin American Perspectives* 29(1): 61–82.

Sassen, Saskia. 1988. *The Mobility of Labor and Capital.* Cambridge: Cambridge University Press.

———. 2001. *Global Cities: New York, London, and Tokyo.* Princeton, NJ: Princeton University Press.

Savigliano, Marta. 1995. *Tango and the Political Economy of Passion.* Boulder, CO: Westview Press.

Schechner, Richard. 2002. *Performance Studies: An Introduction.* New York: Routledge.

Schwarcz, Lilia Moritz. 1999. *The Spectacle of the Races: Scientists, Institutions, and the Race Question in Brazil, 1870–1930.* New York: Hill and Wang.

Sheriff, Robin E. 2001. *Dreaming Equality: Color, Race, and Racism in Urban Brazil.* New Brunswick, NJ: Rutgers University Press.

Simpson, Amelia. 1993. *Xuxa: The Mega-Marketing of Gender, Race, and Modernity.* Philadelphia: Temple University Press.

Skidmore, Thomas. 1990. "Racial Ideas and Social Policy in Brazil, 1870–1940." In *The Idea of Race in Latin America, 1870–1940,* ed. Richard Graham, 7–35. Austin: University of Texas Press.

———. 1993. *Black into White: Race and Nationality in Brazilian Thought.* Durham, NC: Duke University Press.

Smith, Neil. 1996. *The New Urban Frontier: Gentrification and the Revanchist City.* London: Routledge.

Sommer, Doris. 1990. "Irresistible Romance: The Foundational Fictions of Latin America." In *Nation and Narration*, ed. Homi Bhabha, 71–98. New York: Routledge.

Sovik, Liv. 2009. *Aqui ninguém é branco* [Here nobody is white]. Rio de Janeiro: Ed. Aeroplano.

Spivak, Gayatri. 1988. "Can the Subaltern Speak?" In *Marxism and the Interpretation of Culture*, ed. Cary Nelson and Lawrence Grossberg, 272–313. New York: Macmillan.

Stam, Robert. 1997. *Tropical Multiculturalism: A Comparative History of Race in Brazilian Cinema and Culture.* Durham, NC: Duke University Press.

Stoler, Ann Laura. 1995. *Race and the Education of Desire: Foucault's History of Sexuality and the Colonial Order of Things.* Durham, NC: Duke University Press.

———, ed. 2006. *Haunted by Empire: Geographies of Intimacy in North American History.* Durham, NC: Duke University Press.

Stolke, Verena. 2006. "O enigma das intersecções: Classe, 'raça,' sexo, sexualidade. A formação dos impérios transatlânticos do século XVI ao XIX" [The enigma of intersections: Class, "race," sex, and sexuality. The making of transatlantic empires from the sixteenth to nineteenth centuries]. *Estudos Feministas* 14(1): 15–42.

Tota, Antonio Pedro. 2000. *O imperialismo sedutor: A americanização do Brasil na época da Segunda Guerra* [Seductive imperialism: The Americanization of Brazil in World War II]. São Paulo: Cia das Letras.

Twine, Frances Winddance. 1998. *Racism in a Racial Democracy: The Maintenance of White Supremacy in Brazil.* New Brunswick, NJ: Rutgers University Press.

Veltmeyer, Henry, James Petras, and Steve Vieux. 1997. *Neoliberalism and Class Conflict in Latin America: A Comparative Perspective on the Political Economy of Structural Adjustment.* New York: St. Martin's Press.

Vianna, Hermano. 1999. *The Mystery of Samba: Popular Music and National Identity in Brazil.* Chapel Hill: University of North Carolina Press.

Vidal-Ortiz, Salvador. 2010. "Blurring the Boundaries of Being, the Field, and Nation: Santeria in the Bronx, Puerto Rico." In *Fieldwork Identities in the Caribbean*, ed. Erin Taylor. Coconut Creek, FL: Caribbean Studies Press.

Viotti da Costa, Emília. 1985. *The Brazilian Empire: Myths and Histories.* Chicago: University of Chicago Press.

Waldinger, Roger. 1996. *Still the Promised City? African-Americans and New Immigrants in Postindustrial New York.* Cambridge, MA: Harvard University Press.

Wardlow, Holly. 2006. *Wayward Women: Sexuality and Agency in a New Guinea Society.* Berkeley: University of California Press.

Weitzer, Ronald. 2000. *Sex for Sale: Prostitution, Pornography, and the Sex Industry.* New York: Routledge.

Whitehead, Stephen M., and Frank J. Barrett, eds. 2001. *The Masculinities Reader*. Malden, MA: Blackwell.

Winant, Howard. 1994. *Racial Conditions*. Minneapolis: University of Minnesota Press.

———. 1999. "Comparing Contemporary Racial Politics in the U.S. and Brazil." In *Racial Politics in Contemporary Brazil*, ed. Michael Hanchard. Durham, NC: Duke University Press.

Xavier, Ismael. 1997. *Allegories of Underdevelopment: Aesthetics and Politics in Modern Brazilian Cinema*. Minneapolis: University of Minnesota Press.

Yúdice, George. 2003. *The Expediency of Culture: Uses of Culture in the Global Era*. Durham, NC: Duke University Press.

Index